EXPLAINING BEHAVIOR

an introduction to psychology

David S. Dustin
James M. Johnson
State University of
New York at Plattsburgh

Daniel N. Robinson,
Consulting Editor

Dickenson Publishing Company, Inc.
Encino, California, and Belmont, California

Figure 2–7. From J. P. Scott. Critical periods in behavioral development. *Science*, 1962, *138*, 949–958. Copyright 1962 by the American Association for the Advancement of Science, and used by permission.

Figure 1–4. Reproduced with permission from the Rosenzweig P-F Study, Children's Form. Copyright 1948 by Saul Rosenzweig.

Figure 2–5. From M. V. Morphett and C. Washburn. When should children begin to read? *Elementary School Journal*, 1931, *31*, 496–503. Copyright 1931 by the University of Chicago.

Figure 3–17. From "The generalization of conditioned responses: I. The sensory generalization of conditioned responses with varying frequencies of tone," by Carl Iver Hovland, which appeared in *The Journal of General Psychology*, Vol. 17, 1937, 125–148, as reanalyzed in Hilgard, Atkinson, and Atkinson, *Introduction to Psychology* (5th ed.), Fig. 807, p. 194.

Figure 6–4. Reproduced by permission of the American Optical Company.

Figure 7–7. From Wilbert J. McKeachie and Charlotte L. Doyle, *Psychology*, Second Edition, 1970, Addison-Wesley, Reading, Mass.

Figure 8–3. From *The Structure and Meaning of Psychoanalysis*, by William Healy, Augusta Bronner, and Anna Mae Bowers. Copyright 1930 and renewed 1958 by Alfred A. Knopf, Inc. Reprinted by permission of the publisher.

Figure 8–8. From *Psychology: A Scientific Study of Man*, 3rd edition, by F. H. Sanford and L. S. Wrightsman, Jr. Copyright 1970 by Wadsworth Publishing Company, Inc. Reprinted by permission of the publisher, Brooks/Cole Publishing Company, Monterey, California, and Mrs. Ann Sanford.

Figure 9–6. From *Diseases of the Nervous System* by S. E. Jellife and W. A. White. Copyright 1935, Lea & Fediger, Philadelphia.

ISBN-0-8221-0119-X

Library of Congress Catalog Card Number: 73-88125

Printed in the United States of America

Printing (last digit): 9 8 7 6 5 4 3 2

CONTENTS

chapter two

Developmental Explanations   27

chapter three

Learning and Cognitive Explanations   49

chapter six

Perceptual Explanations   127

chapter seven

Motivational Explanations   151

chapter eight

Personality
Explanations   173

chapter nine

Clinical
Explanations   197

Preface

Undoubtedly the first thing the student will notice about this book is its brevity. While some textbook authors apparently assume that the more information they cram in the better, in our experience this approach often leads to intellectual indigestion. Therefore, we have included in this book only the most fundamental principles and terms in psychology, so that students will not get lost in a glut of less important material.

A question of many students about to begin this book is, "What is psychology all about?" At first glance, psychology may seem to be no more than a series of completed studies, fascinating in their human interest and final in the explanations they provide. But we feel that the student who stops there, who remains a passive consumer of psychology books and articles, has not reached the heart of psychology because he, himself, has never tried to explain behavior in a scientific way. We don't suggest, of course, that the beginning student is ready to don a long white coat and diagnose patients, and we don't recommend that he set up his own full-scale research laboratory just yet. But we do believe that a first course in psychology is not too early for the student to begin brewing up speculations, hunches, and hypotheses about behavior in his own intellectual cauldron.

Two kinds of information should help the student to improve his skill at explaining behavior: a knowledge of explanatory principles that psychologists have found useful, and an understanding of how to determine whether a given explanation does in fact fit the behavior at hand. This book attempts to provide, in brief form, both kinds of information.

Some of the major explanatory principles in psychology are summarized in Chapters 2–9. To make these principles easier for the reader to pinpoint, they are italicized. In striving for brevity and clarity, we have oversimplified and over-generalized many of these principles. The student interested in adding detail to the generalizations presented here can do so by consulting his instructor and by taking more advanced psychology courses.

The basic rules for psychological research—for determining whether a possible explanation is correct—are presented in Chapter 1. There, again, we have attempted to give the student a brief, working knowledge of the subject without going into the many details that the professional psychologist needs to know.

What is the best way to study this book so as to learn what it has to offer? First, there is an application-type question following each italicized principle. We encourage the student to venture a written answer to each of these questions. We feel this is well worth the effort because it will tell him whether or not he understands what he has just read. If he cannot answer it, that means he should go back and reread the preceding paragraphs—with special emphasis on the itali-cized phrases—until he can answer it. A list of correct answers is provided in the back of the book.

At the end of every chapter is a "Behavior to Explain." The student who tackles these should realize clearly that there is no one correct explanation for any of these behaviors. What is called for here is speculation about some of the many possible explanations. The more text principles the student is able to use in these explanations, the better he will understand and remember those principles.

If the student meets a term he doesn't understand, it can probably be found in the glossary. And, if he wishes to look further into some of the more popular topics in psychology, he will find in the back of the book a list of short but lively readings in popular periodicals.

Many people have helped to create this book. All our colleagues in the psychology department at Plattsburgh State University College have generously contributed encouragement and ideas. Our students have helped by using prelimi-nary versions of the book. Elaine Linden of Dickenson Publishing Company has proven a most helpful editor. Joyce Armstrong bore much of the burden of typing the manuscript. But the final responsibility for the finished product lies with the authors. The first author (D.S.D.) was primarily responsible for Chapters 1–7, and the second author (J.M.J.), for Chapters 8 and 9.

D. S. D.
J. M. J.

chapter one

Explaining Behavior

Psychologists explain behavior through the process of psychological studies. This chapter begins with three examples of psychological studies—and then shows why these studies were done as they were.

SOME EXAMPLES OF PSYCHOLOGICAL EXPLANATION

Example 1

Early in his career, Sigmund Freud developed the hypothesis that bringing back to consciousness guilty impulses and painful memories that neurotic patients have "repressed" or pushed out of consciousness leads to reduction of their neurotic symptoms. From that time on, Freud attempted to treat his patients by talking with them to help them become aware of this repressed material. Every case that Freud treated was in effect a test of his hypothesis. That is, if this therapy led to improvement in the symptoms, Freud's hypothesis was supported. If it did not, the hypothesis was not supported.

One case which Freud reported in detail is the case of "Little Hans" (Freud, 1959). The major neurotic symptom of four-year-old Hans was his irrational fear of horses. He was afraid to go outside his house for fear horses in the street would bite him; sometimes he even expressed the fear that a horse would come right into his bedroom and attack him. For a number of reasons, Freud suspected that Hans was really afraid of his father, that he had repressed this fear, and that this repression was causing his neurotic fear of horses.

FIGURE 1-1. Sigmund Freud, 1856–1939. The Bettmann Archive.

So, in his treatment of Hans, Freud attempted to make him aware of this repressed emotion by simply telling him that he was afraid of his father. And what was the effect of this treatment? The day following the interview with Professor Freud, Hans seemed somewhat less anxious. His father reported to Freud that Hans stood before the front door of their apartment house for an hour, sometimes starting to run inside when he saw a horse and cart approach, but then changing his mind and going back outside. Although his anxiety seemed somewhat lessened, it did not disappear entirely until several months later.

It is unclear what to conclude from this result. One possibility is that Freud's hypothesis is incorrect. Another is that the hypothesis is correct, but that Freud simply failed to remove Hans' repression completely in that one short interview. Years afterward, Freud decided that the removal of repression had failed to decrease patients' symptoms too often for the hypothesis to be correct.

Example 2

Psychologists have done a large amount of research on the "need for achievement," which is abbreviated "n Ach." The early research on this subject was done entirely on college students. Then, a few years ago, psychologists Joseph Veroff, John Atkinson, Sheila Feld, and Gerald Gurin (1960) thought it would be valuable to gather some basic information about the n Ach of the entire United States population. They had no particular hypotheses in mind.

The researchers selected a random sample of 1,609 adults and measured the n Ach of their subjects by asking them to make up stories about six pictures.

One of the relationships they investigated was that between n Ach and years of schooling. They found that, for both men and women, n Ach tended to be higher the more years of school the subject had completed.

Veroff et al. mentioned three possible interpretations of this finding: (1) people with different amounts of schooling reacted differently to the pictures for reasons having nothing to do with n Ach; (2) schooling influences n Ach; or (3) n Ach influences schooling. They concluded that their results did not allow them to choose among these possible interpretations.

Example 3

It has often been reported that people in crowds show an extraordinary amount of conformity: when one person in a crowded theatre shouts "Fire!" others take up the cry; when a few fans start tearing down the goalposts at the end of a football game, others soon join them.

On thinking about this, one of the present authors (Dustin) wondered whether the distractions that usually are present in crowd situations—the noise and the milling people—might not make it difficult for the individual to think for himself, thus causing him to conform to the actions of others. The hypothesis that resulted from this line of reasoning was that crowd distraction influences conformity.

To test this hypothesis, Dustin (1968) did an experiment on 60 volunteers from an introductory psychology class. He gave these subjects some multiple-choice problems to solve. One answer to each problem was marked with a check and subjects were told that this was the answer most students choose. In fact, however, this was not true; subjects were told this simply to find out how often they would conform to the answers they thought others had chosen.

Half the subjects—15 men and 15 women—worked the problems in presence of recorded crowd noise, played at a high volume. Another 15 men and 15 women worked the problems in a room with no noise at all.

It was found that the men who worked the problems in the presence of the crowd noise chose the checked answers significantly more often ($p <$ .05) than the men who worked them without noise. The corresponding difference for the women was smaller and not statistically significant. Dustin concluded that his hypothesis was supported for the men but not the women.

Using the above three cases as our examples, we will now describe the following steps in explaining behavior:

1. Stating an hypothesis.
2. Designing a study to test the hypothesis.
3. Choosing methods of observation or measurement.
4. Analyzing the results.
5. Reporting the results.

STATING AN HYPOTHESIS

As every psychologist knows only too well, it is easy to make the mistake of trying to study too much at once. To avoid this, researchers usually narrow down the field they wish to study by selecting one—or at most, a few—hypotheses.

While there are many interesting aspects of neurosis, Freud limited himself to studying only a few hypotheses about it, including the hypothesis that "amount of repression influences degree of neuroticism." While there are many fascinating questions that could be asked about crowd behavior, Dustin confined his study to the single hypothesis that "amount of crowd distraction influences amount of conformity." Although Veroff and his colleagues did not specifically state any hypotheses, they may well have had in mind several, including the hypothesis that "n Ach is positively related to years of schooling."

As illustrated by these examples, an hypothesis is simply a guess about the truth. *A causal hypothesis takes the form "X influences Y," while a noncausal hypothesis takes the form "X is related to Y."* Don't let the fact that an hypothesis takes the form of a statement make you think that it is proven fact. Not at all. All hypotheses, even those based partly on observation, require testing.

QUESTION 1.

A. Make up a causal hypothesis to explain suicide, and write it below.

B. Make up a noncausal hypothesis to explain suicide, and write it below.

This is a good place to introduce some terms: variable, independent variable, and dependent variable. *A variable is an aspect of something that can change.* Some examples are given in Table 1-1.

TABLE 1-1 EXAMPLES OF VARIABLES

Hair color	(black, brown, yellow, red, or white)
Brightness of a light	(dim to bright)
Attitude toward war	(negative to positive)
Sex of a person	(male or female)
n Ach score	(low to high)
Years of schooling	(0 to about 20)
Amount of conformity	(low to high)
Repression of fear	(not repressed or repressed)

QUESTION 2.   List below all the variables in the following hypothesis: "Amount of frustration influences amount of aggression."

Independent and dependent variables are the "cause" and "effect" variables in causal hypotheses. In the hypothesis "amount of crowd distraction influences amount of conformity," the dependent variable is "amount of conformity," because that it is the variable that—according to the hypothesis, at least—depends on or is influenced by the other variable. And "amount of crowd distraction" is the independent variable, because the hypothesis states that it does not depend on its partner. This and other examples of independent and dependent variables are shown in Table 1-2.

TABLE 1-2 INDEPENDENT AND DEPENDENT VARIABLES

	INDEPENDENT VARIABLE (CAUSE)		DEPENDENT VARIABLE (EFFECT)
HYPOTHESIS 1	amount of crowd distraction	influences	amount of conformity
HYPOTHESIS 2	amount of repression	leads to	degree of neuroticism
HYPOTHESIS 3	amount of frustration	influences	amount of aggression

In the hypothesis "n Ach is related to years of schooling," there are no independent or dependent variables because this is not a causal hypothesis.

QUESTION 3.   Write "independent variable" or "dependent variable" beside the phrases to which they apply.

A. Hypothesis: The number of other bystanders who are present influences the likelihood that a bystander will help in a crisis.

_____ Number of other bystanders present.

_____ Likelihood that a bystander will help in a crisis.

B. Hypothesis: Students' attitudes toward religion are related to their college majors.

_____ Students' attitudes toward religion.

_____ College major.

DESIGNING A STUDY

The investigator must design his study so that the observations he makes will adequately test his hypothesis. This means that these observations must be relevant to three elements of the hypothesis: (1) inner mental processes, (2) influence or relationship between variables, and (3) generalization.

Making Observations Relevant to Inner Mental Processes

Most psychologists have in the back of their heads a model of the human subject that, in very simplified form, looks like Figure 1-2.

This diagram shows that the factors we theorize to be inside the subject—learning, motivation, perception, thinking, and many others—are influenced by environmental stimuli or S (such as the lights he sees, the sounds he hears, the odors he smells), which in turn influence his responses or R (his physical actions or behaviors, such as running, kissing, speaking).

It is a widely accepted rule in psychology that only those factors that are open to observation by all—namely, stimuli and responses—can be studied scientifically. How, then, can we find out about all those intriguing inner mental processes? We can't study them directly, because they are not observable by all. Although the subject himself may be able to observe them, no one else can. *What the psychological researcher has to do to study an inner mental process is to find stimuli and responses that seem related to it.* Verbal report—obtained simply by asking the subject to tell about his inner mental processes—is one kind of response that may be observed, but it is not the only one, and very often not the best one.

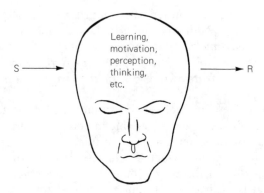

FIGURE 1-2. **The psychologist's model of a subject.**

Table 1-3 summarizes how Freud, Veroff et al., and Dustin translated the inner mental processes involved in their hypotheses into observable terms.

TABLE 1-3 TRANSLATIONS OF INNER MENTAL PROCESSES INTO OBSERVABLE TERMS

THEORETICAL (INNER MENTAL PROCESS)	OBSERVABLE
Freud: removal of repression	Freud told Hans he was afraid of his father (a stimulus for Hans).
	Hans behaved more aggressively toward his father afterward (a response).
Veroff: need for achievement	References to achievement in the stories subjects wrote about pictures (a response).
Dustin: mental distraction	Crowd noise (a stimulus).

QUESTION 4. Describe a stimulus and a response that would be reasonable bases for theorizing that a subject was angry (inner mental process).

A. Stimulus:

B. Response:

Making Observations Relevant to Relationship or Influence

Although somewhat more evidence is required to show that X influences Y than to show merely that X is related to Y, both procedures include the following three steps: *(1) either create or find ready-made two or more conditions in which variable X differs; (2) control other variables—that is, keep them the same in these two or more conditions; (3) measure variable Y in the two or more conditions.*

These three steps were carried out in each of the studies described at the beginning of this chapter. In Freud's study, the X variable (amount of repression) was varied because Hans was first in a "repressed" condition and later—as a result of Freud's therapeutic efforts—in a somewhat less repressed state. And, because the subject was the same person in these two conditions, many aspects of the subject were controlled. That is, in both conditions the subject was four years old, highly intelligent, Viennese, and so on. Finally, Freud measured the Y variable, and found that Hans seemed somewhat less afraid of horses after the repression was removed than before. The three steps of Freud's study are outlined in Table 1-4.

TABLE 1-4   DIAGRAM OF FREUD'S "LITTLE HANS" STUDY

	CONDITION 1		CONDITION 2
1. VARY X	Hans's fear repressed	$\neq$	Hans's fear less repressed
2. CONTROL OTHER VARIABLES	S age 4, intelligent	$=$	S age 4, intelligent
3. MEASURE Y	Afraid of horses	$\neq$	Less afraid of horses

In the Veroff study, the researchers made use of an already-existing difference on the X variable: they found subjects who already differed in amount of schooling. One of the variables that was controlled in this study was sex of subject. This was done by analyzing the results first for men only, then for women only. The Y variable in this study was, of course, the n Ach score. This study is diagrammed in Table 1-5.

TABLE 1-5   DIAGRAM OF THE VEROFF STUDY

	CONDITION 1		CONDITION 2		CONDITION 3
1. VARY X	Grade school only	$\neq$	Some high school	$\neq$	Some college
2. CONTROL OTHER VARIABLES	Ss all men (or all women)	$=$	Ss all men (or all women)	$=$	Ss all men (or all women)
3. MEASURE Y	Mean n Ach	$\neq$	Mean n Ach	$\neq$	Mean n Ach

Finally, the Dustin study is diagrammed in Table 1-6.

TABLE 1-6   DIAGRAM OF THE DUSTIN STUDY

	CONDITION 1		CONDITION 2
1. VARY X	Crowd noise	$\neq$	No noise
2. CONTROL OTHER VARIABLES	Experimental room; instructions; 50% men, 50% women	$=$	Experimental room; instructions; 50% men, 50% women
3. MEASURE Y	Mean conformity score	$\neq$	Mean conformity score

A term that the reader is likely to meet frequently is "control group." In the Dustin study, the no-noise group was a control group because it showed the influence only of the variables that were controlled (see Table 1-6), without any noise being present. This control group was essential. Only by comparing it with the noise group could the researcher find out how much of the effects were due to noise alone.

QUESTION 5.   Suppose you wanted to find out whether amount of alcohol consumed influenced how much a student learned from studying a passage in a textbook. List three steps that would have to be carried out in order to find out whether one of these variables in fact influences the other, and describe briefly how you would carry out each of them.

Once the above three steps have been carried out, how does the researcher draw conclusions about influence or relationship? If he finds that the Y variable differs "significantly"—that is, more than can be accounted for by chance alone—in the two or more conditions, then he can conclude that X is related to, and might possibly be influencing, the obtained difference on Y.

Furthermore, all variables that were controlled in the study are not related to the obtained difference on Y and cannot possibly be causing it. This doesn't necessarily mean that the controlled variables have no effect on Y. It simply means that whatever effect they have is the same in the various conditions of the study, and thus these variables cannot be responsible for the differences in Y that were obtained among those conditions.

Making Observations that Permit Generalization

Every study is, of course, carried out on a specific group of subjects. But researchers typically wish *to generalize* their *findings—that is, to draw conclusions about groups of people (called populations) that are broader than the specific group they used in their study (called a sample).* From the one neurotic child he studied, Freud drew some conclusions about the population of neurotics in general and other conclusions about the population of children in general.

Specific finding:
Hans afraid of father

Generalization:
All boys afraid of father

FIGURE 1-3.   An example of generalization.

Veroff concluded that his results applied to the population of United States adults in general, not just to the sample that had been interviewed. Dustin did not specify in his report how far he felt the results from his sample of 60 subjects could be generalized; some possibilities would be to generalize them to the entire introductory psychology class from which the sample was drawn, to the entire student body of that college, to college students everywhere, or to people in general.

QUESTION 6.   Suppose that a study of 50 foremen at the Ford Motor Company showed a relationship between the amount of concern a foreman showed for his men and the productivity of those men.

A.   What is the sample of subjects in this study?

B.   State one generalization that might be drawn from the above results.

C. In the generalization you just made, what is the population?

Although most researchers generalize the results of their studies to some extent, many fail to design their studies in such a way as to warrant their generalizations. *The way to warrant generalizations about subjects is to select the sample of subjects in such a way that it will be representative of—that is, similar to—the population to which you wish to generalize. One way to do this is to choose the sample from the population in a random manner—that is, in some manner that gives every kind of person in the population an equal chance of being chosen.* While random selection sometimes produces an atypical sample, usually it gives a highly representative one. Drawing names from a hat is a random method of selecting a sample from the population of names in the hat because each name has an equal chance of being chosen. Selecting every tenth name from a complete student directory is a random method of drawing a sample from the student body of a college. Assigning a number to every person in a population and then selecting those people who have the first 40 numbers that appear in a table of random numbers is a random method of selection. But choosing your ten best college friends as subjects for an experiment is not a random method of selection because you probably like some kinds of people more than others, and therefore your friends are probably not representative of the entire student body.

In the light of the above, we can see that there was little evidence for generalization in the Freud or Dustin studies but good evidence in the Veroff study. For example, Freud had no evidence that Hans was representative of neurotics in general, or of children in general. Indeed, Hans might have been unusual in some way so that Freud's findings for him would not apply to the typical neurotic or to the typical child. Veroff and his colleagues, however, took pains to provide a sound basis for generalization. They did this by selecting their 1,600 subjects in a random manner from the entire population of U.S. adults.

QUESTION 7.   Suppose you wanted to study the effectiveness of methadone treatment for institutionalized heroin addicts. You have room for only 35 addicts in your methadone program.

A. What would be the sample of subjects in your study?

B. What is the population in which you would be interested in this study?

C. To permit generalization, you would probably want to select the sample of subjects in what general manner?

D. Describe a specific selection procedure of the kind you mentioned in (c), above.

CHOOSING METHODS OF OBSERVATION OR MEASUREMENT

All the research principles described so far are to no avail if the researcher cannot find a way to measure the necessary variables accurately. An accurate method of measurement is one that is (1) objective, (2) reliable, and (3) valid.

Objectivity of Measurement

Objectivity refers to whether an observation lies in the realm of fact, or whether it exists only in the biased, subjective perception of a particular observer. Because objectivity is theoretical in nature, it cannot be observed directly; there are, however, observations that may be made which are indirectly related to it. *The standard method of finding out the objectivity of a method of measurement is to have two observers independently apply that method to the same subjects at the same time. If their observations agree closely, the measure is highly objective; if they do not, the measure has low objectivity.* Veroff checked the objectivity of his n Ach scoring procedure by having the stories that had been written by a subsample of 30 subjects scored independently by two different observers. The two sets of scores showed a correlation of about .80, which indicates—as will be explained later in this chapter—that they were very similar, and that therefore the scoring was highly objective.

QUESTION 8.   Describe what you would have to do to find out the degree of objectivity of the conformity measure that was used in the Dustin study.

One important step the researcher can take to increase objectivity is to use unbiased observers. This is one reason why it is risky to use measurement procedures that require the subject to provide information about himself. Subjects tend to be biased about themselves; they tend to see themselves as more intelligent, more courageous, more admirable in every way than they really are. And the same is true of those who are close to the subjects, such as their friends and relatives.

Researchers are apt to be biased observers, too, unless special precautions are taken. The researcher is biased because he wants the results of the study to support his hypothesis. For example, Dustin was hoping to find more conformity in the crowd-noise subjects than in the no-noise subjects. As a result, unless precautions had been taken, there was the danger that when Dustin scored the subjects' problem booklets, he would see more conformity in the crowd-noise subjects than actually existed, and less in the no-noise subjects than was there.

Fortunately there are ways of eliminating experimenter bias. One way is for the researcher to recruit observers who do not know what his hypothesis is; another is for the researcher to act as observer himself, but in such a way that while he is observing, he does not know what condition each subject is in. Dustin did this by shuffling all the problem booklets so that while he was scoring them he didn't know which booklets belonged to crowd-noise subjects and which ones belonged to no-noise subjects.

The above considerations are summarized in the following principle: *Objectivity of measurement is maximized by the use of unbiased observers. A researcher is apt to be a less biased observer than a subject if the researcher is not aware of the hypothesis being tested or not aware of the experimental condition of each subject he observes.*

QUESTION 9.   Suppose you wanted to test the hypothesis that women stand closer to others they are talking to than men do.

A. Describe a method of measuring the dependent variable in this hypothesis that would probably have *low* objectivity.

B. Describe a method of measuring the same variable that would probably have *high* objectivity.

Reliability of Measurement

The term reliability, as used in psychology, means less than the layman would guess. *A method of measurement is reliable to the extent that it gives similar scores each time it is used on the same subjects.* Suppose someone decided to measure intelligence by counting the number of gray hairs on a person's head. If he got very similar scores when he counted the same subjects' gray hairs twice, his intelligence measure would be highly reliable. Of course it would probably not be measuring intelligence, but that has nothing to do with reliability; instead, that is a matter of validity, as we shall see shortly.

The n Ach test used by Veroff has been checked for reliability several times. One researcher gave two different forms of the test to the same subjects at the same time. When he compared subjects' scores on these two forms, he found a correlation of .64, which indicates that the scores were fairly similar and that therefore the test was fairly reliable.

Dustin did not attempt to find out the reliability of his conformity measure. If he had wished to do this, the appropriate procedure would have been to give the same measure twice to the same group of subjects. Either two different versions would be given at the same time, or the same version would be given at two different times.

QUESTION 10.   Suppose that you developed a measure of how effective a high school teacher is at maintaining classroom discipline.

A.   Describe a procedure for testing the reliability of this measuring instrument.

B.   If you applied the procedure you just described, what kind of result would indicate high reliability? Low reliability?

C. Suppose you discovered later that your measure didn't really do a very good job of measuring a teacher's classroom discipline. What would this discovery imply about the reliability of the measure?

Validity of Measurement

A method of measurement is valid to the extent that it measures what it is supposed to measure. If Hans' father was correct when he reported that Hans' fear decreased the day after his interview with Freud, then his report was a valid measure of Hans' fear. If the n Ach scores of Veroff's subjects accurately reflected how much achievement motivation they had, then the n Ach measure was valid in that study.

QUESTION 11.   What would it mean to say that the "Jones Test of Marital Happiness" is reliable but not valid?

Now that we have described objectivity, reliability, and validity—the three standards by which every measure is judged—it is time to outline some of the types of measures that are available to test hypotheses.

Some Commonly Used Measures

Some types of measures that typically use the subject himself or someone close to him as the observer are the interview, the rating scale, and the inventory.

INTERVIEW   In most interviews, the subject is asked questions about himself—his experiences, his goals for the future, his attitudes, and so on. Note that these are all factors that would be very difficult for the interviewer to observe directly.

RATING SCALE   Rating measures ask people to rate themselves or others on a scale. For example, the recommendation forms used by most colleges include questions such as the following:

Please rate the applicant on each of the following characteristics by making a check in the appropriate column:

	TOP 5%	TOP 10%	TOP 25%	TOP HALF	BELOW TOP HALF	NO INFO
CREATIVITY						
RESPONSIBILITY						
ABILITY TO GET ALONG WITH OTHERS						

INVENTORY   *An inventory consists of a number of items, usually a large number, that ask the subject about himself.* There are many kinds of inventories: medical inventories ask what diseases you have had, and attitude inventories ask about your attitudes. Probably the best-known psychological inventory is the Minnesota Multiphasic Personality Inventory (MMPI), which consists of several hundred items of the following kind:

I sometimes think I am going crazy.   True_____   False_____
I like to watch sporting events.   True_____   False_____
I find it easy to meet new people.   True_____   False_____

Other psychological inventories use these types of items:

When I have a project due at a certain deadline, I usually:
_____   start on it early so there is plenty of time to do it and revise it.
_____   wait till the last minute because I always work better under pressure.

QUESTION 12.   Make an inventory of three items for the purpose of measuring attitudes toward pollution. Write the three items below.

Some measures that use the researcher as the observer are naturalistic observation, projective tests, ability tests, physiological measures, and the Skinner box.

NATURALISTIC OBSERVATION   This simply means observing subjects in their natural environment. Examples are a developmental psychologist taking notes on the activities of a kindergarden class and an anthropologist taking notes on the behavior of members of a primitive society.

PROJECTIVE TEST   *A projective test is one in which the subject is asked to interpret an ambiguous stimulus.* Since there is little in the stimulus itself to guide the interpretation, *it is assumed that the subject's interpretation must stem from his own personality and thus reveals aspects of that personality.* The n Ach test, in which subjects write stories about pictures, is one example of a projective measure.

FIGURE 1-4. **A sample picture from Rosenzweig's Picture Frustration (P-F) Test (children's form), which is an example of a projective test.**

Another projective measure is the well-known Rorschach test, which requires the subject to tell what he sees in a series of inkblots.

A third projective measure is the sentence completion test, which requires the subject to complete phrases such as the following:

I often think about   _____

When I go to a party   _____

It should be noted that the stimuli used in a projective test are not problems—that is, they have no right or wrong answers. They are, rather, stimuli that
may be interpreted in a variety of ways.

QUESTION 13.   Invent a brief projective test that might be used to
measure aggressiveness, and describe it below.

ABILITY TEST   An ability test does use problems, the responses to
which can be considered correct or incorrect, better or worse. Examples are school
exams, IQ tests, and measures of physical ability, such as the 100-yard dash and
the walk-a-straight-line test for drunken drivers.

PHYSIOLOGICAL MEASURES   There are available several physiological measures of emotional arousal. Because they use the researcher as observer,
they are more objective than the alternative of asking the subject to report his
emotions. Among these are measures of heart rate, blood pressure, and brain waves.

SKINNER BOX   Finally, it should be mentioned that researchers have
devised countless procedures to measure particular physical movements. Many
of these have been used only in a single study; others are in widespread use.
One of the most widely used is B. F. Skinner's procedure for measuring the level
of a rat's bar-pressing activity, which is a response used in many learning experiments. The rat is placed in a soundproof box with a bar protruding from one
wall. If the rat exerts enough pressure on the bar, it activates a microswitch which
in turn advances a counter outside the box. In order to observe responses, all
the researcher has to do is look at the counter. Clearly this measure has high
objectivity; any two observers would agree closely as to the number of bar-presses
a rat had made.

Here, then, are some of the types of measuring procedures that are used
by psychologists. The researcher chooses the one he thinks will measure the variable he wants to study with the highest possible objectivity, reliability, and validity.

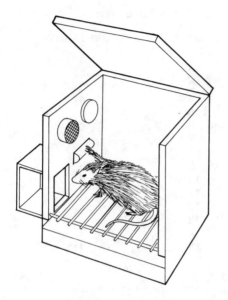

FIGURE 1-5. **A rat pressing the bar in a Skinner box.**

ANALYZING THE RESULTS

After the measurements have been made the researcher is usually confronted with a large set of numbers or other data. The problem then is to make sense of those data. While there is much to be known about data analysis, we will discuss only three methods: mean, correlation, and significance. These are terms that the reader will meet especially frequently in psychology.

Mean

The mean is what is usually called the average. To find the mean of a group of scores, sum all the scores and then divide by the total number of scores. For an example, let us calculate the mean of the conformity scores for the male subjects in Dustin's crowd noise experiment, which are shown in Table 1-7. To find the mean for the crowd noise men we first add their 15 conformity scores together: 5 plus 4 plus 3, and so on. The total turns out to be 65. Then this total is divided by the number of scores (15), giving a mean conformity score of 4.33. When the same procedure is followed for the no-noise men, their mean conformity score turns out to be 3.67.

TABLE 1-7   CONFORMITY SCORES FOR THE MEN IN THE DUSTIN EXPERIMENT

CROWD-NOISE MEN		NO-NOISE MEN	
SUBJECT #	CONFORMITY	SUBJECT #	CONFORMITY
1	5	1	3
2	4	2	5
3	3	3	4
4	6	4	4
5	4	5	3
6	5	6	4
7	3	7	4
8	4	8	3
9	3	9	3
10	4	10	5
11	5	11	4
12	5	12	3
13	4	13	3
14	6	14	3
15	4	15	4
	total = 65		total = 55

$$\text{mean} = \frac{65}{15} = 4.33 \qquad\qquad \text{mean} = \frac{55}{15} = 3.67$$

QUESTION 14.   A sample of college women report that they dated the following numbers of men last year: 3,5,2,3,3,4,1. What is the mean of these scores?

Correlation Coefficients

A correlation coefficient is a number that describes a relationship between two variables. In the Dustin study, only one variable—conformity—was measured, so no correlation coefficient could be calculated. Suppose, however, that Dustin had also measured the IQ of every subject. Then he would have been able to calculate a correlation between conformity and IQ.

We will now describe the various kinds of relationships that can be found and the correlation coefficients that correspond to them.

A relationship is as strong as it can get (perfect) and positive if, when the scores on one measure increase by equal steps, the scores on the other measure also increase by equal steps. It is not necessary that the steps on the two scales be the same size. This is illustrated in Figure 1-6.

SUBJECT	MEASURE 1	MEASURE 2
A	1	1
B	2	2
C	3	3
D	4	4

SUBJECT	MEASURE 1	MEASURE 2
A	6	30
B	8	35
C	10	40
D	12	45

FIGURE 1-6. **Strong (perfect) positive relationships; *r* = 1.00**

It is possible to compute a number which describes a relationship precisely. This number is called a correlation coefficient and is symbolized by the small letter "r." A perfect positive relationship gives a correlation coefficient of 1.00.

The relationships in figure 1-7 are still positive, because there is still a tendency for high scores on one measure to go with high scores on the other and low to go with low. But this tendency is weaker than before because the scores on measure 2 no longer increase by equal steps. The correlation coefficient computed from each of the tables in Figure 1-7 is .60. The exact number of this correlation coefficient is not important for our purposes. All we need to observe is that this number is positive because the relationships are positive, and it is lower than before because the relationships are weaker than before.

SUBJECT	MEASURE 1	MEASURE 2
A	1	2
B	2	1
C	3	4
D	4	3

SUBJECT	MEASURE 1	MEASURE 2
A	6	35
B	8	30
C	10	45
D	12	40

FIGURE 1-7. **Weak positive relationships; *r* = .60**

There is no relationship in figure 1-8, because there is no systematic association between the two sets of scores. That is, as measure 1 increases, there is
no overall tendency for measure 2 to either increase or decrease. The correlation
coefficient computed from such a set of numbers turns out to be 0.00.

SUBJECT	MEASURE 1	MEASURE 2
A	1	2
B	2	4
C	3	1
D	4	3

FIGURE 1-8. No relationship; r = 0.00

Weak negative relationships are shown in Figure 1-9. These should not
be confused with zero relationships. In a negative relationship, scores on the two
measures are definitely related, but in a negative direction. That is, *high* scores
on one measure tend to go with *low* scores on the other. The relationships in
this figure are exactly the reverse of those in Figure 1-7, and the correlation coefficient is also the reverse.

SUBJECT	MEASURE 1	MEASURE 2
A	1	3
B	2	4
C	3	1
D	4	2

SUBJECT	MEASURE 1	MEASURE 2
A	6	40
B	8	45
C	10	30
D	12	35

FIGURE 1-9. Weak negative relationships; r = -.60

Strong negative relationships are shown in Figure 1-10.

SUBJECT	MEASURE 1	MEASURE 2
A	1	4
B	2	3
C	3	2
D	4	1

SUBJECT	MEASURE 1	MEASURE 2
A	6	45
B	8	40
C	10	35
D	12	30

FIGURE 1-10. Strong (perfect) negative relationships; r = -1.00

In summary,

1.   *A relationship is positive if there is a tendency for subjects who score higher on one measure to also score higher on the other; it is negative if the tendency is for the subjects who score higher on one to score lower on the other.*

2.   *A relationship is strong if this tendency is a strong one, and weak if this tendency is weak.*

3.   *Correlation coefficients are positive for positive relationships and negative for negative ones.*

4.   *Correlation coefficients are larger for stronger relationships and smaller for weaker ones.*

QUESTION 15.   Here are two possible sets of results of a study on conformity and IQ:

SET A				SET B		
SUBJECT	**CONFORMITY**	**IQ**		**SUBJECT**	**CONFORMITY**	**IQ**
1	2	100		1	2	130
2	3	110		2	3	140
3	3	110		3	3	120
4	4	120		4	4	120
5	4	120		5	4	130
6	4	120		6	4	110
7	5	130		7	5	120
8	5	130		8	5	100
9	6	140		9	6	110

A.   Describe the relationship in Set A: (Circle one.)

1.   Positive

2.   Negative

B.   Describe the relationship in Set B: (Circle one.)

1.   Positive

2.   Negative

C.   Which set shows the stronger relationship? (Circle one.)

1.   Set A

2.   Set B

D.   The correlation coefficient for one set is $-.92$ and that for the other is 1.00. Draw lines to connect the matching correlation coefficients and sets below.

r	Set
$-.92$	A
1.00	B

Statistical Significance

Dustin found that his two noise conditions produced a difference in mean conformity score for the men as well as for the women, as shown in Table 1-8. Are these two differences statistically significant or are they due to chance alone?

TABLE 1-8 **MEAN CONFORMITY SCORES IN THE DUSTIN STUDY**

	CROWD NOISE	NO NOISE	DIFFERENCE	P OF DIFFERENCE	DIFFERENCE SIGNIFICANT?
Men	4.33	3.67	.66	.04	Yes
Women	4.27	4.13	.14	.64	No

We will not attempt to explain the rather complex methods by which psychologists estimate the probability that a finding is due to chance. However, it is useful for the reader to know that *if the probability that a finding is due to chance turns out to be equal to or less than .05 ($p \leq .05$), it is standard practice among psychologists to conclude that the finding is "statistically significant"—that is, not due to chance.* The highest possible probability is 1.00, and the lowest is 0.00. Thus the probability indicated above is .05 out of a maximum 1.00, which is equivalent to 5 out of 100. This principle is shown in Table 1-9.

TABLE 1-9 **DRAWING CONCLUSIONS ABOUT STATISTICAL SIGNIFICANCE**

P (PROBABILITY THAT THE FINDING WAS DUE TO CHANCE ALONE)	CONCLUSION	P (PROBABILITY THAT THE FINDING WAS DUE TO CHANCE ALONE)	CONCLUSION
1.00		.05	
.90		.04	
.80		.03	
.70	Finding is *not* statistically significant (it may be due entirely to chance)	.02	Finding *is* statistically significant (it is not due entirely to chance)
.60		.01	
.50		.009	
.40		etc.	
.30			
.20			
.10			
.09			
.08			
.07			
.06			

When Dustin applied appropriate tests of statistical significance, he found that the probability that the conformity difference for the men was due to chance was about .04, while the probability for the women was about .64. Thus he concluded that the difference for the men was significant while that for the women was not.

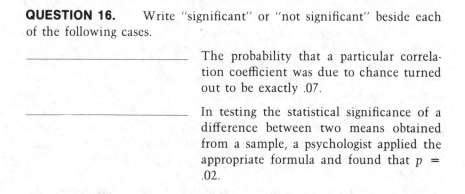

QUESTION 16.   Write "significant" or "not significant" beside each of the following cases.

_____   The probability that a particular correlation coefficient was due to chance turned out to be exactly .07.

_____   In testing the statistical significance of a difference between two means obtained from a sample, a psychologist applied the appropriate formula and found that $p = .02$.

REPORTING THE RESULTS

After the results of a study have been analyzed, the final step is to report any significant findings to other psychologists. This is usually done by reading a paper at a psychology convention, or by publishing an article in one of the many psychology journals.

One reason reporting findings is an important part of science is that it permits others to repeat the study if they wish, thereby checking the objectivity and reliability of the results. Therefore it is essential that the report describe what the researcher did in such detail that others could exactly duplicate his procedure.

Freud, Veroff et al., and Dustin all published reports of their findings. Freud reported the case of Little Hans in "Analysis of a Phobia in a Five-Year-Old Boy." This article can be found in *Collected Papers of Sigmund Freud*, Volume III, which was published by Basic Books, Inc., in 1959. The detailed nature of this report is shown by the fact that it is 142 pages long!

Veroff, Atkinson, Feld, and Gurin reported their study in an article entitled "The use of thematic apperception to assess motivation in a nationwide interview survey," which was published in *Psychological Monographs*, Vol. 74, 1960. Their report, which covers much more than the relationship between n Ach and years of schooling, is 32 pages long.

Dustin's article, although only two pages long, is also fairly detailed. It is printed in modified form in the Appendix to this book, so the reader may look at an example of a psychological report.

SUMMARY

The process of explaining behavior through psychological study can be divided into five steps:

1. Stating an hypothesis. While causal hypotheses have independent and dependent variables, these terms are not appropriate for the variables in noncausal hypotheses.

2. Designing a study to test the hypothesis. In order to study an inner mental process, the psychologist must translate it into observable factors—that is, into stimulus or response variables. In order to find out whether X is either related to or influences Y, the researcher must find two or more conditions where X differs, control other variables, and measure Y in those two or more conditions. If Y differs significantly, then X is related to the obtained difference in Y, and may be causing it. In order to warrant generalizations, the investigator must select a sample that is representative of the population to which he wishes to generalize. One way to do this is to select that sample from the population by some random method.

3. Choosing methods of observation or measurement. Measures should have high objectivity, reliability, and validity. One way of maximizing objectivity is to use unbiased observers. Among the many kinds of psychological measures are the inventory and the projective test.

4. Analyzing the results. Terms used frequently in data analysis are "mean," "correlation coefficient," and "statistical significance."

5. Reporting the results. The report should include a detailed description of what the researcher did, so that others may duplicate the study if they wish.

BEHAVIOR TO EXPLAIN

Heroin addiction is a critical national problem. Addiction not only cripples the addict himself but also may force him to steal from others to support his habit.

While there certainly are environmental pressures that influence heroin use, it is also true that in the same environment one person becomes a junkie while another person is unscathed. What personality factors explain drug addiction?

1. Develop an hypothesis about a personality factor that helps to explain drug addiction.

2. Describe all the steps you would take to test this hypothesis.

chapter two

Developmental
Explanations

ANCIENT RIDDLE: What goes on four feet, on two feet, and three, but the more feet it goes on the weaker it be?

ANSWER: Man. [In infancy he crawls on all fours, in adulthood walks erect on two feet, and in old age uses a cane to support himself.]

AN OVERVIEW OF THE DEVELOPMENTAL PROCESS

Why do people and animals behave in the ways—altruistic and selfish, intelligent and stupid, turned-on and turned-off—that they do? This is the basic question of psychology and will appear again and again in this book. The specific factors that determine behavior and how these various determinants fit together are diagrammed in Figure 2-1. This figure shows the process of organismic development: the organism, with its heredity and current adaptations, interacts with the environment. This interaction produces further adaptations in the organism, so

27

that it is somewhat different the next time it interacts with the environment. The three determinants of behavior that are shown in Figure 2-1—heredity, environment, and adaptation—will now be described briefly.

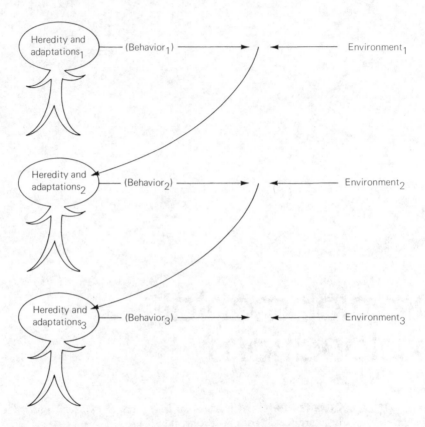

FIGURE 2-1.   The interaction of heredity and environment in the development of the organism.

Heredity

There are 23 pairs of complex molecules called chromosomes in every one of the billions of cells that make up your body (except the reproductive cells—the male's sperm and the female's eggs—which contain 23 unpaired chromosomes). And the 23 pairs in each cell are identical to the 23 pairs in every other cell, whether it be an eye, skin, bone, muscle, or brain cell. Genes, which are considered the basic units of heredity, are simply tiny segments of a chromosome.

Where did you get these chromosomes? One in every pair came from your father, and the other came from your mother. And by means of your reproductive cells, you will pass on half of each of your 23 pairs to each of your children. Your children will not be genetically identical to each other, however, because you will contribute a different reproductive cell and therefore a somewhat different set of 23 unpaired chromosomes to each child. The only case in which the heredity of two children is identical is that of identical twins. They are genetically identical because they come from a sperm cell and an egg cell that joined and produced a fertilized egg that, in its first cell division, divided into two separate organisms, each with a complete and identical set of chromosomes.

What do your chromosomes do? They carry instructions that guide your biological functioning. And since the biological functioning of, for example, sense organs, nerve cells, and muscles affects psychological functioning, your chromosomes also influence your psychological functioning.

One more important point needs to be made about heredity: not all of its effects are present at birth. Many inherited characteristics show up only later in development. *This unfolding of largely inherited characteristics with age is called maturation.* We all know about physical characteristics that undergo maturation: hair color sometimes changes from early to late childhood; the sex organs become fully functional at adolescence; some children look more and more like a particular relative as they grow older. It seems reasonable to expect that psychological characteristics, too, will be found to be greatly influenced by maturation.

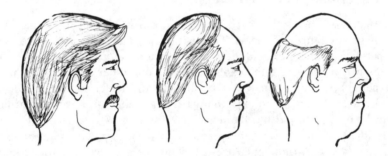

FIGURE 2-2. Baldness occurs primarily through maturation. This means that it is a largely hereditary characteristic that doesn't "unfold" or become apparent until the individual gets older.

Notice that the scientific term maturation does not mean the same thing as the every-day term mature. "Mature" is usually used to describe an individual who is especially "grown-up" or "wise," no matter whether this is due to maturation or to experience.

QUESTION 1.   Suppose you knew the following things about certain behaviors. In which of these hypothetical cases is the behavior most clearly due to maturation? (Check one.)

_____   This behavior is mostly inherited, and it is present at birth.

_____   This behavior is mostly inherited, and it appears at one year of age.

_____   This behavior is mostly learned, and it appears at one year of age.

Environment

The human organism comes in contact with several different kinds of environment during its development. Its first environment is the mother's body, and many aspects of that environment are important for its development. If the mother is undernourished, the fetus growing inside her will be undernourished too. If the mother is using drugs, such as thalidomide (the infamous sedative, now banned) or heroin, the fetus may be affected. And if the mother's body contains certain microbes, such as those for German measles, the fetus may be damaged.

At birth the infant has to adapt to the physical environment of the outside world. For example, the newborn baby must quickly get used to the greater brightness and the cooler temperatures of its new environment.

As the child grows up, the social environment becomes more and more important. First it is the family to which the child must adapt. Then, the school. And beyond that, society at large, with its political, religious, occupational, and other systems.

Psychological Adaptation

Figure 2-1 shows that each time the organism comes in contact with the environment, it changes or adapts. Through learning and other adaptive processes, each experience changes the individual's perceptions, motives, and habits—in other words, his personality—to some extent. As he grows older and acquires more and more experiences, adaptations make up a larger and larger part of his personality.

Let's use Figure 2-1 to explain a particular behavior. Assume that behavior 3 in the figure is compulsive hand-washing: at this particular point in his life the individual begins to wash his hands many times a day, sometimes only a few minutes apart. Although Figure 2-1 won't help to explain this behavior in any detailed way, it does show the kinds of factors that need to be considered in explaining it. (1) Heredity may be a factor. Although it does not seem very likely that there are genes that directly determine how often we wash our hands, there may very well be genes that influence other factors—such as nervousness—that in turn influence compulsive hand-washing. (2) The individual's current environmental situation could be important. For instance, there may be some stressful or threatening aspects of this environment that produce, in this particular kind of person, compulsive behavior. (3) The other important factor is the adaptations the individual has accumulated over the years. For instance, perhaps he has previously learned to respond to stressful situations with compulsive behavior.

SORTING OUT THE EFFECTS OF HEREDITY AND ENVIRONMENT

People often assume that the effects of heredity and environment are separate and distinct. When a mother says that "Junior's athletic ability comes from his father's side of the family," she seems to be saying that the fact that Junior made the varsity football team is entirely due to heredity. And when the same mother explains that Junior's five fumbles in the recent football game were due to the fact that the other team was "playing dirty," she seems to be saying that his poor performance was due entirely to environmental factors.

We want to emphasize strongly that it is *not* true that heredity is entirely responsible for some characteristics and environment is entirely responsible for others. Instead, *every behavior is due both to heredity and to environment.* This is evident from the very nature of heredity and environment. Heredity is a set of possible plans or blueprints while environment provides the building materials. The biological structure that results is caused by *both* the blueprints and the building materials; this structure would be different if either different blueprints had been used or different building materials had been available.

Even though heredity and environment always work in partnership, it is possible to sort out their effects to some extent. *The tools for separating the effects of heredity and environment are the research methods described in Chapter 1.* Thus, to find out the effects of environment on a particular behavior, the researcher must vary environmental factors while controlling heredity and then measure the behavior of the subjects in the various environmental conditions.

QUESTION 2.   What would be the procedure for finding out the effects of heredity on a particular behavior?

We will illustrate how heredity-environment studies are done on animals by describing a study of maze-learning behavior in rats (Cooper and Zubek, 1958). In this study, the researchers used two strains of rats: bright and dull. These strains have been created over many generations by interbreeding rats that perform well in learning mazes and interbreeding those that perform poorly on this kind of task. Each succeeding generation of "bright" rats has proven better and better at learning mazes and each generation of "dull" rats has proven worse and worse. Of course the very fact that it is possible to breed rats for maze-learning ability demonstrates that there is some genetic basis for this behavior.

The researchers separated some of these bright and dull rats from their mothers immediately after weaning, and reared one group of them for 40 days in a normal laboratory environment—individual cages containing a food box and a water pan. At the end of the 40 days, this group of rats was tested for ability to learn a variety of mazes. The mean number of maze-running errors made by the bright and dull rats in this group is shown in Table 2-1. In reading this table, remember that lower error scores indicate better performance.

TABLE 2-1 **EFFECTS OF HEREDITY ON MAZE-LEARNING FOR RATS REARED IN NORMAL LAB ENVIRONMENT**

	CONDITION 1		CONDITION 2
Independent variable (heredity)	Bright rats	$\neq$	Dull rats
Controlled variable (environment)	Normal lab	=	Normal lab
Dependent variable (mean # of errors)	117.0	$\neq$*	164.0

*p < .05.

Source: From R. M. Cooper and J. P. Zubek. Effects of enriched and restricted early environments on the learning ability of bright and dull rats. *Canadian Journal of Psychology*, 1958, *12*, 159–164. Used by permission.

Can we conclude from these results that heredity alone causes maze-learning performance? No, we cannot, because these maze-learning scores were undoubtedly influenced by the environmental variable, too. True, the environment was controlled in this study, but that doesn't mean that it had no influence on the results. It only means that the influence it had was the same in both conditions of the study. If the same experiment were done in a different environment, the results might very well be different.

And this is what the researchers did. They repeated the experiment with another group of bright and dull rats, rearing these subjects in an "enriched" environment—a group cage containing ramps, mirrors, swings, marbles, barriers,

TABLE 2-2 **EFFECTS OF HEREDITY ON MAZE-LEARNING FOR RATS REARED IN ENRICHED LAB ENVIRONMENT**

	CONDITION 1		CONDITION 2
Independent variable (heredity)	Bright rats	$\neq$	Dull rats
Controlled variable (environment)	Enriched environment	=	Enriched environment
Dependent variable (mean # of errors)	111.2	=*	119.7

*p > .05.

Source: From R. M. Cooper and J. P. Zubek. Effects of enriched and restricted early environments on the learning ability of bright and dull rats. *Canadian Journal of Psychology*, 1958, *12*, 159–164. Used by permission.

slides, tunnels, bells, teeter-totters, and springboards that were set in different positions every few days. When the maze-learning of these rats was tested, the results were as shown in Table 2-2.

As we suspected, maze-learning behavior is influenced by environment as well as by heredity. While bright rats perform better than dull ones when both have been reared in a normal environment, there is no significant difference between the performances of the two groups when reared in an enriched environment.

While it is possible, through inbreeding, to obtain large numbers of animals with almost identical heredity, it is of course impossible to do this with humans. Therefore studies of the influence of heredity and environment on human behavior must be designed somewhat differently than animal studies. The main difference is that in human studies the unit is not the individual subject, but a *pair* of subjects. For example, one researcher (Kallmann, 1946) wanted to find out to what extent one particular kind of mental illness—schizophrenia—is influenced by heredity. He began by obtaining records on a large number of schizophrenic individuals, each of whom had an identical twin. He then obtained information on their twins, as well as on any nontwin brothers and sisters, to find out how often they, too, showed a history of schizophrenia. His findings are shown in Table 2-3.

TABLE 2-3   EFFECTS OF HEREDITY ON SCHIZOPHRENIA

	CONDITION 1		CONDITION 2
INDEPENDENT VARIABLE (similarity of heredity)	Pairs of identical twins	$\neq$	Pairs of non-twin siblings
CONTROLLED VARIABLE (similarity of environment)	Most pairs reared in same family	$=$	Most pairs reared in same family
DEPENDENT VARIABLE (similarity on schizophrenia)	% *schizophrenic* 1st members of pairs: 100% 2nd members of pairs: 85%		% *schizophrenic* 1st members of pairs: 100% 2nd members of pairs: 14%

Source: After F. J. Kallmann. The genetic theory of schizophrenia. *American Journal of Psychiatry*, 1946, *103*, 309–322.

These findings show that individuals who are exactly the same in heredity (identical twins) also tend to be very similar with regard to schizophrenia; and subjects who are less similar in heredity (nontwin brothers and sisters) are less similar to each other with regard to schizophrenia. The conclusion, then, is that heredity does seem to influence schizophrenia. These findings, of course, do not rule out the possibility that environmental factors may also influence schizophrenia.

QUESTION 3.   Design a human study to find out whether environment influences schizophrenia. Diagram your study below, showing the independent variable, control variable, and dependent variable.

Now that the general point has been made that all behavior is influenced by both heredity and environment, we will discuss some important illustrations of this principle: instinct, maturational readiness, and the critical period.

Instinct

Instinctive behavior is (1) stereotyped behavior (2) that is more complex than a single muscle movement. Although (3) the behavior itself is not learned, (4) the stimuli that control it may be influenced by experience. For instance, the nut-burying behavior of the squirrel is instinctive. If squirrels raised apart from other squirrels are given nuts for the first time, they go through a fixed sequence of burying behaviors, even if they happen to be on a bare, hard floor. First they make digging movements, then they push the nut down with their nose, and finally they make covering motions. This burying behavior is stereotyped in the sense that it runs its course in a rigid, mechanical way, even when it serves no purpose. It is clearly more complex than a single muscle movement. And it is unlearned, as shown by the fact that it occurs without previous experience with nuts or with other squirrels.

FIGURE 2-3.   Migrating ducks, an example of instinctive behavior.

Although no one has yet found that experience influences the stimuli controlling nut-burying behavior in squirrels, there are instinctive behaviors for which such an environmental influence has been found. One example is the migratory behavior of the indigo bunting, a songbird that spends the summer in the Eastern United States and the winter in the Caribbean. An interesting fact is that if this bird is caged, during migration seasons it becomes restless at night and hops toward the side of the cage that corresponds to its normal direction of migration—south in the fall and north in the spring. Therefore, in the research we are about to describe, the investigator (Emlen, 1972) was able to use the direction in which the bunting hopped in its cage as a measure of the direction of its migratory tendency.

In one of his early studies, this researcher put some buntings under the artificial sky of a planetarium during August and September. He found that the birds tended to hop toward the southern part of this artificial sky, no matter whether this was actually south or north. Apparently, then, the birds told direction by the visible pattern of stars. But this is not very surprising; many instinctive behaviors require environmental stimuli to direct them, and it has long been suggested that star patterns might direct the flight of migrating birds.

The next question was how the ability to navigate by the stars develops in these birds: is it innate or is it influenced somehow by experience? To find out, the same investigator took ten baby buntings and raised them in the laboratory so that they never saw the sun or the stars. Another eight birds were, during rearing, exposed to the normal night sky of August and September. At the end of the rearing period, both groups of birds were tested for direction of hopping under the planetarium sky, which this time was oriented to correspond with true directions. The surprising finding was that none of the birds raised without seeing the night sky hopped in any consistent direction, while seven of the eight birds that had received this experience hopped in the normal southerly direction. These results clearly indicate that, contrary to the common belief that instincts cannot be influenced by environmental factors, the celestial stimuli that control migration in buntings depend upon experience for their effectiveness.

QUESTION 4.   Suppose that you were studying the striking behavior of rattlesnakes. What four things would you have to find to be true of this behavior before you could conclude that it was instinctive?

One special kind of instinctive behavior that zoologists and psychologists have become intrigued with in recent years is the attachments that many kinds of baby animals normally form to other members of their own species. For example, baby ducklings and goslings normally follow their mother wherever she goes, and baby animals of other kinds also stay close to their mothers. And when these animals become adult, they of course make sexual responses toward other members of their species.

These following and sexual behaviors are definitely instinctive: they are stereotyped, complex, and unlearned. But for some species, the stimuli that produce these behaviors are not innately determined. Instead, for these species, controlling stimuli are acquired through a process known as imprinting. *In imprinting, the animal will become permanently attached to whatever kind of object (within certain limits) it experiences first during a certain early period of its life.* Consider, for example, the behavior of the Mallard duckling. Normally, the first object the duckling sees is its own mother, and it therefore becomes imprinted to her and follows her. But what if the duckling were isolated from its mother and instead presented with a wooden decoy, or a box, or a human? When this experiment is carried out, the duckling becomes imprinted to the substitute object and remains "attached" to that kind of object ever afterward, even in preference to its own mother.

Another example of imprinting is described in the following account:

A number of years ago I was given a female lamb taken from its mother at birth. My wife and I raised it on the bottle for the first 10 days of life and then placed it out in the pasture with a small flock of domestic sheep. As might have been expected from folklore, the lamb became attached to people and followed the persons who fed it. More surprisingly, the lamb remained independent of the rest of the flock when we restored it to the pasture. Three years later it was still following an independent grazing pattern. In addition, when it was mated and had lambs of its own it became a very indifferent mother, allowing its offspring to nurse but showing no concern when the lamb moved away with the other members of the flock (Scott, 1945).

QUESTION 5.   Some children took over the feeding of a nestful of baby birds when the birds' mother disappeared. (1) Under what conditions would you expect the birds to become imprinted to the children? (2) What would you expect some of the effects of such imprinting to be?

Do instincts occur in humans? Some scientists have suggested that they do: for example, Lorenz (1966), among others, argues that man's aggressiveness is an instinct. However, these scientists seem to mean something different than we do by the term instinct. It seems unlikely that the kind of stereotyped, unlearned behavior described in our definition will be found in man, whose behavior is generally so flexible and so strongly influenced by learning.

Maturational Readiness

Organisms are more susceptible to certain environmental influences at some maturational stages than at others. "Maturational readiness" is one case of this kind, and the "critical period" is another.

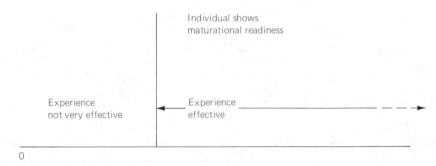

FIGURE 2-4. Maturational readiness.

Maturational readiness means that there are particular points in maturation when the organism becomes ready to benefit from particular kinds of training experiences. Before these points are reached the training will be of little value, but any time afterward it will be effective. This is diagrammed in Figure 2-4.

Some behaviors that seem to depend on maturational readiness are the swimming of salamander tadpoles, the walking of human infants, and the reading of children. One well-known study (Gesell and Thompson, 1941) dealt with stair-climbing in two female identical twins, referred to in the research reports as T and C. When the study began, T and C were about 11 months old and approximately equal in general motor development. Then began a six-week period during which twin T was given a daily 10-minute practice session climbing a set of four stairs that the experimenters had set up in the nursery. During this first period, C received no stair-climbing practice at all. When both twins were tested at the end of the six weeks, T climbed the stairs in 25 seconds, while C could do no more than put one knee on the first tread. Then T's training stopped, and it was C's turn to receive training. At the end of only two weeks of training, C was scaling the steps in just 10 seconds. Why was C able to climb so much faster after only two weeks of training than T could after six weeks of training? Undoubtedly it was because C was several weeks older when her training began and more maturationally ready to benefit from it.

The concept of maturational readiness has also been applied to reading. In one of the classic studies on reading readiness (Morphett and Washburne, 1931), 141 first-grade children were given an intelligence test at the beginning of the school year and their mental ages determined. The group was then placed in a reading program and after six months their progress was measured. The researchers found a positive relationship between children's mental age at the beginning of the year and the degree to which they had benefitted from the reading program. Figure 2-5 shows what percentages showed satisfactory reading progress at the time of testing.

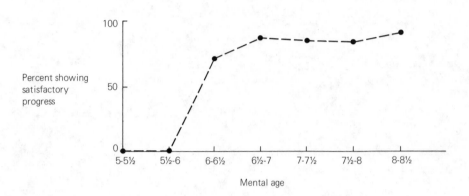

FIGURE 2-5.   Reading readiness. (Morphett and Washburne, 1931.)

These authors concluded that it is not worthwhile to teach reading until a child reaches the mental age of 6.5. From what we know about the interplay of heredity and environment, however, we would expect that environmental factors, such as the particular reading program used, would also influence the time at which a child learns to read. And more recently, in fact, reading programs have been developed that successfully teach reading to children with mental ages lower than 6.5.

QUESTION 6.   The concept of maturational readiness can also be applied to toilet training. With this in mind, complete each of the following statements.

A. It has been found that when mothers begin bowel training very early (before the child is five months old), the training takes about: (Circle one.)

1. Five months
2. Ten months

B. It has been found that when mothers begin bowel training very late (at 20 months or later), the training takes about: (Circle one.)

1. Five months
2. Ten months

Critical Periods

We have seen that the concept of maturational readiness emphasizes a lower limit: if certain environmental factors occur before the beginning of the appropriate maturational period, they will not have much influence on development because they occur too early. In contrast, *a critical period has both a lower*

FIGURE 2-6.   The notion of a critical period.

and an upper limit: if certain environmental factors occur either too early or
too late in maturation, they will not have much influence on development. This
is illustrated in Figure 2-6.

One kind of behavioral phenomenon for which a critical period is important is imprinting. This was clearly demonstrated by a study (Hess, 1959) in which
the experimenter attempted to imprint mallard ducklings of various ages to something other than the usual mother duck. He kept the ducklings completely isolated
for the first few hours after hatching, then set them on a circular runway around
which a wooden model of a *male* mallard was moving, making a very unducklike
sound—"Gock, gock, gock." After this imprinting experience, each duckling was
tested by being placed halfway between the "gocking" male model and the type
of stimulus that most young ducklings follow—a model of a female duck making
a realistic call. Then the researcher observed which model the duckling moved
toward. He found that the success of imprinting, indicated by a choice of the

FIGURE 2-7.   **Puppies reacting to leash training according to their experience during the critical
period (about 3 to 10 weeks of age). At left: reaction of a puppy that had had contact with
people for one week during the peak of the critical period. At right: reaction of a puppy that
had contact only with other dogs prior to the end of the critical period. This puppy shows an
extreme fear reaction and refuses to follow. (J. P. Scott, 1962.)**

male model in the test situation, was clearly related to the age of the duckling. The training experience was most effective for ducklings between 13 and 16 hours of age. They chose the male model much more often than either younger or older ducklings did, showing that there is a critical period for this behavior.

There also seems to be a critical period for the development of normal social behavior in monkeys, which includes defense against attack, sexual behavior, and caring for an infant by a mother (Harlow and Harlow, 1962). Although there is no known lower limit for this critical period, there is an upper limit of about six months of age. A monkey isolated during early life will, if he is placed in the company of other monkeys before he is six months old, eventually develop normal social behavior. However, if social experience is delayed beyond this limit, no amount of later experience can make him normal.

QUESTION 7.   Indicate whether the following case is or is not an example of a critical period by circling the appropriate phrase after it.

In the development of the human embryo inside the uterus, abnormal environmental conditions tend to do the greatest damage to whatever kinds of tissue are currently growing most rapidly. For example, German measles is most likely to damage the hearing apparatus of the embryo if the mother catches this disease during the second or third month of pregnancy, a time when the hearing apparatus is growing especially quickly. (Circle one of the following sentences.)

1.   This is an example of a critical period.
2.   This is not an example of a critical period.

Having described how heredity, environment, and adaptation work together to produce developmental trends, we now turn to the trends themselves. How can developmental trends be measured, and what kinds of trends are generally found?

DEVELOPMENTAL TRENDS

Methods of Measuring Developmental Trends

There are two good ways of measuring trends in development: the longitudinal method and the cross-sectional method. *The longitudinal method is to follow the same people over a period of time, applying the measure to them at two or more different ages. The cross-sectional method is to apply the measure to different people of different ages at the same time.*

An example should make the distinction between these two methods clearer. Suppose a psychologist wanted to find out how children's feelings toward

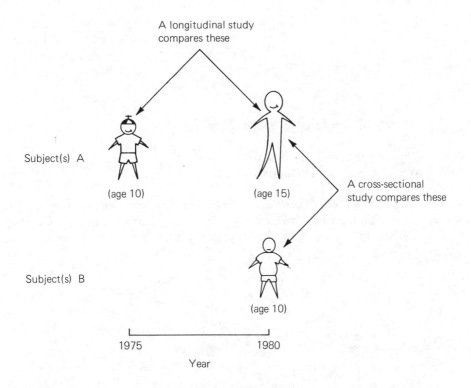

A longitudinal study
compares these

Subject(s) A

(age 10)   (age 15)

A cross-sectional
study compares these

Subject(s) B

(age 10)

1975   1980

Year

FIGURE 2-8.   The longitudinal versus the cross-sectional method of studying development.

their parents change from age 10 to age 15. Applying the longitudinal method, he would select a group of 10-year-olds and measure their feelings toward their parents, then wait five years until the same subjects reached age 15, at which time their feelings toward their parents would be measured once again. The cross-sectional approach would be to find a group of 10-year-olds and another group of 15-year-olds, then apply the measure to both groups at the same time. This is shown in diagrammatic form in Figure 2-8.

QUESTION 8.   Identify each of the following studies by writing "longitudinal" or "cross-sectional" in front of it.

_____   A study was made on the development of self-esteem from age 5 to age 10, which took one year to complete.

_____   A study was done in which the number of intelligence-test questions answered correctly by a group of 20-year-olds was measured. Then, 10 years later, the same people were found and given the same measure again.

_____ A developmental psychologist measured the extent to which eight different groups of children—first-, second-, third-, and fourth-grade boys and girls—preferred "masculine" and "feminine" toys.

Kinds of Developmental Trends

Probably the most general trends in development are those toward (1) quantitative change and (2) qualitative change.

QUANTITATIVE CHANGE *The development of many physical and psychological characteristics follows a typical growth curve, which rises sharply at first, then gradually levels off.* The general shape of this growth curve is shown in Figure 2-9.

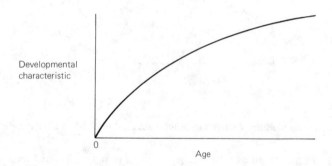

Developmental
characteristic

0   Age

FIGURE 2-9. **The typical growth curve.**

One example is the growth of weight in humans from their beginning in the mother's uterus, until they reach full size at about age 25. This particular growth curve, shown in Figure 2-10, has a dip in the middle that is not typical of growth curves in general.

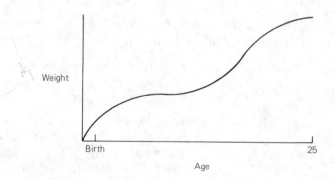

Weight

Birth   25

Age

FIGURE 2-10. **The growth of human weight with age.**

QUESTION 9.   The development of intelligence (number of intelligence-test questions answered correctly, not IQ) follows a typical growth curve. That being so, which of the following trends is most likely to be true of intelligence? (Circle trend A, B, or C.)

MEAN # OF INTELLIGENCE-TEST ITEMS CORRECT

AGE	TREND A	TREND B	TREND C
10	50	50	50
20	150	100	60
30	190	150	100
40	200	200	200

QUALITATIVE CHANGE   That development involves growth is obvious. Not quite as obvious is the fact that development also involves qualitative change. That is, development is not something simply getting bigger, like a balloon that keeps the same form even when inflated. Instead, there are important changes in form and organization that occur during developmental growth, as when a tadpole develops into a frog. Two ways in which the developing organism changes qualitatively are through (1) differentiation and (2) moving from one stage to another.

Differentiation   *Differentiation is the process of one, unitary entity separating into several relatively distinct and independent entities.*
One kind of differentiation occurs in the physical development of the human infant. In its early life, the infant will make a total body response to a stimulus. If something touches its left hand, for example, it responds by moving its whole body. Later, when the infant has developed further, its responses are more differentiated; that is, each part of its body responds independently. If the left hand is stimulated now, only that hand will move.
Differentiation also occurs in the development of skills. The budding basketball player begins by learning one, basic lay-up shot. Later, differentiation occurs when he develops several different variations on this basic shot: a lay-up in which the shot is delayed, a lay-up in which the shot is faked on one side, then made on the other, and so on.

QUESTION 10.   The concept of differentiation also applies to the development of the young child's emotions (Bridges, 1932). That being the case, in which of the following ways must emotion develop? (Circle 1, 2, or 3.)

1. In the newborn, the only emotion is general excitement. Later, the positive (delight, affection) and negative (anger, fear) emotions become distinct.

2.   In the newborn, there seem to be both positive and negative emotions. Later, these merge into general excitement.

3.   In the newborn, there seem to be both positive and negative emotions, and there is no change in this emotional repertoire as the individual grows older.

Stages   Another kind of qualitative change occurs when the organism moves from one stage to another. Take, for example, the stages of intellectual development. From one point of view intelligence grows in a continuous way: the older the individual gets, the more intelligence-test items he answers correctly. However, closer inspection reveals that there are some sharp differences between the *kinds* of intelligence shown by people in different periods of life. The differences between intellectual stages have been described by the famous Swiss psychologist Jean Piaget (Pee-ah-*jay*), who has devoted most of his life to research on this topic. We will describe a few of them below.

According to Piaget, a sharp intellectual change that typically occurs during the second year is the development of "object identity." *A child who has developed object identity perceives objects as stable in two ways: (a) he realizes that an object that looks somewhat different because it is seen from two different viewpoints is in fact the same object, and (b) he realizes that an object that disappears from sight does not stop existing.* Piaget's observations led him to claim that very young children do not have either of these kinds of object identity and must develop them. What kinds of evidence does Piaget have for this claim? Here are two examples. Piaget once noticed his 11-month-old daughter, who was sitting in a child's swing, looking down at her foot. First she looked straight down at it through the leg hole of the swing, then she looked at it over the side; back and forth she went from one viewpoint to the other. Piaget concluded that she was getting used to the idea that the appearance of an object (her foot) depends upon one's viewpoint, and thus was developing the first aspect of object identity mentioned above. At about the same time, Piaget noticed his daughter engrossed in play with a toy duck. Suddenly the duck became hidden under a sheet, and the infant immediately turned to other activities. She made no effort to retrieve the duck, although it would have been easy to do. Piaget concluded from this observation that when the duck disappeared from her sight, it no longer existed as far as she was concerned, and that is why she didn't try to recover it. In other words, she had not yet developed the second aspect of object identity.

QUESTION 11.

A.   What will happen when a child who has not yet developed object identity sees its uncle play the following trick: he picks up a ball, moves his hand behind a footstool, and when his hand emerges on the other side, there is no ball in it. (Circle 1, 2, or 3.)

1.   The child will look behind the footstool.

2. The child will make no attempt to get the ball.

3. The child will look to see if his uncle is hiding the ball in his hand.

B. What will happen if the same child is used to seeing a far-away clock tower from his house. Then one day while he is out for a ride in his stroller, he sees the same tower from close up. How will he probably react? (Circle 1 or 2.)

1. As though he recognized the tower.

2. As though he did not recognize the tower.

At about age seven another sharp intellectual change occurs. This is the development of conservation, of which there are several kinds that develop at slightly different times. The type we shall describe is called conservation of quantity. *A child has developed conservation of quantity when he realizes that changing the shape of a substance does not change its quantity.* Piaget has demonstrated, by an experiment that has become famous, that children under the age of about seven do not understand this. Two tumblers (A and B in Figure 2-11) are filled with water until the child is satisfied that they contain exactly the same quantity of water. Then, in front of the child, all the water in tumbler A is poured into a tall, thin container, C, and the child is asked whether the amounts of water in B and C are the same or different.

The child who has not yet developed conservation of quantity reacts to this simple problem in a way that is rather amazing, because it is so different

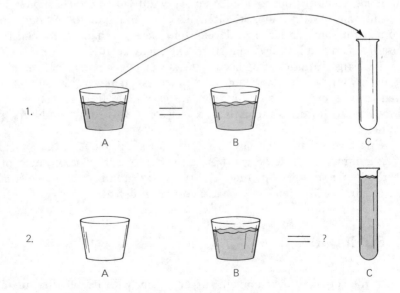

FIGURE 2-11. **Piaget's experiment on conservation of quantity.**

from the adult reaction. For one thing, he looks long and hard at the two containers, as though he thought it necessary to mentally calculate the volume of water in them in order to solve the problem. For another, he usually gives the wrong answer. Either he says that there is more water in C because it is taller or he says that there is more in B because it is wider.

Most children over seven, in contrast, react to this problem just as an adult would. They give the right answer with hardly a glance at the containers.

QUESTION 12.   A child who has not yet achieved conservation of quantity gets a present of a box full to the brim of modeling clay. He takes it all out and kneads it into one huge pancake. Then it is time to put it away. Which is he more likely to think? (Circle 1 or 2.)
1.   The clay will fit perfectly in the box.
2.   The clay will be either too large or too small to fit perfectly in the box.

Of course Piaget's stage theory of intellectual development is not the only stage theory in psychology. There are many others, including Freud's theory of personality development, but they will not be discussed here.

Individual Differences in Development

Although psychologists often focus their attention on average developmental trends, you must not conclude that every individual does or should develop at the same rate. As psychologists often have to point out to anxious mothers, it is normal for some children to develop more slowly than others and there is no cause for worry unless development is extremely retarded.

The large variation that occurs in rate of development can be observed clearly in any first-grade classroom. The new first-grade teacher should not be surprised to find, even for children who are very close in age, great differences in ability to read, to dress themselves, to get along with other children, and in every other way.

A few years later, the boys who are just reaching age nine and playing their first summer of Little League baseball differ greatly in how much of their growth they have attained, in their ability to pay attention to the instructions of their coach, and in their emotional maturity in defeat.

SUMMARY

In the course of development the organism, with its heredity, its maturation, and its previous adaptations, interacts with the environment, and this interaction produces further adaptations in the organism.

Although every behavior is due to both heredity and environment, it is possible to separate their effects to some extent using the research tools described in Chapter 1. Some examples of the close partnership of heredity and environment are instinctive behavior (some of which is subject to imprinting), maturational readiness, and the critical period.

The developmental trends that result from heredity, environment, and adaptation can be studied by two methods—the longitudinal and the cross-sectional. Such studies show that quantitatively, many characteristics develop according to a typical growth curve. Development also involves qualitative changes, such as differentiation, and a progression from one stage to another as exemplified in the development of object identity and conservation of quantity.

BEHAVIOR TO EXPLAIN

Some people seem to have zero conscience. For example, Herman Goering, the Nazi leader, showed sadistic brutality toward his mother and sisters when he was a boy, and, in adulthood, toward the inmates of the concentration camps. Furthermore, he showed no guilt about his brutal acts.

At the other extreme are individuals who have extremely strong consciences. They take great pains not to hurt anyone in the slightest and become distraught when they imagine that they have accidentally done so. How can these differences in strength of conscience be explained?

1. Think of all the principles you can that might help to explain the strength of a person's conscience.

2. State an hypothesis involving a developmental explanation of strength of conscience.

3. Describe a study that could be done to test your hypothesis, including both the design and the measuring instruments you would use.

chapter three

Learning and Cognitive Explanations

Many psychologists see the adaptive processes as a series of stairs, each one built upon those below it. The lowest stair is simple stimulus-response learning. Higher stairs represent more and more complex adaptive processes, such as language, memory, and problem-solving. These latter are called cognitive processes, because they involve thinking.

LEARNING

It is amazing what organisms can learn. Consider circus performers: the trapeze artists who arrive at the same spot at exactly the same instant; the juggler who twirls a half-dozen plates simultaneously without dropping one; the acrobat who leaps into the air, spins like a wheel, and lands squarely atop his partner's

49

shoulders; the seal that blows a series of horns to play "God Bless America."
All these behaviors are learned; most people (or seals) could probably learn them,
if they practiced enough.

FIGURE 3-1. **An example of learned behavior. Photograph by Harold M. Lambert. Frederick
Lewis.**

But learning is not only a matter of acquiring tricks. Organisms also learn their everyday ways of adapting to the world. The wife of one of the authors recently learned to avoid a certain skating rink, because she felt nauseated whenever she went there. Last winter her husband learned to leave his car windows slightly open after using the car on a cold day to prevent frost from forming on the inside of the windshield.

The term learning is abstract; learning is a mental process and no one can look inside the mind of another to see learning occurring there. There are, however, certain observable variables that are usually linked to this inner mental process. One of the major variables thought to produce learning is practice. And the behavioral result of learning is usually considered to be a change in behavior. Thus, in observable terms, *learning may be defined as (1) a change in behavior, for better or worse, (2) that follows practice.* Let's see how this definition fits the above examples. The woman's avoidance of the skating rink resulted from one occasion when she discovered a puddle of vomit in a corner of the rink and immediately experienced a strong feeling of nausea. This was the practice or experience that led to the learning. The resulting changes in behavior are two: first, she tried to avoid that skating rink for the rest of the winter; and second, she felt some degree of nausea the few times she did return there. In the second example, the practice was the man's experimenting with leaving his car windows open a crack when he arrived at work in a cold winter morning and finding that the windshield no longer was frosted over when he got in the car at 5 P.M. The behavioral change was that the man began leaving his windows open a few inches whenever he parked his car in the winter.

Although learning usually involves changes for the better, this is not always so; we can learn bad habits as well as good ones.

QUESTION 1.   According to the above definition, which of the following are examples of learning? (Check each one that is.)

_____   A little girl had several bad spills on her new bicycle. So her father put on a pair of training wheels and she rode the bike that way for a few weeks. When the training wheels were removed a month later, the little girl rode it without falling at all.

_____   A piano student made numerous mistakes on Chopin's "Polonaise" at his weekly lesson, so he played the piece 10 times a day during the following week. At his next lesson, he hit even more wrong notes in the "Polonaise" than he had the week before.

_____   A college student made lots of vocabulary mistakes during one Spanish class. Discouraged, she didn't look at her vocabulary at all before the next class. At the next class meeting, she made no mistakes at all in vocabulary.

Conditioning

Conditioning is simple, stimulus-response learning. The principles of conditioning are particularly useful to the person who wishes to change someone's behavior, because these principles are well understood and relatively convenient to work with. For that reason, conditioning principles—and related principles of learning—have been widely used by such change agents as parents, psychotherapists, teachers, and animal trainers.

Psychologists have studied two types of conditioning: classical and operant.

CLASSICAL CONDITIONING   Classical conditioning is so called because it was the *first* kind of conditioning to be extensively studied—by the famous Russian physiologist, Ivan Pavlov. In one of his early experiments, Pavlov wanted to find out whether a dog could be conditioned to salivate when a bell rang. Many times in succession Pavlov first rang the bell, then immediately put some meat powder into the dog's mouth. On each of these trials, Pavlov measured how many drops of saliva were produced by the dog's salivary glands after the bell rang, but before the meat powder was given. This salivation was a learned response to the bell itself. As the conditioning trials continued, Pavlov found an increase in salivation to the bell, as shown in Figure 3-3.

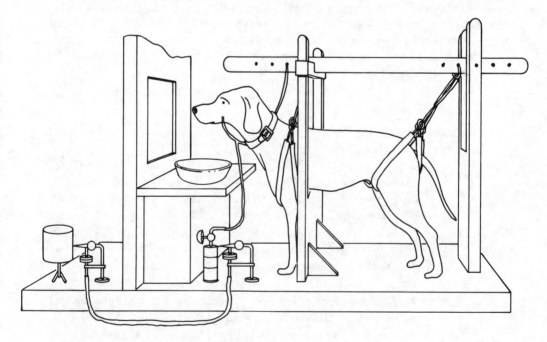

FIGURE 3-2. **Pavlov's apparatus for salivary conditioning.**

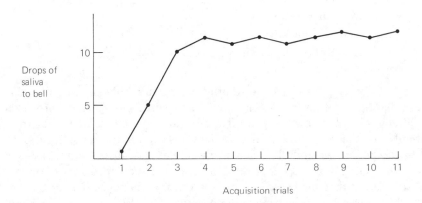

FIGURE 3-3. **The salivary response during classical conditioning.**

This salivary conditioning study may be diagrammed as in Figure 3-4. The solid arrow in that figure indicates a stimulus-response connection that existed at the beginning of the study; the dotted arrow indicates a connection that was learned during the study.

FIGURE 3-4. **Diagrammatic representation of classical conditioning.**

Some terms used in classical conditioning are unconditioned stimulus and unconditioned response, conditioned stimulus and conditioned response. The unconditioned stimulus is the one that produces the response at the beginning of training, and the unconditioned response is the response to it. The conditioned stimulus is the one that later—after conditioning has occurred—comes to produce the response, and the conditioned response is the response to it. Figure 3-4 shows how these terms apply to Pavlov's salivary conditioning experiment.

QUESTION 2.   Classical conditioning can be demonstrated with the knee-jerk response. In such a study, the procedure on each trial is: (1) present a stimulus, such as a flash of light; then (2) tap the knee to produce the knee-jerk. One way to find out whether conditioning has occurred is to omit the tap to the knee on one trial. If the knee-jerk occurs on this trial, it is a response to the light alone, indicating that conditioning has taken place. Write CS (conditioned stimulus), CR, UCS, and UCR in the following spaces to identify each of the elements in knee-jerk conditioning.

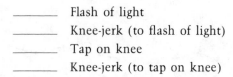

_____ Flash of light
_____ Knee-jerk (to flash of light)
_____ Tap on knee
_____ Knee-jerk (to tap on knee)

Of course, classical conditioning occurs not only in the laboratory but also in real life, whenever a CS and a UCS are paired enough times. For example, an elderly lady we know stepped off a curb and started to cross the street. She suddenly saw that a car was headed straight toward her. In that split second when the brakes screeched and she tried to scramble back to the curb, she was sick with terror. Luckily she was not hit. However, the incident had a curious effect. The lady found that she became distinctly uneasy whenever she put on the dress she had been wearing at the time of her near-accident. Whereas classical conditioning often requires many trials, in this case it apparently occurred in a single trial. This example is diagrammed in Figure 3-5.

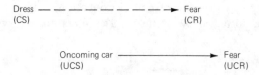

FIGURE 3-5. Classical conditioning of a fear response.

Here is the general rule for classical conditioning: _to classically condition a subject to make a new response to a conditioned stimulus, run a series of trials in which you first present the conditioned stimulus, then present an unconditioned stimulus that produces the desired response. After this procedure has been repeated over enough trials, the conditioned stimulus itself will produce the response._ Although there is no limit to the stimuli that can be used as conditioned stimuli in classical conditioning, the only responses that can be used are those for which unconditioned stimuli are available. This means that good study habits, bar-pressing, and other voluntary behaviors cannot be taught through classical conditioning because there are no unconditioned stimuli that produce them.

QUESTION 3.

A. Shock produces the response of feeling uncomfortable. Describe what a psychologist would have to do to classically condition an overweight patient to feel uncomfortable whenever he sees fattening foods.

B. Identify each of the elements of the classical conditioning situation you described in (a) by writing it in the appropriate space below.

CS _____

CR _____

UCS _____

UCR _____

OPERANT CONDITIONING   The contemporary American psychologist B. F. Skinner has conducted numerous experiments in operant conditioning. One of the best known is training a rat enclosed in a "Skinner box" to press a bar.

FIGURE 3-6. **B. F. Skinner, 1904–   Culver Pictures.**

The procedure is to put a hungry rat into the box, then wait for him to press the bar that protrudes from one wall. In his explorations of the box, the rat will eventually press the bar by accident. When it does, a pellet of food falls into a nearby food trough. The result is that, as time goes by, the rat presses the bar (and receives food) more and more frequently.

An automatic recorder is typically used to record the subject's responses during operant conditioning. In this device, a strip of paper moves continuously underneath a pen and every time a response occurs the pen jumps upward a step, producing the kind of record shown in Figure 3-7. When the subject is not responding, the pen remains stationary; it never moves downward. *On this kind of record—called a cumulative graph—the steepness of the slope indicates how frequently the subject is responding.* The cumulative curve shown in Figure 3-7 is typical of operant conditioning; the slope of the curve gets steeper and steeper as conditioning continues, indicating that the subject is learning to respond more and more frequently.

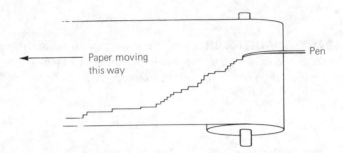

FIGURE 3-7. A cumulative graph.

QUESTION 4.   One patient in a mental hospital expressed feelings more and more frequently during the first half of his therapy hour one day, but in the latter half of the hour he expressed feelings less and less frequently. Which of the following is more likely to be the cumulative graph of this patient's expressed feelings? (Circle one graph.)

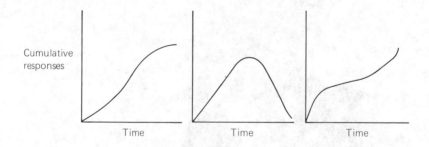

The operant conditioning of bar-pressing behavior may be diagrammed as in Figure 3-8.

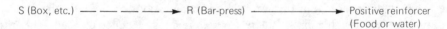

FIGURE 3-8.   Operant conditioning of bar-pressing.

Operant conditioning, too, occurs in the real world. The following is an actual example. One summer the parents of a teen-aged girl encouraged her to practice diving by telling her that every time she dove into the lake from the family cabin cruiser she could have a turn driving the boat. As a result, she dove more and more often. This example is diagrammed in Figure 3-9.

S (Boat, etc.) — — — — ➤ R (Diving) ————————➤ Positive reinforcer
                                                        (A turn driving the boat)

FIGURE 3-9. **Operant conditioning of a diving response.**

Now we will point out the basic characteristics of operant conditioing and show how they contrast with those of classical conditioning.

The Stimulus   The stimulus to which the response becomes "attached" is often difficult to identify precisely in operant conditioning, while it is very easy to identify in classical conditioning. For instance, although it's a safe bet that the bar-pressing response of the rat becomes attached to the general environment of the Skinner box, it would be difficult to specify exactly what aspects of that environment were important—the color of the walls, the texture of the floor, the degree of illumination. In classical conditioning, in contrast, the response is always conditioned to a specific conditioned stimulus, such as the bell in Pavlov's salivary conditioning experiment.

The Response   A second difference lies in the degree of control the trainer has over the response to be conditioned. The operant conditioner may simply wait for the response to occur or he may try to speed things up by instructing a (human) subject to make the response, by increasing the size of a bar so that a rat will bump into it sooner, or by other means. But he can never control the response as completely as can the classical conditioner, who is able to make the response occur whenever he wants simply by presenting the unconditioned stimulus to the subject.

The Reinforcing Stimulus   A third difference is that the operant conditioner uses rewards or punishments immediately after the subject's response, whereas no rewards and punishments are involved in classical conditioning. *In the terminology of operant conditioning, a reward is a "positive reinforcer," and a punishment is a "negative reinforcer."*

QUESTION 5.

A. List two common stimuli that are positive reinforcers for most people.

B.   List two common stimuli that are negative reinforcers for most people.

Reinforcers may be used in several different ways in operant conditioning. If a positive reinforcer is presented following each occurrence of a particular response, that response will occur more and more frequently. This is the procedure that occurred in the examples of the rat being conditioned to bar-press and the girl being conditioned to dive from the boat. On the other hand, if a positive reinforcer is regularly withdrawn following a response, that response will occur less and less frequently. An example is a mother withdrawing her son's evening television-watching privileges every time he comes home late for supper.

If a negative reinforcer is regularly presented following a response, that response will occur less and less frequently: a mother may spank her son when the boy tells her that he knocked down a smaller boy in school. However, use of punishment presents several problems, which are apparent in this example. First, punishment may have undesired side effects: the boy may become afraid of his mother, and unwilling to confide in her. Second, even if the punishment does decrease the boy's fighting at school, it will not necessarily help him to handle his anger in constructive ways. While punishment may teach organisms what *not* to do, it cannot teach them what *to* do. For this reason, many psychologists believe that punishment can lead to permanent improvement in behavior only when it is combined with positive reinforcement of desired behavior.

Another reinforcement procedure in operant conditioning is to regularly withdraw a negative reinforcer following a response; this should result in an increased frequency of that response. For example, suppose that every time a college student telephones his parents, he feels relieved of the responsibility of writing them a letter that week. If writing letters to his folks is an onerous task for this student, he will probably phone them more and more frequently.

In summary, *to use operant conditioning to train a subject to make or not to make a particular response to a stimulus, (1) wait until the response occurs in the presence of that stimulus, either with or without encouragement from you, and immediately afterward (2) present or withdraw a positive or a negative reinforcer.*

QUESTION 6.   Suppose that you wanted to condition an eyeblink response to a tone. One stimulus that will produce an eyeblink is a puff of air in the eye. One stimulus that is rewarding to the subject is an M&M candy. How would you condition this response using (1) classical conditioning and (2) operant conditioning? (Note: The eyeblink responses conditioned by these two methods will be somewhat different. The classically-conditioned eyeblink is a very rapid, reflex response. The eyeblink resulting from operant conditioning is a slower, voluntary response.)

A. Classical conditioning method:

B. Operant conditioning method:

Secondary Reinforcement

We have seen that if a bell is repeatedly paired with meat powder, a dog will become conditioned to salivate to the bell alone. In this procedure, the meat powder is a primary or unlearned UCS, sometimes called a primary reinforcer. After the salivary response to the bell has become strong, the bell itself may be used as a USC in further conditioning. That is, if this bell is paired repeatedly with some other stimulus—such as a light—the salivary response will eventually become conditioned to the light. Here the bell is a secondary reinforcer.

The general principle is this: *any stimulus can be made a reinforcer through association with a reinforcer.* This principle is of considerable practical importance in real-life operant conditioning. It means that instead of relying solely upon primary reinforcers such as food and water, which are effective only when the subject is hungry or thirsty, "trainers" may also use secondary reinforcers, such as praise, trophies, and grades, which are more widely effective.

QUESTION 7. Suppose that you are beginning to train a young puppy. So that you will not have to carry pellets of dog food (primary reinforcers) around in your pocket to use in this training, you want to make the words "good dog" into a secondary reinforcer for this puppy. How could you do this?

Shaping

Shaping is a special operant conditioning procedure that is used at the beginning of training in cases where the response to be conditioned occurs infrequently or not at all. Nearly all researchers use shaping to get the rat to begin pressing the lever in the Skinner box. Although it would be possible to use straightforward operant conditioning for this purpose, progress would be slow because untrained rats do not press the bar very often. This means that the experimenter probably would have to wait a long time before the first bar-press occurred and could be reinforced.

The shaping procedure consists of reinforcing closer and closer approximations to the desired response. Because the shaper must "play it by ear," the specific sequence of responses that is reinforced during shaping is different for different subjects. However, a typical sequence might go like this. First a rat gets a pellet of food for merely facing the bar; after this response is reinforced a half dozen or so times, it will no longer be reinforced. At this point, the rat will probably repeat this response a few more times, then make some other responses. Perhaps one of these will be touching the bar with its nose. Since this clearly is a step closer to bar-pressing, the alert shaper will reinforce this response the first time it occurs and several times thereafter. Then he will stop reinforcing this response and wait for a still-closer response to occur. After several more steps, the rat finally presses the bar. At that point, the researcher shifts to the regular operant conditioning procedure of waiting for the response to occur and then reinforcing it.

Shaping could also be applied to the problem of getting the girl to dive off the boat. In actuality, the girl's parents were able to use the straightforward operant conditioning procedure because the response did occur occasionally, giving them the opportunity of reinforcing it. But what if the response had never occurred? What if, for example, the girl had been afraid to dive off the deck because it was too high above the water? If that had happened, shaping would have been necessary. It might have gone something like this: First the parents could have had the girl dive from the rung of the boat's ladder that was right at water level. After this response had been reinforced several times, they might have had her dive from halfway up the ladder. During this stage, they would no longer reinforce dives from the lower level, but always require that the "more advanced" response occur before giving the positive reinforcer. Next, the parents might have reinforced only dives from the next-to-the-top rung of the ladder. And finally, they would reinforce only dives from the deck.

QUESTION 8.   Shaping was used to get a mental patient who had not said a word to anyone in nineteen years to talk again (Isaacs, Thomas, and Goldiamond, 1960). Sticks of chewing gum, which the patient liked very much, were used as the reinforcing stimuli. The first response that was reinforced was silent movement of the lips. After several more steps, each of which took considerable time, the patient was saying the word "gum" distinctly. After this response had been reinforced several times, the psychologist thought it was time to move on to another response.

A. Which of the following responses would it be better to reinforce next? (Circle 1 or 2.)

    1. An indistinguishable croak.

    2. The words "Give me gum, please".

B. What would the psychologist have to do in order to move on to this next response? (Check all the things he would have to do.)

_____ Reinforce the response you chose in (a) whenever it occurred.

_____ Continue reinforcing the response "gum" whenever it occurred.

_____ Use two sticks of gum as a reinforcer, instead of the one stick he was using before.

_____ Switch to candy instead of gum as the reinforcer.

Extinction and Spontaneous Recovery

Extinction is a way of weakening a previously learned response; not just any way (for example, punishment is not extinction), but only the particular way described in this section. The extinction procedure is somewhat different in classical and operant conditioning.

EXTINCTION IN CLASSICAL CONDITIONING   *A response that was acquired through classical conditioning is extinguished by continuing to present the conditioned stimulus, but no longer following it with the unconditioned stimulus. The eventual result is that the response stops occurring to the conditioned stimulus.*

To extinguish the dog's salivary response to the bell, Pavlov continued ringing the bell from time to time, but no longer presented the meat powder afterward (Figure 3-10). The result was that fewer and fewer drops of saliva occurred after the bell (Figure 3-11).

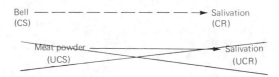

FIGURE 3-10. **Procedure for extinguishing a response acquired through classical contitioning.**

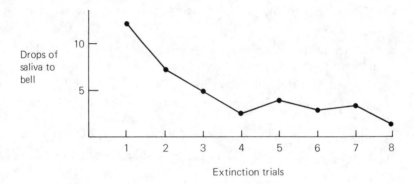

FIGURE 3-11.   Results of the extinction procedure.

QUESTION 9.   How would you attempt to extinguish the elderly woman's conditioned fear response to the dress she was wearing when she was almost run over? (Circle 1 or 2 in each pair of alternatives below.)

A.   1.   Continue showing her the dress.
        2.   Put the dress out of her sight.

B.   1.   Continue reminding her of the near-accident.
        2.   Avoid reminding her of the near-accident.

C.   1.   Give her a painful electric shock whenever she shows fear of the dress.
        2.   Do not use any punishment.

EXTINCTION IN OPERANT CONDITIONING   *A response that was acquired through operant conditioning is extinguished by allowing the response to continue to occur but no longer reinforcing it..*

To extinguish bar-pressing behavior, one should allow the rat to continue pressing the bar but no longer give it food when it does (Figure 3-12). The result should be that the rat presses the bar less and less frequently (Figure 3-13).

FIGURE 3-12.   Procedure for extinguishing a response acquired through operant conditioning.

Cumulative responses

Time during extinction

FIGURE 3-13. **Results of the extinction procedure.**

What about the girl who learned to dive off the boat? Her parents could have extinguished her diving behavior by continuing to go out in the boat with her, thus permitting the diving to occur but no longer reinforcing it. If other reinforcers had become important in the situation—e.g., if the girl had learned to enjoy the praise that followed each dive—then they too would have to be removed before the response would extinguish.

QUESTION 10. A small boy cried when his parents left him alone in his bedroom at night. At first the parents unwittingly reinforced this crying behavior by returning to comfort him whenever it occurred. As you would expect from what you know about operant conditioning, the youngster cried more and more often at bedtime and longer and longer each time. Finally the parents decided that, in order to keep their sanity, they had to try to extinguish their son's bedtime crying. How should they go about this?

A. Circle 1 or 2.

　1.　Move his bed to the guest room, where he didn't cry as much.

　2.　Leave his bed where it was.

B. Circle 1, 2, or 3.

　1.　Comfort him when he cried at bedtime.

　2.　Ignore him when he cried at bedtime.

　3.　Spank him when he cried at bedtime.

SPONTANEOUS RECOVERY　　The extinction curve is not all downhill. *Whenever the subject whose behavior is being extinguished is given a rest period, the response recovers some, but not all, of its lost strength. This is called* *spontaneous recovery.* For example, when a dog whose salivary response is being extinguished is placed back in the apparatus at the beginning of each day, its salivation to the CS is somewhat greater than it was at the end of the previous day's trials. (See Figure 3-14)

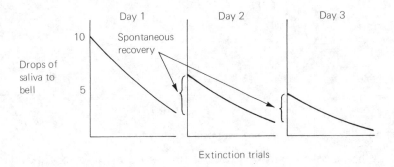

FIGURE 3-14. **Spontaneous recovery of a classically conditioned response.**

The same reaction occurs when a researcher extinguishes a rat's bar-pressing behavior. Every morning when the animal is put back in the Skinner box, its rate of bar-pressing is initially somewhat higher than it was at the end of the previous day's extinction trials. (See Figure 3-15.)

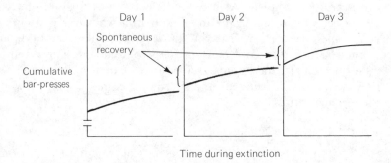

FIGURE 3-15. **Spontaneous recovery of a response acquired through operant conditioning.**

To take an example from real life, if our elderly woman succeeds in extinguishing her fear of the dress she was wearing at the time of her near-accident, she should not be surprised if this fear response recurs later on. But this is no reason to become discouraged. If she will simply repeat the extinction procedure several more times, she will eventually extinguish the response so completely that it will no longer recover spontaneously.

QUESTION 11.   Suppose that a student is trying to extinguish his roommate's practical jokes by simply not reacting—either negatively or positively—when they occur. At first, the roommate played about ten practical jokes a week, but after several months of extinction, the rate had decreased to about one a week. Then came Christmas vacation. During the first week after vacation, how many practical jokes did the roommate probably play? (Circle one answer.)

0

1

3

10

Intermittent Reinforcement in Operant Conditioning

Of course there is no statute that says a trainer must always use continuous reinforcement—that is, reinforcement for every single correct response. In fact, as we will soon see, there is an important advantage, especially in the later stages of conditioning, in using intermittent reinforcement—reinforcement for only some of the correct responses.

There are many different ways in which intermittent reinforcements may be scheduled. One way is to deliver the reinforcer after a set number of responses has occurred. Another is to reinforce the first response that occurs after a set time period. Although this procedure does have some effects in classical conditioning, its main usefulness seems to be in operant conditioning. *In operant conditioning, intermittent positive reinforcement during acquisition has the advantage of increasing the number of trials it takes the subject to stop responding during subsequent extinction.* Or, as psychologists usually put it, "intermittent reinforcement increases resistance to extinction." One possible explanation for this is that the intermittently reinforced subject is not expecting reinforcement as frequently as the continuously reinforced subject, so that when extinction begins, it takes him longer to realize that reinforcement has stopped.

For example, suppose that an experimenter continuously reinforced the bar-pressing of the rats in group A, but reinforced every third bar-press of the rats in group B. Then, after using these schedules of reinforcement for several days, the researcher began the extinction procedure. The result would probably be that the bar-pressing of group A would extinguish more quickly than that of group B.

An apt example from real life is that of the compulsive gambler. His gambling has been reinforced (by winning) only intermittently, which is probably one reason this behavior is not extinguished by long losing streaks.

FIGURE 3-16. Behavior learned under intermittent reinforcement is slow to extinguish. Photograph by Jay Florian Mitchell. Frederic Lewis.

For maximum efficiency, intermittent reinforcement should be used only during the later stages of operant conditioning. In the beginning every response should be reinforced; later, after the response is occurring frequently, the trainer can switch to intermittent reinforcement, reinforcing perhaps every third response or perhaps the first response that occurs after every one-minute period. Still later the trainer might reinforce every fifth response or the first response that occurs after every two-minute period. In this way reinforcement can gradually be made to occur less and less often.

This procedure was used by the parents of the girl who spent the summer diving off the family boat. At first her parents let her drive the boat after every single dive. Later they gradually increased the number of times she had to dive into the water before they would give her the wheel.

QUESTION 12. Young John was an incessant talker. Once he talked to a psychologist for 17 minutes without taking a single pause as long as three seconds. At the request of John's mother, the psychologist decided to try using operant conditioning to decrease John's long-windedness. He found that John, although not much interested in candy or ice cream, was really "turned on" by caps. So the psychologist decided to use a roll of caps as the reinforcing stimulus. (It is difficult to understand why he didn't use just a few caps for each reinforcement, instead of an entire roll.) The response he decided to reinforce was that of pausing for at least three seconds during conversation (Whaley, Sibley, and Risley, 1971).

A. Which of the following should the psychologist do during the early conditioning trials? (Circle 1, 2, or 3.)

1. Give John a roll of caps after every three-second pause.
2. Give John a roll of caps after every other three-second pause.
3. Give John a roll of caps after every tenth three-second pause.

B. Later in conditioning, the psychologist decided to switch to intermittent reinforcement. Which of the above three schedules did he probably use in the next stage of conditioning? (Circle 1, 2, or 3.)

1.
2.
3.

QUESTION 13. In the operant conditioning of bar-pressing, as well as of many other responses, all three of the procedures listed below are typically used. What is the order in which these would have to be used? (Indicate their order by writing 1, 2, or 3 in front of each one below.)

_____ Continuous reinforcement
_____ Shaping
_____ Intermittent reinforcement

Stimulus Generalization

If learning were completely specific—that is, if what we learned was to make very specific responses to very specific stimuli—we could never use our past learning. The reason is that no new stimulus can ever be *exactly* the same as any we previously have learned to respond to.

The most primitive way in which organisms go beyond specific stimulus-response learning is that they show *stimulus generalization. This means that when a new stimulus is similar to one the subject previously has learned to respond to, he tends to confuse the two and make the learned response to the new, similar stimulus. The more similar the new stimulus is to the old one, the stronger the response to it will be.* Stimulus generalization occurs in both classical and operant conditioning.

Generalization was demonstrated very nicely in a study (Hovland, 1937) that used the galvanic skin response (GSR). The GSR is a momentary increase in the electrical conductivity of the skin, and, for unknown reasons, indicates a momentary increase in emotion. In the first stage of this study, classical conditioning was used to "attach" the GSR to a particular tone. This was done by first presenting the tone, then giving the subject a mild but painful shock. The GSR produced by the shock gradually became conditioned to the tone. In the second stage, the experimenter sounded a variety of tones, and measured the subject's GSR's to them. The results are shown in Figure 3-17. The important thing to notice is that the closer a tone was to the original training tone, the larger the GSR it produced. The tones three steps above and below the training stimulus produced the smallest GSR's. Tones two steps and one step away produced larger GSR's, and a tone identical to the one used during conditioning produced the largest GSR of all.

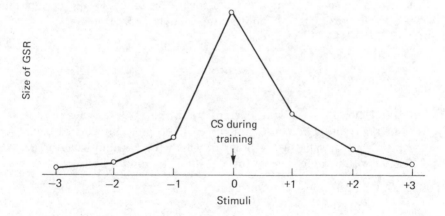

FIGURE 3-17. Generalization of the galvanic skin response (GSR).

FIGURE 3-18.   An example of stimulus generalization.

Generalization also occurs with responses learned through operant conditioning. A rat trained to press the lever in one particular Skinner box would probably press at a lower rate in another box that differed in color, size, odor, or in any other way. For another example, the girl's diving response might occur in other, similar situations. The more similar another situation in all its aspects—boat, lake, people, and so on—to the one in which she learned this response, the more likely it is that the response would generalize to it.

QUESTION 14.   A one-year-old boy had an experience with a white rabbit that made him afraid of it (Watson and Rayner, 1920). How much fear would you then expect him to show to each of the following stimuli? (Write 1 beside the stimulus you would expect him to be most afraid of, 2 beside the next-most-feared stimulus, and so on.)

_____   A white wool shirt

_____   The white rabbit

_____   His white building blocks

_____   A white fur muff

Discrimination Training

Discrimination training is a procedure for teaching a subject who is generalizing—that is, making the same response to two similar stimuli—to respond differently to them. This is ordinarily done by presenting the two stimuli and conditioning the response to one of them, but extinguishing it to the other. This can be done in both classical and operant conditioning.

The dog that Pavlov conditioned to salivate to the bell would probably also salivate—although to a lesser extent—to the sound of a triangle (the musical instrument). The discrimination procedure would be to present these two sounds to the dog in random order, and always present the meat powder after the bell, but never present it after the triangle. The result would probably be that the animal would discriminate between bell and triangle better and better; that is, its salivary response to the bell would get stronger, while its salivary response to the triangle would get weaker.

An example of discrimination training in operant conditioning would be training a rat to press a bar when a light was on, but not to press it when the light was off. This would be done by giving the rat food for bar-presses that occur when the light is on, but not for those that occur when it is off.

FIGURE 3-19. Baseball players must learn to discriminate between pitches that are in the strike zone and those that are outside it. Photograph by Harold M. Lambert. Frederick Lewis.

One interesting application of discrimination training was teaching pigeons to inspect pill capsules for a drug company (Verhave, 1966). This is a discrimination problem because the pigeons had to respond to capsules of the wrong shape or color in one way (rejecting them), while responding to the acceptable ones in another way (allowing them to pass). A psychologist built an endless belt to move the capsules one at a time past the pigeon's viewing window. During the first stage of the training project, the pigeon was reinforced with food only when it responded to a *red* capsule by pecking the reject button. Rejections of *white* capsules were not reinforced. After one week of this discrimination training, the pigeons were responding correctly 99% of the time. Sad to say, however, the drug company never put the idea to use because it was afraid of what its competitors and customers might think of using pigeons as inspectors.

QUESTION 15.   An elementary school class has a pet turtle, which all the students have learned to play with. Outside of school this behavior generalizes to all turtles, and several of the pupils have gotten hurt playing with snapping turtles they have found. Explain how the teacher could solve this problem through discrimination training.

COGNITION

The term cognition refers to the higher mental processes, such as language, remembering, and problem-solving. Although such processes seem to have their foundation in simple kinds of learning, they involve much more complex and extensive inner mental processes than do conditioning, stimulus generalization, and discrimination learning. In recent years psychologists have become more and more interested in these more complex aspects of behavior.

Language

Scientific interest in language has come to a boil in the last few years. There is an enormous amount of current theoretical and research activity in language, but we will be able to consider only a few of the most fundamental principles.

Probably most of man's achievements—his machines, his art, his cities and nations—would have been impossible without language. What is there about language that makes it such a powerful tool? Its potency probably lies in two characteristics that, at first glance, may not look very important: first, language is a system of related categories, and second, it is a set of symbols that stand for those categories.

LANGUAGE AS A SYSTEM OF RELATED CATEGORIES   As we noted earlier, man would not benefit from past experience if he learned only to respond to specific stimuli because he would never encounter exactly the same stimuli again. We have seen that one solution to this problem is stimulus generalization, such as occurs when a child who has been bitten by one German Shepherd subsequently avoids all German Shepherds. But this is not always sufficient; often the organism must learn to respond in the same way to rather *dissimilar* stimuli. For example, it might be useful for the child just described to also learn to be careful of Cocker Spaniels, Pekingese, Saint Bernards, and other dogs that are very different from German Shepherds. This is called concept learning.

FIGURE 3-20.   **The concept of "crime."**

In theoretical terms, concept learning is learning to abstract out those characteristics that are essential to the particular concept or category and to ignore the nonessential characteristics. In observable terms, *concept learning is learning to respond in the same way to stimuli that are examples of the particular concept, in spite of their many differences.* Except for names of specific objects, such as "John Q. Jamieson," and "West 23rd Street," all of the words in all languages refer to concepts. Consider, for example, the concept referred to by the word "red." Although a red ball and a red sunset are different in many ways, a person who has learned this concept can abstract out the redness of these two stimuli, and on this account consider them to be in the same category. A more abstract concept is that referred to by the word "justice." Only a person who had learned this concept would see any similarity between a judge fining a man for speeding and a dog biting a man who had just kicked him.

QUESTION 16.   Write "generalization" or "concept" in front of each of the following examples.

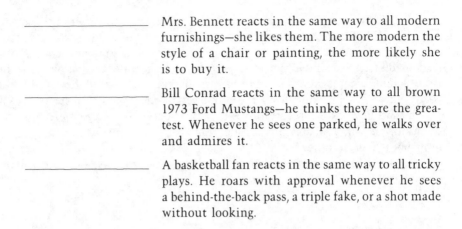

Mrs. Bennett reacts in the same way to all modern furnishings—she likes them. The more modern the style of a chair or painting, the more likely she is to buy it.

Bill Conrad reacts in the same way to all brown 1973 Ford Mustangs—he thinks they are the greatest. Whenever he sees one parked, he walks over and admires it.

A basketball fan reacts in the same way to all tricky plays. He roars with approval whenever he sees a behind-the-back pass, a triple fake, or a shot made without looking.

Thus our language provides us with a large number of concepts or categories into which we may mentally "file" every new experience. An earthling seeing a Martian for the first time might categorize him as "green," "short," "three-eyed," and "friendly."

Linguistic categories are not separate and independent of each other; quite the contrary, there are numerous and complex relationships among them. These relationships help us to respond appropriately to the environment. For a simple example, suppose that a naval officer has learned the concepts "mutiny" and "severe punishment," "justified protest," and "encouragement." Furthermore, there are definite relationships among these concepts in his mind. He sees "severe punishment" as the appropriate way for him to react to "mutiny," and "encouragement" as the appropriate reaction to "justified protest." Now suppose that some sailors stage a sit-in on this officer's ship to protest racial discrimination. How will he react? If he puts this incident into the category of "mutiny," he will react in one way; if he puts it into the category of "justified protest," he will react quite differently.

LANGUAGE AS A SET OF SYMBOLS   In addition to providing us with a system of related concepts, language also provides symbols to represent these concepts. A symbol is something that stands for something else. Thus the word "dog" is a symbol that stands for a category of four-footed animals, and the word "red" is a symbol that stands for the category of visual experiences produced by certain wavelengths of light.

Why are linguistic symbols useful? An obvious reason is that they facilitate our communication with other people. Not so obvious is the fact that they also facilitate our own thinking. That is, we sometimes use words in the same way admirals use the miniature warships that symbolize their fleet. With these symbols, an admiral can explore the consequences of various battle strategies before giving the actual orders to the fleet. In the same way, we can use words to help us mentally explore various solutions to a problem before actually trying one of them.

When we apply our linguistic systems to the real world, it can be critically important what categories we place a particular stimulus in. If these categories are appropriate, they may lead to effective responses. If inappropriate, they may lead to disaster. Consider the example of a young child who is walking home from school alone when a stranger stops his car and asks if he would like to go get an ice cream cone. Will the child get in the car or will he refuse? It all depends on how the child categorizes the situation. If the category "friend" comes to mind, he will probably make one response; if he thinks "enemy," he will probably make the other.

As we shall see, linguistic symbols and category systems are important in memory and in problem-solving.

Memory

Learning is of no use without remembering, as all of us are well aware whenever we struggle to recall the answer to an exam question, search our memory for the name of a person who acts as though he knows us, or wonder what it was that our wife told us not to forget at the store.

In the psychological laboratory, memory is typically studied by having subjects learn lists of nonsense syllables—such as DAK, KUG, and ZOS—then waiting for an interval of time, and finally measuring how well they can remember the nonsense syllables.

FIGURE 3-21. A memory drum, often used in studies of human memory. The material to be memorized appears in the window as the drum revolves.

There are several different ways of measuring memory. *In a recognition test, the correct answer is supplied, mixed in with one or more incorrect answers, and the subject must select it. In a recall test the subject must produce the answer himself.*

QUESTION 17. Write "recognition test" or "recall test" in front of each of the following examples:

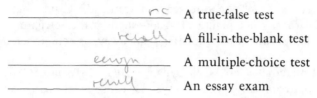

_rc_	A true-false test
recall	A fill-in-the-blank test
recogn	A multiple-choice test
recall	An essay exam

Memory experiments typically show that the amount of material remembered decreases rapidly right after learning, then more slowly later on, as shown in Figure 3-22. Although the forgetting curve looks very much like the extinction curve, the reader will notice that there is a distinct difference between the two processes. During extinction the subject practices the response, while during forgetting he does not.

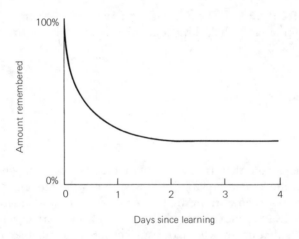

FIGURE 3-22. **A typical memory curve.**

The main reason psychologists study memory is to find out what factors influence it. Many laymen believe that forgetting is caused by disuse—that is, by the amount of time that passes without practice of what is learned. Although time alone may play some part in forgetting, there is evidence to indicate that it is not very important. For example, Skinner once trained a pigeon to peck at a disk in a Skinner box, then removed the bird from the apparatus for six years. When, at the end of that time, he placed the same pigeon back in the box, it quickly resumed disk pecking. And you, yourself, know that if you once have learned to ice skate or play ping pong, you can pick up the sport again years later and very quickly regain your earlier skill.

A more important determinant of memory is the amount of original learning. *The more often material has been practiced, the better it will be remembered.* Thus you will probably remember the name of a new acquaintance a long time if, when you first meet him, you say his name often: "I'm glad to meet you, Mr. Claybrook," "How are you enjoying the party, Mr. Claybrook?" "Is your wife here tonight, Mr. Claybrook?" "I hope to see you again, Mr. Claybrook." On the other hand, material that is not practiced at all—such as the telephone number that you find in a phone directory and dial right away—is remembered only a few seconds.

Meaningful material—such as the syllables DIG, CAR, and SOS—is much easier to remember than nonsense syllables. Why? Because meaningful words have been practiced frequently in the past, whereas nonsense syllables have not.

If the material to be remembered is not very meaningful itself, the learner may make remembering easier by associating that material with something that is meaningful. For example, it would be difficult for beginning music students to remember that the lines of the treble clef are e, g, b, d, and f, but it is easy for them to remember the meaningful sentence "*Every good boy does fine.*"

QUESTION 18.   Describe at least two ways a person could use the above principle to help him remember his social security number.

Another factor that is important in memory is this: when the subject tries to do what he learned previously, how strong is the tendency for the correct response to occur, and how strong are the tendencies for other, incorrect responses to creep in? One way to maximize the tendency for the correct response to occur is to make the situation in which the subject has to remember the material as similar as possible to the situation in which he originally learned it. For example, one study (Abernethy, 1940) showed that students who were tested in the same classroom in which they had learned the material scored higher than their classmates who were tested in a different room.

Of course remembering will be poor if there exists a strong tendency for an incorrect response to occur. This can happen due to the generalization of responses that the subject learned either before or after he learned the material he is trying to remember. *If memory is impaired due to material learned before the material to be remembered, that is called proactive inhibition; if it is impaired due to material learned after the material to be remembered, that is called retroactive inhibition.* This is illustrated in Figure 3-23.

	TIME 1	TIME 2	TIME 3	TIME 4
NO INHIBITION:	Rest	Learn 2	Rest	Measure retention of 2 and obtain high score
PROACTIVE INHIBITION:	Learn 1	Learn 2	Rest	Measure retention of 2 and obtain low score
RETROACTIVE INHIBITION:	Rest	Learn 2	Learn 3	Measure retention of 2 and obtain low score

FIGURE 3-23. **Proactive and retroactive inhibition.**

Suppose that six years ago, when he lived in Chicago, a man learned to turn *right* at a Sunoco station to get to a friend's house. Before that, he had lived in Boston, where he turned *left* at a Sunoco station to get to church on Sunday morning. And for the past five years he has been living in Dallas, where he goes *straight* past a prominent Sunoco station on his way to work. Now suppose that this man revisits his former neighborhood in Chicago and tries to find his way back to his friend's house. There are two incorrect responses that could occur when he arrives at the Sunoco station: he could turn left, as he had learned to do in Boston (proactive inhibition), or he could go straight, as he learned to do more recently, in Dallas (retroactive inhibition). Either of these incorrect responses would, of course, constitute poor remembering.

QUESTION 19. In a classic experiment (Jenkins and Dallenbach, 1924), college men learned lists of nonsense syllables and then either slept in the lab or went about their regular college routine until it was time for their memories to be tested. The finding was that subjects remembered fewer nonsense syllables if they had gone to classes during the delay interval than if they had slept. What kind of inhibition does this demonstrate? (Circle one.)

1. Proactive inhibition
2. Retroactive inhibition

Problem-solving

It was recently reported in the newspapers that thieves had surprised a night watchman and locked him in the trunk of a car that was parked nearby. Since the trunk was airtight, the victim's problem was to find air to breathe until the next morning when he would undoubtedly be found. There was no way of making a hole to the outside. If you were this watchman, how would you solve the problem?

Solving problems is quite different from simple conditioning. Whereas in conditioning psychologists usually find a gradual improvement in performance with practice, in problem-solving they often find two kinds of behavior that are very different from gradual learning. Some people solve the problem almost immediately (this is called insight); others get bogged down and never make any progress at all. Luckily, the night watchman solved his problem quickly. His solution was to breathe the air he released from the spare tire that was in the trunk with him.

Many characteristics of problem-solving behavior can be explained by the theory that *problem-solving involves the generalization of previously learned responses to the present problem.* If the responses the subject has learned to similar situations in the past are ones that will solve the problem, the result is insight. Possibly the night watchman in the preceding example was a SCUBA diver in his spare time, and therefore was accustomed to getting air to breathe from a container of compressed air. On the other hand, when previously learned responses are not the ones required by the problem, the person may be unable to solve it. Someone whose only experience with tires was in using them to support automobiles would not be as likely to think of using them as a source of oxygen.

Many trick problems are based on this principle of generalization. One evening at supper the eight-year-old daughter of one of the authors asked him, "How do you spell 'shop'?" Wondering what was up, he replied "s-h-o-p." "Now say it." "Shop." "Now spell it. . . . Say it. . . . Spell it. . . . Say it." Then she asked quickly, "What do you do when the light is green?" And just as quickly her father replied "STOP." Why did he give give this incorrect answer? Because his daughter had "set him up" by creating in him a strong tendency to say, in response to her questions, words similar to "shop."

Another example is the nine-dot problem, shown in Figure 3-24. The task is to connect the nine dots by drawing four straight lines. You are not allowed to retrace a line, or lift the pencil from the paper. Most people have great difficulty with this problem because they have a strong tendency—undoubtedly learned in the past—to stay within the boundaries of the square. But to solve the problem, you must draw some lines that extend outside these boundaries. Now can you solve it?

QUESTION 20.   Suppose that some subjects were given a simple problem: to hammer a nail into a wall so that a pendulum could be hung from it. The only available solution was to use a nearby lead weight as a hammer. For group A, this lead weight had a string tied around it, and in a previous task they had used it as a pendulum. For group B, there was no string around the weight and they previously had used it to pound stakes into the ground. For group C, there was no string tied to the weight and they had had no previous experience with it. How quickly would you expect each group to arrive at the solution of using the weight to

pound in the nail? (Answer by drawing a line from each group to a prediction.)

Group   Prediction
A   Would probably solve it most quickly
B   Would probably solve it second most quickly
C   Would probably solve it least quickly

FIGURE 3-24. **The nine-dot problem.**

SUMMARY

Learning may be defined as a change in behavior that follows practice.
Two simple kinds of learning are classical and operant conditioning. In classical
conditioning, a conditioned stimulus is paired with an unconditioned stimulus
(either primary or secondary). In operant conditioning, a positive or negative
reinforcer (either primary or secondary) is regularly given or taken away following
a particular response. When the response to be learned ordinarily occurs infre-

quently, the early stages of operant conditioning may be speeded up by the use of shaping.

In both kinds of conditioning, extinction occurs when the response is no longer reinforced, spontaneous recovery occurs when the subject is given a rest during extinction, intermittent reinforcement during training leads to slower subsequent extinction, stimulus generalization occurs when stimuli similar to the one used in training are presented to the subject, and discrimination training may be used to teach the subject to stop generalizing.

"Cognition" refers to the higher mental processes, such as language, remembering, and problem-solving. Language is useful because it provides many interrelated concepts, as well as symbols that stand for those concepts. Memory, which may be measured by recognition tests and by recall tests, is influenced more by practice and by stimulus generalization—in the form of proactive and retroactive inhibition—than by disuse. Problem-solving is also greatly influenced by the generalization of responses learned in the past. If these responses are appropriate, the individual will solve the problem quickly; if not, he may never solve it.

BEHAVIOR TO EXPLAIN

Some college students are extremely dependent on their professors, staying after class to talk with them on the slightest pretext and asking their opinion about every little detail of a term project. How may this behavior be explained?

1.   Think of all the principles you can that might help to explain this behavior.

2.   State an hypothesis involving a learning or a cognitive explanation of this behavior.

3.   Describe a study that could be done to test your hypothesis, including both the design and the measuring instruments you would use.

chapter four

Social Explanations

No man is an island. . .—John Donne, 1624.

The individual's behavior is powerfully influenced by other people. It is this influence that the social psychologist studies.

It is possible to consider much of the field of social psychology as merely an extension of learning principles. From this viewpoint, other people are just one of the many different kinds of stimuli that we have learned to react to in certain ways. However, social stimuli are of such special importance that we have chosen to devote a separate chapter to their effects.

Before looking into some of the ways in which other people influence the individual, it is necessary to be clear about what aspects of the individual they influence. A major influence of others is on the individual's attitudes and this area is the social psychologists' main interest. *A person's attitude toward a particular object or idea includes his (a) feelings, (b) cognitions (what he knows or thinks), and (c) behavioral tendencies with respect to that object or idea.*

This definition makes it clear that the concept of attitude encompasses nearly all aspects of the individual's reactions to an object or idea and thus overlaps other psychological categories such as motive, perception, and learning. A student's attitude toward Shakespeare may include feelings of liking and admiration, the cognitions that Shakespeare lived in England several centuries ago and wrote many famous plays, and the behavioral tendency to register for the Shakespeare course offered at his college.

FIGURE 4-1. Frederick Lewis.

Another example of an attitude is shown in the following prejudiced statement:

I have a little dislike for Jewish people. I don't think they are as courageous or as interested in humanity as they ought to be. They accent the clannish and the material. It may be my imagination, but it seems to me you can see their eyes light up when you hand them a coin. I avoid the Jewish clothiers because they have second-rate stuff (Adorno, Frenkel-Brunswik, Levinson, and Sanford, 1950).

All three components of attitudes are represented in this statement. Feeling: "I have a little dislike for Jewish people." Cognition: "They accent the clannish and the material," and "You can see their eyes light up when you hand them a coin." Behavioral tendency: "I avoid the Jewish clothiers. . ."

QUESTION 1.   What is your own attitude toward Communism? Briefly describe the three components of this attitude.

A person's feelings, cognitions, and behaviors tend to be consistent with each other. For example, the prejudiced individual who made the statement quoted above is consistently negative toward Jews. His feelings are negative, his cognitions are negative, and his behavioral tendencies are negative.

QUESTION 2.   Person A gets disgusted every time he sees a bottle that someone has tossed beside the road but this doesn't bother person B at all.

A. These different responses indicate that A and B differ in: (Circle one.)
   1. Cognitions
   2. Feelings

B. If you asked A and B how dangerous it is for the roadsides to be littered with bottles, which would probably say it was more dangerous? (Circle one.)
   1. A
   2. B

C. The different responses referred to in question (b) indicate that A and B differ in: (Circle one.)
   1. Cognitions
   2. Feelings

D. Which of these two people probably switched to using low-polluting, nonleaded gasoline in his car first? (Circle one.)
   1. A
   2. B

E. The difference mentioned in question (d) is a difference in: (Circle one.)

1. Cognitions
2. Behavior
3. Feelings

We turn our attention now to some of the obvious and not-so-obvious ways that individual attitudes (as these are defined by the social psychologist) can be influenced by other people.

HOW IMPORTANT IS SOCIAL INFLUENCE?

People influence each other more than they realize. Past social influences have made each individual the kind of person he is now, and present social influences are constantly molding him further. To put the question in its most extreme form, what would you be like if, from an early age, you had grown up alone, without parents, friends, or society to train you? If you survived at all, you might be like the wild, naked boy who once was found living in a French forest (Itard, 1962). He bit and scratched like a wildcat to avoid being captured. When taken to the home of a psychologist to be studied and cared for, he swayed back and forth ceaselessly like some animal in a cage. Although this particular behavior eventually disappeared, some of his "wildness" never did leave him. He never gave up walking like an ape, using both his hands and his feet. He never developed much sensitivity to heat or cold; he would squat for hours on the cold winter ground, and several times he was seen in the kitchen, reaching into a pot of boiling water for a potato. Although it is difficult to understand how lack of social influence could be responsible for some of these strange behaviors, apparently it was.

Each of us continues to be influenced by others in ways large and small. For example, don't you act differently when you share an elevator with strangers than when you have the elevator all to yourself? With strangers present, many people develop an urgent interest in looking at the carpet, the ceiling, the floor indicator—anything far away from the stranger's eyes.

A particularly noticeable kind of social influence is influence toward conformity—toward adopting the feelings, cognitions, and behaviors of others. We can observe conformity everywhere. Most of the people sitting in a Methodist church on a Sunday morning will be dressed conservatively, will share many of the same cognitions, and may even adopt a uniform feeling toward the minister's sermon that morning. Members of a hippie commune may all wear long hair and unconventional clothes, share cognitions about the immorality of the establishment and the power of love, and indulge in marijuana and yoga. Conformity even occurs with respect to setting off bombs, according to a statement made by the head of the New York City bomb squad a few years ago:

This particular year is by far our busiest. . . . Bombings, like anything else, are fashionable or nonfashionable, in vogue or not in vogue. It's a little more serious than that. They're catching. So if you have a series of bombings, they encourage further bombings. People who are a little mentally unstable or perhaps inclined to this sort of thing say, "Now is the time, everybody's doing it." So they get out and do their thing (Greene, 1970).

The great strength of social pressures to conform has been demonstrated by one of the most famous experiments in social psychology—Solomon Asch's conformity experiment (1956). Because this is such an important study, we will go into it in some detail.

Asch knew, from previous studies, that when people are asked to select answers to very difficult questions they will choose answers known to have been given by others. But what if the questions were made very easy, so that the correct answers were obvious? Is the tendency to conform so strong that it can lead people to give incorrect answers even in this situation? To find out, Asch put pairs of cards, like those shown in Figure 4-2, in front of the subject, and asked him to judge which of the three lines on the righthand card was the same height as the line on the lefthand card.

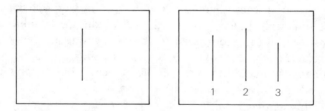

FIGURE 4-2. A line-judging problem like those in the Asch conformity study.

None of Asch's line problems was very difficult. College students who worked them without any social influence nearly always chose the correct answer. In Asch's experiment, however, strong social pressure was brought to bear. The following paragraphs describe the experiment as it appeared to a typical subject, called Hank.

Hank was recruited by a friend who said he was in the same study. When he arrived at the appointed place, Hank found six other men, including the friend who had recruited him, waiting outside the laboratory door. The experimenter soon arrived and let them all into the room. They seated themselves in chairs arranged as shown in Figure 4-3, and Hank got seat number six, the next-to-the-last seat. The experimenter explained the line-judging task and said that, for the sake of convenience, he wanted the subjects to call out their answers aloud, in numerical order. The instructions seemed clear to Hank, but some of the others asked some questions.

FIGURE 4-3. Seating arrangement in the Asch experiment. Photo by William Vandivert.

Then the experimenter put up the first pair of cards, and the judging began. On the first trial, the others gave the correct answer, and Hank did too. Also on the second trial. But on the third trial all the other subjects gave the same wrong answer and they continued to agree on wrong answers on 12 of the 18 trials. Strangely enough, the experimenter didn't look surprised at these wildly incorrect judgments (and neither he nor the subjects showed any reaction to whatever answer Hank gave).

The truth was that Hank was the only real subject in the group. All the other men had met with the experimenter in advance and had been coached

FIGURE 4-4. Reactions of one subject in the Asch conformity experiment. Photo by William Vandivert.

on when to give wrong answers and how to play their parts realistically. In other words, the seven other "subjects" were really accomplices of the experimenter, playing a part in order to put social pressure on the one real subject—Hank—to find out how he would react.

Hank—and the other real subjects in the many groups that were run—certainly did react. One such subject said afterward, "Either those guys were crazy or I was—I hadn't made up my mind which." Another reported, "I felt they'd think I was a wet blanket, or a sore thumb" (Asch, 1956). Many said they had thought that the others had misunderstood the instructions or that perhaps there was some optical illusion.

What about Hank's and the other subjects' conformity? On the trials when the others all gave the wrong answer, the typical subject also gave the wrong answer about one-third of the time. It was not always the same wrong answer the others had given, but even another wrong answer seems to show social influence when the task is as easy as this one. Although the average subject stuck to his guns almost two-thirds of the time, even one-third conformity on problems as easy as these was surprising to Asch.

Now Asch knew how much total conformity was produced by the entire experimental situation, but he didn't know the separate effects of each of the important variables in that situation. Take, for example, the variable of majority size. He knew how much conformity a majority of six accomplices produced, but what are the effects of using more or fewer accomplices than that? To find out, Asch did a follow-up study using majority size as the independent variable and keeping the rest of the situation the same as before. What he found was quite interesting. While amount of conformity did increase as the majority increased from 1 to 3, it then remained fairly steady as the majority continued increasing up to 16. This is shown in Figure 4-5. It is puzzling that conformity

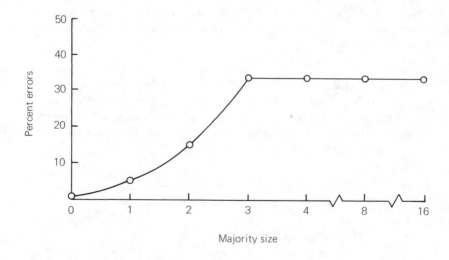

FIGURE 4-5. **Effect of majority size on conformity (idealized curve).**

should reach its peak with a majority of three; why this happens is still not known.

Until now we have been talking about the situation where the subject is alone against the world. But what if the subject were given one "partner" who always gave correct answers? *Asch found that, when he used six accomplices giving wrong answers and one accomplice giving the correct ones, the amount of conformity shown by the subjects dropped drastically.* In this situation, the average subject made only 5.5 percent errors, compared to nearly 33 percent errors without a partner.

QUESTION 3.   A few years ago, a young lady went to a dinner party wearing a short miniskirt, only to find that all the other women were wearing long midis. As the evening progressed, she felt more and more embarrassed. Finally, she went around looking for someone she knew, found one, and spent the rest of the evening, happy and relaxed, wearing her friend's midilength coat.

Assume Asch's findings apply to this behavior. What could the hostess of this dinner party have done to make the young lady feel at ease without having to wear a coat all evening?

One other variable Asch studied was the difficulty of the task. Apparently, *when the task is more difficult for the subject, he is more likely to conform to the majority.* Asch found that when the "incorrect" lines were only 1/4" longer or shorter than the "correct" lines, subjects conformed more often than when the difference was 3/4".

QUESTION 4.   A student and his friends are rehashing an exam they just finished taking. On one particular question, the student chose one answer and all his friends chose another. In which of the following conditions is he more likely to decide that his friends' answer was right? (In each pair, circle 1 or 2.)

A.   1.   He had studied very hard for the exam.
         2.   He hadn't studied very hard for the exam.

B.   1.   He is a very good student.
         2.   He isn't a very good student.

C. 1. The question concerned a point that had been heavily stressed in the course.
   2. The question concerned a point that had been mentioned only in passing in the course.

Now that you have some appreciation of the power of social influence in producing conformity, we turn our attention to some of the more fundamental reasons why people are influenced so strongly by others.

WHY ARE PEOPLE INFLUENCED BY OTHERS?

Three basic reasons people are influenced by others are: (1) reinforcement (they want the reinforcement of having others like them); (2) information (they believe that others are better informed than they are); and (3) consistency (they want their feelings, cognitions, and behaviors to be consistent with each other). To illustrate, a sheep rancher's negative attitude toward American bald eagles may become more positive if (1) he becomes friends with a group of conservationists who are strongly against shooting eagles and he adopts their attitude so that they will like him. Or (2) he might hear an expert argue that eagles are not a menace to livestock and adopt his attitude because he considers it better informed than his own. Or (3) someone might persuade him to help rescue an injured eagle, a behavior that is not consistent with his present negative attitude toward eagles. After this rescue expedition, in order to restore psychological consistency, his attitude toward eagles would probably become more positive. These three basic reasons for social influence are discussed in more detail below.

Others Control Reinforcements

The stronger the positive or negative reinforcers another person uses to pressure an individual to conform to his wishes, the more likely it is that that individual will conform. Sometimes these reinforcers are tangible ones, such as money, food, physical punishment, and so on. For instance, an American priest just back from missionary work in Jamaica said that he had found the Jamaicans easy to convert. "They are very poor," he said, "and the poor are more easily swayed. Some of them probably joined us because of the fringe benefits—food and care." (Press-Republican, 1968). Presumably, if the Jamaicans were better off, the food offered by the missionaries would not be as strong a reinforcer for them and they would be more difficult to influence.

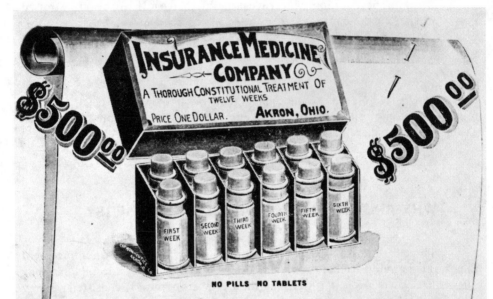

FIGURE 4-6.   The Bettmann Archive.

Negative reinforcers can be influential as well. One black teenager, talking about the looting of shops that occurred during the 1967 Detroit riot, said: "All the guys who'd been sittin' on us—especially those shopkeepers who charged us 60 cents for a 49-cent half-gallon of milk—they got some dues paid" (Lukas, 1967). Perhaps the punishment of having their stores looted influenced some shopkeepers to lower their prices after the riot.

Other social reinforcers are more subtle: for example, the liking, respect, and approval of people one cares about.

QUESTION 5. In a particular Job Corps training camp, the trainees were breaking the rules frequently. One plan was that each trainee who broke the rules would be disciplined by a committee of fellow trainees. Assuming that the disciplinary committees were equally well informed, which kind of committee do you think would produce better discipline in the camp? (Circle 1 or 2.)

1. One from his own barracks.

2. One from another barracks.

Liking is an important social reinforcer; the need to be liked can lead us to agree with others. At the same time, agreement can lead to liking others. These two relationships between liking and agreement will now be discussed in some detail.

First, *the need to be liked can lead to agreement.* An example comes from a well-known study done many years ago at Bennington College (Newcomb, 1943). One of the main issues of the day was President Franklin D. Roosevelt's use of the powers of the federal government to try to bring this country out of the Great Depression. The well-to-do families from which most of the Bennington girls came were vehemently against F. D. R. and his "New Deal." The political climate at Bennington, however—probably due to the liberal views of most of the faculty members and student leaders—was enthusiastically in favor of the New Deal.

Of course the Bennington girls held their parents' conservative views when they first arrived at college, but in the course of four years most of them showed a drastic change in their feelings, cognitions, and behaviors until many of them became "parlor pinks," as some parents expressed it. A small group of Bennington students, however, in contrast with the majority, remained just as conservative in their senior year as they had been as freshmen.

QUESTION 6. What do you think were the differences between the Bennington girls who gradually came to agree with the dominant attitude at the college, and those who did not? (Match amount of change with description of the girls by drawing a line from one to the other below.)

Amount of Change	*Description of Girls*
These girls did not become any more liberal at Bennington.	During college these girls maintained close ties with their parents, writing them often and making frequent visits home.
These girls did become more liberal at Bennington.	During college these girls were less interested in maintaining their family ties than they were in being liked and respected by the college community.

The liking-agreement relationship can work the other way too; that is, *agreement can lead to liking.* We all have noticed how friendly people suddenly become when they find they have something important in common. One of the authors remembers living in Cleveland in 1948, a year the Cleveland Indians had a red hot baseball team. As the summer wore on, and the Indians got closer to the pennant, Clevelanders became more and more friendly toward each other. The day the Indians won the American League pennant, downtown Cleveland was crowded with cars. All the car windows were open and the occupants—total strangers who ordinarily wouldn't have anything to say to each other—were talking with people in the other cars about their team. The same kind of thing happens when fellow Americans meet in Europe or fellow residents of New Hampshire meet in California. In foreign surroundings what little these people have in common seems very important, and they often act like long-lost friends.

Of course there is another side to this coin: disagreement or dissimilarity can cause dislike. In East Africa today there is much hatred of the "Asians" who came there from India centuries ago and who—although a small minority—dominate East African commerce. Probably one reason these people are hated so much by the Africans is that their customs and clothes are so different from the native ones. There are tall Sikh men wearing beards and turbans, Hindu women wearing bright saris, and other groups of Asians with other, equally "mysterious," customs (Fellows, 1967).

QUESTION 7.   Imagine that you are applying for a job and are eager to have the employer like you. What should be the effect of behaving in the following ways in your job interview? (Write "like most" where you think the employer would like you the most and "like least" where you think he would like you the least.)

_____   In the interview, you emphasize matters on which you find you and the employer agree.

_____ In the interview, you emphasize some matters on which you and the employer agree and others on which the two of you disagree.

_____ In the interview, you emphasize matters on which you find you and the employer disagree.

Others Have Useful Information

Even when there is no possibility that the other person will reinforce you for it, you may still adopt his feelings, cognitions, or behaviors if you believe that they are better informed or more useful than your own. Notice that two things are necessary for this kind of influence: you must believe that you do not already have accurate or useful information, and you must also believe that the other fellow does.

The most obvious instance of this type of influence is when someone is openly trying to convince you of something—Ed McMahon is recommending that you buy Budweiser, Senator Fulbright is arguing earnestly that the Vietnam war should be stopped, a friend is telling you that you ought to let your hair grow longer. (Although your friends can also use reinforcements to influence you, we are talking here only about the usefulness of their information.) In all these examples, the central question is credibility—can you believe what they are telling you? _The more credible a communicator, the more influence he will have._

A few years ago, when the future of movies was in doubt, subjects in one experiment (Hovland and Weiss, 1951) read a passage arguing that, although the movie theatre industry had been hurt temporarily by the popularity of television, it would recover and in fact prosper in the future. Some of the subjects were told that this passage had appeared in _Fortune_ magazine, while others were led to believe that it had appeared in a movie gossip column. The subjects were more influenced by the article when they thought that it had appeared in _Fortune_, presumably because _Fortune_ was a more credible source. After all, _Fortune_, being a highly respected business magazine, would probably know more about the economics of movie theatres and, moreover, would have fewer selfish reasons to plug the movie industry than a movie columnist would.

QUESTION 8. You are trying to decide whether to buy a VW bug or a Ford Pinto. On the basis of credibility only, in which of the following cases will you be most influenced in favor of the Pinto? (Circle 1, 2, or 3.)

1. A car salesman at the Ford dealership recommends that you buy a Pinto.

2. A used car salesman who has both VWs and Pintos in his lot recommends that you buy a Pinto.
3. Your five-year-old daughter begs, "Daddy, please buy a Pinto!"

FIGURE 4-7. Frederick Lewis.

QUESTION 9.   In the preceding question, in which case was reinforcement (either delivered or anticipated) most important? (Circle one.)
1   2   3

You also get useful information by watching what other people do when
they are not making any attempt to influence you. For example, when a person
is not sure of his own feelings, cognitions, and so on, he often looks at other
persons and adopts their feelings or cognitions. This kind of influence on emotional
response has been studied especially carefully. The principle that emerges from
these studies is this: *when people are experiencing an emotion but can't identify
it, they look at others who are in the same situation and adopt their emotion*
(and, accordingly, their behavior).

You may wonder why anyone should ever be unclear about what emotion
he is feeling. There is evidence indicating that, contrary to common belief, different emotions do not actually feel very different.

In a study (Schachter, 1959), one group of college women was deliberately
frightened fairly severely by being told that they would be given strong electric
shocks which "will be quite painful but, of course, will do no permanent damage."
Another group of women was frightened only mildly by being told that the shocks
would be so faint that they would not hurt at all.

After these explanations, the high-fear group was presumably experiencing
strong emotion as well as some uncertainty about what that emotion was. The
experimenter then explained that there would be a short delay while he got ready
for the experiment. Then he posed the crucial question: Would the subject prefer
to wait alone or with some other subjects who were taking part in the same
experiment? Because waiting with the others would presumably give the subject
an opportunity to observe what emotion the other subjects showed, and because
the high-fear group presumably had a strong need to do this, it was predicted
that the high-fear group would show more desire to wait with others.

As predicted, about two-thirds of the high-fear subjects chose to wait with
others, while only about one-third of the low-fear subjects did so. The results
of this study can also be explained rather easily in other ways. However, Schachter's
explanation gained additional support from two further studies.

QUESTION 10.   The same experimenter did a follow-up study
(Schachter, 1959) in which he used two groups of subjects, both of them
in the high-fear condition. One of the groups was given, as before, a choice
between waiting with other subjects who were in the same experiment,
or waiting alone. The second group had to choose between waiting with
some students who were not connected with the experiment, or waiting
alone. In which condition would you expect subjects to show the stronger
preference to wait with others? (Circle 1 or 2.)

1.   When the others were subjects in the same experiment.

2.   When the others were not connected with the experiment.

In a third study (Schachter and Singer, 1962) done to test the same hypothesis, the emotion was produced in the subjects by an injection of epinephrine, a drug that increases heart rate and produces other symptoms of emotional excitement. Some of the conditions of this study were the following:

1. One group of subjects was injected with the drug, then given an accurate description of the effects the drug would have. Thus when the drug took effect, these subjects would experience an emotion for which they had an adequate identification.

2. A second group was also injected with the drug but given no description of its effects. Thus they would experience an emotion but have no adequate definition of it.

3. A third group was given an injection of salt solution, which produces no emotional effects.

After receiving one of these three treatments, each subject sat in a waiting-room for 20 minutes with another subject (actually an accomplice of the experimenter) who acted in a rather madcap, euphoric way: he practiced shooting crumpled sheets of paper into the waste basket, floated paper airplanes around the room, made a tower of manila envelopes, and twirled a hula hoop on his arm. During this time, close observations were being made of the extent to which the real subject imitated these behaviors.

QUESTION 11.   In the study described above,

A. Which of the three groups of subjects showed the greatest tendency to imitate the accomplice's euphoric behaviors? (Circle 1, 2, or 3.)
    1. Drug; accurate description of effects.
    2. Drug; no description of effects.
    3. Salt solution.

B. When the subjects were asked afterward to describe their emotions, which group reported that they were happiest (most euphoric)? (Circle 1, 2, or 3.)
    1. Drug; accurate description of effects.
    2. Drug; no description of effects.
    3. Salt solution.

Some Changes Restore Psychological Consistency

Whenever a psychological change occurs in an individual as a result of others' reinforcements or information, or for some other reason, other changes tend to follow that restore psychological consistency. It is these secondary, consistency-restoring changes that are the subject of this section. The best known and probably the most exciting of the many theories about psychological consistency is the theory of cognitive dissonance, proposed by social psychologist Leon Festinger.

It is obvious that when a person's attitudes change, a change in his behavior will probably follow. Not so obvious is the basic hypothesis of dissonance theory which holds that the reverse is also true. *According to dissonance theory, after a person has behaved in a way that is inconsistent with his attitudes, the unpleasant psychological state of "dissonance" occurs. In order to get rid of this dissonance, his attitudes tend to change so as to become more consistent with the behavior.* For example, a few years ago a man did some work for the presidential campaign of Richard Nixon, just to help out his wife. This behavior was not consistent with the man's attitudes because he preferred another presidential candidate. The more work he did for Nixon, however, the more pro-Nixon he became. By election day, he liked Nixon better than the other candidate and voted for him. The three stages in this example of dissonance are shown in Figure 4-8.

Benjamin Franklin writes that he once made use of the principle of dissonance, although of course he does not call it that. Upon discovering that a certain influential man opposed him, Franklin decided to try to make a friend of the man. This is how he did it:

Having heard that he had in his library a certain very scarce and curious book, I wrote a note to him expressing my desire of purusing that book and requesting he would do me the favor of lending it to me for a few days. He sent it immediately and I returned it in about a week (Franklin, 1906).

It worked. The man soon became Franklin's fast friend, presumably because the favor he had done was inconsistent with his original negative attitude toward Franklin, dissonance resulted, and his attitude changed in order to restore psychological consistency.

If the reader is having difficulty making sense out of dissonance theory, it may be helpful to interpret it in the following way: after the individual has committed the inconsistent act (worked for Nixon, done Franklin a favor), he wonders why he did it, and finally decides that the only way he can explain it is that his attitude must have been different (more pro-Nixon, more pro-Franklin) than he had thought.

QUESTION 12.   A high school student has a negative attitude toward war.

A. Describe an event that would be likely to create dissonance in this student over the topic of war:

B. Describe a likely outcome of this dissonance:

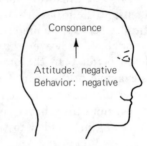

1. Before worked for Nixon

Consonance

Attitude: negative
Behavior: negative

2. Just after began work for Nixon

Dissonance

Attitude: negative
Behavior: positive

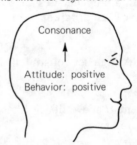

3. Some time after began work for Nixon

Consonance

Attitude: positive
Behavior: positive

FIGURE 4-8. **An example of cognitive dissonance.**

Degree of inconsistency between behavior and attitude is not the only variable that has to be considered in predicting dissonance and the resulting attitude change. Another important variable is the amount of justification the individual had—threats, rewards, and so on—to engage in the inconsistent behavior. *There has to be some minimum level of justification to motivate the individual to commit the inconsistent act at all. But above that minimum, the weaker the justification, the greater the resulting dissonance and attitude change.*

For example, if the man had been paid royally for working for Nixon, little dissonance and attitude change would have resulted. If Benjamin Franklin had offered to threaten or reward the influential gentleman in an attempt to persuade him to lend the book, he probably would have been less successful in changing the man's attitude toward him.

In understanding this principle, too, it is useful to imagine how the subject sees the situation. If, when he wonders why he committed the inconsistent act, he can say "I did it for the money," or "I did it because I was being blackmailed," that is sufficient to explain the behavior, and no attitude change is necessary. Only if such justifications are lacking is the individual forced to the conclusion that he must have done it because his attitude is different than he had thought.

QUESTION 13.   In one experiment (Aronson and Carlsmith, 1963), children were told not to play with a particular toy they liked very much while the experimenter was out of the room. One group of children were threatened mildly, being told that the experimenter would be "annoyed" if they played with the toy; another group was threatened more strongly, being warned that the researcher would be "very angry" if they played with it. As a result of this threat, none of the children did play with the toy while the researcher was away, a behavior that was inconsistent with their positive attitude toward the toy. When he returned to the room, the experimenter measured once again the subjects' attitudes toward the forbidden toy.

A.   In which general *direction* would you expect the attitudes of all the subjects to change after they had resisted the temptation to play with the toy? (Circle 1 or 2.)

1.   They should like the toy more than they did before.

2.   They should like the toy less than they did before.

B.   Which group would you expect to show *greater* attitude change in the direction you indicated? (Circle 1 or 2).

1.   The mild-threat group.

2.   The strong-threat group.

GROUPS

For all that has been said so far in this chapter, it would be possible for a reader to think that everyone influences everyone else equally. This, of course, is not true. People have the most influence on others who are in the same groups they are in. We will make only a few of the most basic points about group goals and group structure.

Group Goals

People are more likely to behave in a cooperative and friendly way if they have common goals than if they have different goals.

The Scanlon Plan, a unique incentive plan that has been adopted by some small industrial companies (Lesieur, 1958), provides factory workers with a common goal. The key idea of this plan is to set a standard for labor costs and then to keep a monthly check on these costs. If labor costs for any month fall below the standard that has been set—that is, if the workers increase their productivity—part of the resulting profit is distributed among the workers as a bonus to that month's paycheck. In this way all the production workers in the company are given a very strong and immediate common goal—to increase the plant's productivity.

To get an idea of the degree of cooperation this kind of common goal can produce, let us look at the relations between the engineers who drew the blueprints for the Lapointe Machine Tool Company and the machinists who had to follow their blueprints. Before the Scanlon Plan was adopted at Lapointe, there was friction between these two groups. Whenever the machinists would ask a question about how to build a particular machine, the engineers would reply unsympathetically, "Just follow the blueprints." As a result the machinists began to take great satisfaction in always following the blueprints right down to the last detail, even when they could easily see that the plans were wrong and the machine would never work. After the Scanlon Plan was instituted at the Lapointe Company, this in-fighting stopped. In fact, the engineers became so cooperative that they even volunteered to give up a vacation so that they could get blueprints ready in time to prevent the machinists from being laid off for lack of work. Although some experts question whether the Scanlon Plan would work in all kinds of industries, ten companies that did adopt it increased their productivity an average of about 20 percent the first year, and another 20 percent the second.

QUESTION 14.   Two groups of boys who are camping near each other have become hostile, calling each other names and staging destructive raids on each other's cabins (Sherif, Harvey, White, Hood, and Sherif, 1961). Suppose you wanted to make them friendly. Which of the following methods would best illustrate the principle described above? (Circle 1 or 2.)

1. Arrange a situation in which both groups "happen" to be picnicking in the same area and, when all the boys are famished, the truck that is supposed to get the food for both groups is found to have a dead battery.
2. Arrange for the two groups to eat all their meals together, so that they will get a chance to know each other better.

Group Norms and Roles

To help them achieve their common goals, the members of a group typically—through the liberal use of social influence on each other—arrive at a large number of norms. *A social norm is a rule for feelings, cognitions, and behaviors that is subscribed to by most of the members of a group.* Some norms are consciously recognized by the group members and others are not; some are obvious and others are extremely subtle, some are agreed upon, others only implied. Driving on the righthand side of the road is a norm (as well as a law) in the United States; loyalty is a norm in all groups, we suspect; and watching the television program "Sesame Street" before supper is a norm in at least one family we know.

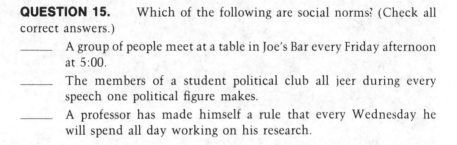

> **QUESTION 15.**   Which of the following are social norms? (Check all correct answers.)
>
> _____ A group of people meet at a table in Joe's Bar every Friday afternoon at 5:00.
>
> _____ The members of a student political club all jeer during every speech one political figure makes.
>
> _____ A professor has made himself a rule that every Wednesday he will spend all day working on his research.

In addition to norms that apply to everyone in a group, there are also norms that apply only to certain individuals. *A group of norms that make up one coherent set of duties and privileges is called a role.* Take the role of folksinger at a picnic. He is usually expected to bring his own guitar, to leave it in its case until the food has been mostly eaten, to know a great many songs, to play requests, and so on. One person may play several different roles in a group. The guitar-player at the picnic may be the same person who organized the frisbee game and cooked the hotdogs.

> **QUESTION 16.**   Is the behavior described in each of the following sentences part of the italicized role? (Write yes or no before each sentence.)
>
> _____ A *father* disciplines his son.
>
> _____ A *protestant minister* is not married.
>
> _____ A woman *jockey* lets men hold doors for her.

Every group, no matter what its goals, needs one or more people to take charge. That is, it needs people to fill its leadership roles.

The Role of Leader

According to available research, *a leader is most effective when he does two things: (1) sees to it that the group is well organized, either by the leader or by the members, and (2) shows consideration for the members.* Organizing

FIGURE 4-9. **An example of social norms. Frederick Lewis.**

a group refers to such things as making sure the important jobs get assigned and
making sure standard operating procedures are set up and followed. Consideration
includes being warm and friendly and being willing to listen to the group members
and to let them participate in making decisions.

The importance of the leader doing both of these things is shown in a
classic social psychological experiment (White and Lippitt, 1960). In this study,
fifth-grade boys were grouped into three clubs, each with an adult male leader.
Each club received different kinds of leadership at different times.

In "laissez-faire" leadership the adult just stood around doing nothing.
The result, as you might guess, was an enormous amount of horseplay by the
boys.

In "autocratic" leadership the adult made sure that activities were organized, but he showed little consideration—he made all the decisions and gave
all the orders himself. Although the boys did a lot of work under this kind of
leadership, their hearts didn't seem to be in it. If the leader left the room for
a moment, they stopped working until he returned. Furthermore, they showed
signs of resentment and aggression.

It was only in the "democratic" leadership condition that the adult leader both attended to organization and showed consideration. He made sure the group was organized by conducting democratic meetings in which the boys made their own decisions. As you would expect, this last kind of leadership had the best results. The boys were productive, even when the leader was out of the room, and they showed none of the resentment and hostility that was characteristic under autocratic leadership.

It is not always possible for leaders to allow group members to make as many of the decisions as in the "democratic" leadership condition described above. During a crisis, for example, when it is necessary that a decision be made immediately, the group leader often must make it alone. Also, in industry it is generally considered unwise to try to run groups in an entirely democratic way. Nevertheless, even here there is evidence that, within limits, consideration shown by managers and foremen toward their subordinates results in higher productivity.

QUESTION 17.   Imagine that you have just been elected chairman of a group of volunteers that is going to pick up trash along the highway.

A.   The following are statements you might make to the group. Indicate whether each statement shows high or low emphasis on organization and high or low consideration by circling the appropriate terms.

1.   "As your chairman, I've got a plan about how to work the trash pickup. Here's how we'll do it . . ."
   Emphasis on organization: high   low
   Consideration: high   low

2.   "I know you people have some good ideas about how to work the trash pickup. Let's pull your ideas together and come up with a good plan."
   Emphasis on organization: high   low
   Consideration: high   low

3.   "I'll try not to be like some chairmen I've known. I'm going to sit back and keep my mouth shut."
   Emphasis on organization: high   low
   Consideration: high   low

B.   Which of the above statements would you expect to produce the best results? (Circle one.)

    1   2   3

SUMMARY

Social psychologists study the influence of other people upon the individual's attitudes. Conformity is one effect of social influence, and some factors found to be related to conformity are size of the majority, availability of a partner, and difficulty of the task.

The search for basic reasons for social influence has produced three: (1) Conforming behavior often is reinforced by others. For example, agreement often leads to liking, which is a social reinforcer. It is also true that the need to be liked may lead to agreement. (2) Others are often perceived to have more information. For instance, the more credible a communicator, the more influence he has. For another example, when a person is experiencing an emotion that he can't identify, he is likely to look at others in the same situation and adopt their emotion. (3) Some kinds of changes restore psychological consistency. According to dissonance theory, after a person behaves in a way inconsistent with his attitudes —especially if he has minimal justification for this behavior—he will first experience dissonance, then change his attitude.

Individuals are especially susceptible to influence from their groups. Common goals tend to lead to cooperative and friendly behavior, as well as to norms and roles. A particularly crucial role is that of leader; a leader can promote group effectiveness by seeing to it that the group is organized and by showing consideration for the members.

BEHAVIOR TO EXPLAIN

Prejudice toward other groups is rampant in this world. In Northern Ireland, Catholics and Protestants hate each other. In the Middle East, it is the Arabs and the Israelis. In East Africa, the natives have negative attitudes toward the families that came from India several generations ago. Why is prejudice toward other groups so common?

1. Think of all the principles you can that might help to explain this phenomenon.

2. State an hypothesis involving a social psychological explanation of this kind of prejudice.

3. Describe a study that could be done to test your hypothesis, including both the design and the measuring instruments you would use.

chapter five

Physiological Explanations

Suppose a friend of yours were in a serious automobile accident during which his forehead rammed against the dashboard. When he left the hospital a few weeks later, he found that he could no longer concentrate or even do simple problems. He also complained of headaches and dizziness. What was the matter with him?

This is the sort of case that makes us want to know more about the internal mechanisms of the human animal, especially his nervous system. While other psychologists concentrate on the effects of external stimuli on behavior, the physiological psychologist studies the influence of physiological variables—the subject's internal environment—on behavior.

One physiological factor that is important for behavior is the chemicals that are carried in the bloodstream. Some of these chemicals are manufactured in the body: for example, the sex hormones and adrenalin. Chemicals which originate outside the body—such as nutrients and drugs—are also important for their effects on behavior.

Another important physiological determinant of behavior is the nervous system, which will be our main interest in this chapter. If you could take an X-ray of the human nervous system alone, it would look something like a mass of roots dangling from a sphere the size of a cocoanut, as shown in Figure 5-1. If you could see the color of the nervous system with its protective membranes removed, it would be gray at some places and white at others. And if you could feel it, it would be soft, like putty.

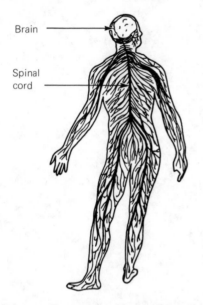

Brain

Spinal
cord

FIGURE 5-1.   The human nervous system.

The problem facing the physiological psychologist is to think of ways to find out how the nervous system takes in information about the world, processes it, and then makes the body behave appropriately. This is a large order and the physiological psychologists would be the first to admit that they have nowhere near filled it yet. There are some things, however, that are quite well understood about the nervous system, and we will focus on those.

THE NEURON AND HOW IT WORKS

The first major discovery was that the nervous system is made up of billions of separate nerve cells called neurons. These neurons do the job of telephone wires, transmitting messages from one part of the body to another. A good way to get an idea of the general organization of the neurons that make up the nervous system is to look at what happens when a person responds to a stimulus. *The sensory parts of the nervous system handle the job of transmitting information about the stimulus up to the brain, while the motor parts of the nervous*

system send back down to the muscles the messages that determine what move-
ments the person makes in response to the stimulus. For example, suppose that
you reach into your pocket and feel about for a dime. When your fingers touch
one, tiny receptor cells in the skin set off nerve impulses in several sensory neurons.
(Without various kinds of sense receptors, you would not be able to see, hear,
smell, feel, and so on because you would have no mechanisms for translating
external stimuli into nerve impulses.) Each of the sensory neurons extend up
the length of the arm and enter the spine. Once inside the spinal cord, these
neurons make contact with several new neurons, setting off impulses in them.
This second group of neurons extend up the spinal cord into the brain. There
the neurons are very short and very numerous and their connections very difficult
to trace.

Once the information is processed by the neurons of the brain, motor
neurons carry appropriate impulses down into the spinal cord. At about shoulder
level these neurons make contact with other motor neurons that transmit the
impulses out to the muscles of the arm and fingers, perhaps causing them to
move so as to grasp the coin, lift it out of your pocket, and drop it into a coffee
vending machine. If your motor nerves were damaged, you would still be able
to feel the coin, but you wouldn't be able to respond to it; without these transmission lines, the brain wouldn't be able to send orders to the muscles and you
would be paralyzed.

> **QUESTION 1.**   What will happen when the following kinds of neurons
> are damaged? (Answer by drawing a line from each kind of neuron to
> an effect.)
>
> *Kind of Neuron Damaged*   *Effect*
> Motor neuron   Person can't move his little finger.
>
> Sensory neuron   Person can't feel his little finger.

Now we shall look more closely at the individual neuron. Although
neurons differ greatly in size and shape, *every neuron has (a) several dendrites*
(pronounced *den*-drites) *that receive impulses from other neurons, (b) a cell body
responsible for nourishment and growth, and (c) one or more long, thin axons
that conduct the impulses away from the dendrites and cell body and toward
other neurons. The ends of an axon do not actually touch the dendrites of these
other neurons, but are separated from them by (d) small gaps called synapses.
A nerve is a bundle of axons from many different neurons.*

> **QUESTION 2.**   The idealized neuron drawn below is magnified many
> times because life-size neurons are barely visible. In the neuron, impulses
> travel from right to left. With that in mind, label the cell body, dendrites,
> axon, and synapses of the circled neuron by writing these terms on the
> lines below.

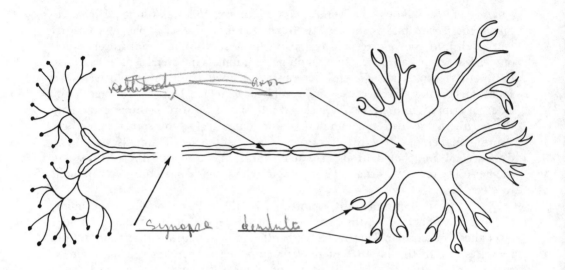

QUESTION 3.   Which would usually have the larger diameter, a neuron or a nerve? (Circle one.)

1. Neuron
2. Nerve

    A neuron works like this: if the sum of the impulses arriving at its dendrites at any moment is great enough, an impulse will be fired off at the beginning of the axon, and will be quickly carried along it to the other end. This impulse in the axon involves the movement of electrically charged chemical particles. *Individual neurons fire according to an all-or-none principle.* If the incoming impulses are above the strength needed to fire the axon, it fires at full strength. If they are not, the axon doesn't fire at all. It cannot fire at partial strength.

    How do nerve impulses get across the synapses that separate neurons? This is done by a chemical transmitter. *A nerve impulse arriving at an axon ending causes a particular chemical to be released there. The chemical moves across the synapse and sets off (or, in some cases, inhibits) an impulse in the next neuron.*

QUESTION 4.   If you attached a sensitive voltmeter to a particular axon, each impulse that passed the voltmeter would appear as a sharp "spike," the height of which would indicate the strength of the impulse. Which of the following records would you be more likely to obtain from such an axon? (Circle A or B.)

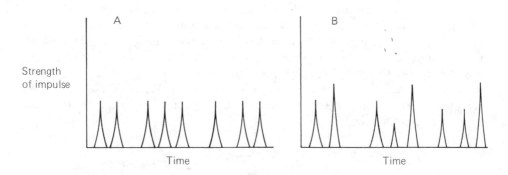

QUESTION 5. What would happen to a nervous system if the chemical that transmits impulses across the synapses were neutralized?

THE NERVOUS SYSTEM: SOME BASIC PRINCIPLES OF OPERATION

An individual neuron is not very versatile. It is like an on-off switch because it either fires completely or not at all. But the *group* of neurons that makes up the nervous system manages very complicated feats. For instance, it transmits information about quality (that it is a sound, not a sight, that we are sensing) and about quantity (that it is a loud sound instead of a soft one). We will now look at some of the basic ways in which the nervous system accomplishes these feats.

How Information about Quality Is Transmitted

Why do some sensory neurons carry "pain" messages and others carry "pleasure" messages? And why do some motor neurons carry orders to avoid and others, to approach? It can't be a difference in the *kind* of impulse that is carried, because all neurons carry the same kind of impulse. The answer seems to be that *the quality of a neural message depends only on where the impulses go in the nervous system*. Normally impulses cannot go to the visual area of the brain unless they begin at the appropriate receptor (eye) and travel over the appropriate sensory neurons. And impulses normally cannot reach the running muscles of the legs unless they begin at the appropriate starting point (motor area of the brain) and travel over the appropriate motor neurons. But if, through surgery, the normal starting points and paths of transmission are bypassed, the quality of the message will still remain the same because its destination remains the same.

A friend of the authors had an ulcerated big toe and doctors had difficulty getting skin grafts to "take." Finally they cut a flap of skin from his second toe, being careful not to detach the blood vessels or nerves, and grafted that flap onto the adjoining big toe. This is shown in Figure 5-2. The graft was a success and now, whenever this individual scratches the grafted skin of his big toe, it feels to him as though he were scratching his second toe. Why? Because the sense receptors in that graft are still attached to the "second toe" areas of the brain, wherever those may be.

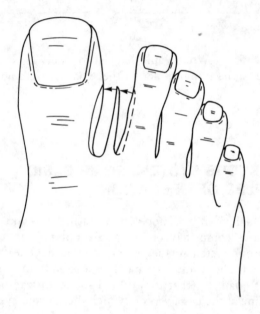

FIGURE 5-2. Grafting a flap of skin from second toe to big toe without cutting nerves.

The same sort of thing happens with motor neurons. This can be demonstrated by applying electrical stimulation to various areas of the brain. (Such stimulation causes nerves to fire but is not painful.) One brain surgeon found that electrical stimulation applied to one particular spot in the brain caused a patient to make a fist with his right hand. Even when the man tried to keep his fingers outstretched, he could not (Delgado, 1969). Clearly his hand closed because the nerve impulses produced by the electrical stimulation went to the muscles that close the hand.

QUESTION 6.   A 60-year-old man had been totally deaf in his right ear for several years. This deafness was due to some problem in the ear itself; there was nothing wrong with any of the nerves extending from the ear to the hearing areas of the brain or with the brain itself. He permitted some surgeons to carefully insert tiny wires among the nerves which led out of his deaf ear and toward his brain. What was the result when they sent small electric currents over these wires? (Circle 1, 2, 3, or 4.)

1. He felt a slight pain.
2. Nothing.
3. He heard sounds.
4. He felt a vibration.

How Information about Quantity Is Transmitted

Our sensory nerves signal mild pain at some times and strong pain at others; our motor nerves carry orders for slight muscle contractions on some occasions and for extreme muscle contractions on others. How does the nervous system transmit information about such quantitative differences?

QUESTION 7.   One logically possible explanation is this: To signal bright light, for example, each neuron leading from the eyes to the brain conducts a series of *strong* impulses and to signal dim light the same neurons conduct a series of *weak* impulses.

A. According to what you have learned in this chapter, can the above explanation be correct? (Circle one.)

    1. Yes
    2. No

B. Why?

Now let's see how the nervous system actually does signal quantitative differences. Suppose that a physiological psychologist attached sensitive voltmeters to two different axons in the same nerve—one axon having a larger diameter than the other. First he stimulated the entire nerve for a few seconds with a weak electric current, then for a few seconds with a stronger current. The resulting impulses in the two axons, as recorded by the two voltmeters, would look something like Figure 5-3. Each sharp point or "spike" in the figure is one impulse passing by the voltmeter.

Several things may be learned from Figure 5-3. First, a continuous stimulation does not produce one long nerve impulse. Instead it causes a series of brief impulses in the neuron. Second, by comparing the left half of Figure 5-3 with the right half, we can see how the nervous system signals quantity. *When the stimulation of a nerve is increased, two kinds of changes occur: (1) the neurons*

*that were firing under the previous level of stimulation now fire more frequently,
and (2) some neurons that previously were not firing at all now begin firing.*
The former effect is apparent in axon A in Figure 5-3. Although the weak stimulation did cause this axon to fire somewhat, stronger stimulation made it fire more
frequently. The latter effect is shown by axon B in the figure. While it did not
fire at all under weak stimulation, it did begin to fire under the stronger stimulation.

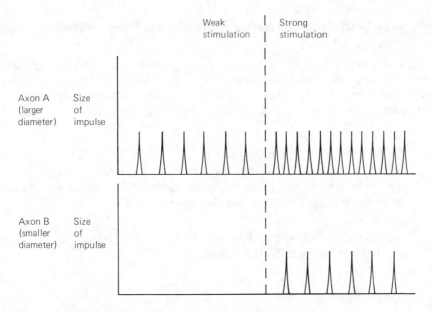

FIGURE 5-3. **Impulses recorded from two axons of different diameter.**

Finally, notice that the strength of the stimulation does *not* influence
the strength of each individual nerve impulse, only the frequency; the spikes
for axon A are all the same height and so are the spikes for axon B. The all-or-none-
principle holds.

QUESTION 8.   Suppose you put a record on the phonograph. At first
it is too loud so you turn down the volume. What happens to the impulses
in the nerves leading from your ears to your brain when you reduce the
volume? (Circle the numbers of all correct answers.)

1. A larger number of neurons fire.

2. A smaller number of neurons fire.

3. Individual neurons fire less often.

4. Individual neurons fire more often.

5. Each impulse gets larger.

6. Each impulse gets smaller.

Duplication in the Brain

In a sense, one could say that every human has two brains. This is because the left and right halves or hemispheres of the human brain, shown in Figure 5-4, are two mirror-image brains that are capable of operating independently, although ordinarily they are kept in close coordination by several connecting cables. The manner in which these two hemispheres work together is different for different kinds of tasks.

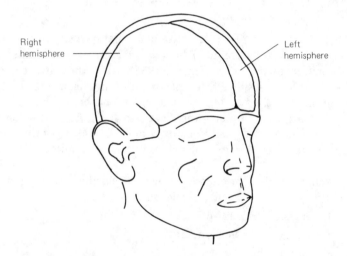

Right
hemisphere

Left
hemisphere

FIGURE 5-4. The two hemispheres of the human brain.

For the tasks of receiving sensory information and sending instructions for motor movements, each hemisphere of the brain is, for most purposes, connected only to the opposite half of the body. For example, one brain surgeon found that electrical stimulation of a particular area of the brain produced a sensation that was, according to the patient, "rather like the feeling of having just been missed by a car"—a shiver of fright—(Delgado, 1969). In accord with the above point, when this area in the left hemisphere was electrically stimulated, the sensation occurred only on the right side of the body. And when the corresponding area in the right hemisphere was stimulated, this sensation occurred only on the left side of the body.

QUESTION 9.   A particular area that is located in the right hemisphere of the brain influences motor neurons. If this area is electrically stimulated, which of the following is most likely to happen? (Circle one.)

1.   The left leg will move.
2.   The right leg will move.
3.   Both legs will move.

For speech, the left brain hemisphere is usually dominant. That is, in most people, the use of language in speaking (not the ability to move the mouth muscles) is controlled only by the left hemisphere. This can be demonstrated in an experimental situation where a brain surgeon applies electric current to certain areas of the left side of a patient's brain. If the patient is in the middle of counting aloud, he pauses during the brain stimulation, being unable to continue. Apparently what happens is that the stimulation interrupts the normal functioning of the speech regions. When the corresponding area of the right hemisphere is stimulated, however, speech is not affected.

QUESTION 10.   To cure a patient's epilepsy, a surgeon cut the connections between her left and right hemispheres, so that neither could send information to the other (Sperry, 1966). After the patient recovered she was tested for any side effects the operation might have had on her behavior. In one test she was blindfolded and a toothbrush—an object she could easily recognize by touch—was placed in her *left* hand. Then the toothbrush was taken away and placed, along with several other common objects, on the table in front of her. Finally, the blindfold was removed.

A.   Where in this patient's brain was stored the information that it was a toothbrush she had felt? (Circle one.)
　　1.   In her left hemisphere
　　2.   In her right hemisphere
　　3.   In both hemispheres

B.   First she was asked to speak the name of the object she had just felt. Was she able to do this correctly? (Circle one.)
　　1.   Yes
　　2.   No

C.   Next she was asked to point to the correct object with her right hand. Was she able to do this? (Circle one.)
　　1.   Yes
　　2.   No

D.   Finally she was asked to point to the correct object with her left hand. Was she able to do this? (Circle one.)
　　1.   Yes
　　2.   No

Still other tasks are handled by both hemispheres at the same time. For example, complex problem-solving seems to go on in the front parts of both hemispheres simultaneously.

THE NERVOUS SYSTEM: WHAT VARIOUS PARTS DO

Now that some of the major principles by which the nervous system operates have been described, it is time to look at what some of the main regions do. We will begin with the lower regions of the nervous system and move up toward the higher ones.

What the Spinal Cord Does

The spinal cord, located inside the bony spinal column, is the main cable connecting the brain with the rest of the body. But the spinal cord does not send all incoming sensory messages up to the brain. *In the case of many of the automatic, unthinking reactions called reflexes, the sensory neurons make contact with the motor neurons right in the spinal cord, without going to the brain.* Such a reflex circuit is shown in Figure 5-5. In this figure the sensory neuron—the lower one—extends into the spinal cord (shown here without the surrounding spine), where a short connecting neuron carries the impulse to a motor neuron, which leads out of the spinal cord to a muscle.

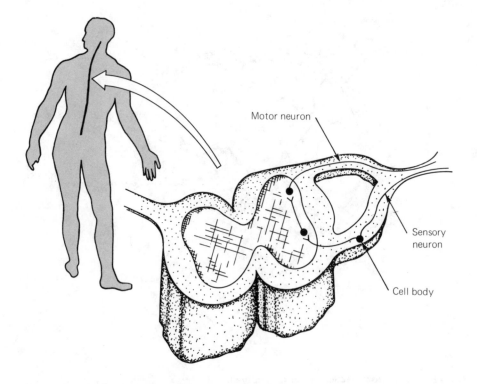

FIGURE 5-5. **A cross section of the human spinal cord.**

QUESTION 11.   In which of the following cases are the sensory-motor connections made right in the spinal cord, and in which does the brain play an important part? (Write "spinal cord" or "brain" in front of each.)

_____SC____ Throwing a baseball toward home plate.

_____Br____ Pulling a burned hand away from a hot stove.

_____Sc____ Getting goosebumps from a cold draft.

_____ Giving an usher your theatre tickets.

_____ Catching yourself when your foot suddenly begins to slip on the ice.

What the Cerebellum Does

If the brain were cut down the middle so as to separate the left and right hemispheres, the cut surface would look like Figure 5-6. At the bottom of Figure 5-6, the spinal cord comes up into the head. One of the first structures growing

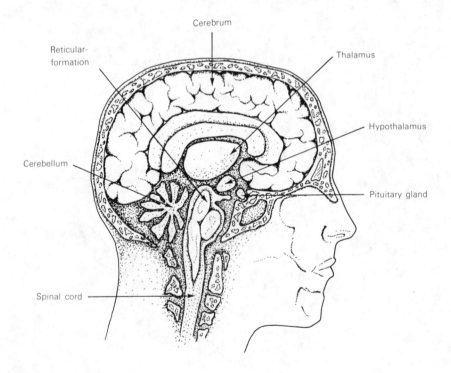

FIGURE 5-6. **A cross section of the human brain.**

out of this cord is *the cerebellum, which is responsible for coordinating the avalanche of sensory information the nervous system receives, so that the complex flow of movements of which most of our behavior consists can proceed smoothly and efficiently.* A pigeon without a cerebellum can still run, eat, and sleep. But it looks drunk. It lurches when it walks and can hardly keep its balance. When it tries to eat its peck is poorly aimed, and each time it tries to correct its error it overshoots the food in the other direction.

QUESTION 12.   Which of the following is the most likely result when a man with a damaged cerebellum is asked to close his eyes and touch his nose with his forefinger three times? (Circle one.)

1. He can't move his arm.
2. He first raises his arm and then bends his elbow, instead of doing both simultaneously.
3. He can't feel when his finger touches his nose.
4. He can't keep track of how many times he has touched his nose.

What Some Regions in the Center of the Brain Do

Many of the regions that lie in the center of the brain, under the helmet-shaped cerebral cortex, are concerned with motivation and emotion. A few of these will be described.

THE RETICULAR FORMATION   The reticular formation, shown in Figure 5-6, is a tangled mass of neurons about the size of your little finger. *Increased stimulation of the reticular formation leads to an increase in the level of activation or alertness of wide areas of the cerebral cortex.* These levels of activation, varying from extreme alertness to deep sleep, can be measured by the electroencephalogram ((EEG), a record of the overall activity of the brain. It is now known that general anesthetics, such as ether, produce their effects by decreasing the activity of neurons in the reticular formation. The brain of an anesthetized patient on an operating table receives just as strong signals from the surgical procedure as it would if he were not anesthetized. The reason he does not feel the scalpel is that his slowed-down reticular formation fails to alert the cortex to pay attention to these stimuli.

QUESTION 13.   If an electrode were implanted in the reticular formation of an animal and high-frequency electrical stimulation were administered, what would be the result? (Circle one.)

1. If sleeping, the animal would awaken.
2. If awake, the animal would go to sleep.
3. There would be no effect.

While the discovery of the reticular formation seems to go a long way toward explaining the continuum of levels of activation, there are a few particular states on this continuum that remain puzzling. One example is REM sleep. *REM sleep is the stage of sleep in which the sleeper shows rapid eye movements (REMs). These eye movements indicate that the individual is dreaming.* At least subjects who are awakened while their eyes are moving rapidly beneath their closed eyelids usually report that they have just been dreaming.

QUESTION 14.   A friend of yours vehemently claims that he never dreams. How could you find out whether or not his claim is correct?

THE THALAMUS   Another area in the center of the brain is the thalamus, which receives most of the incoming sensory information and relays it to the cerebral cortex.

THE HYPOTHALAMUS   The hypothalamus, although no bigger than a lump of sugar in man, controls an amazingly large number of functions, all of which are related to the functioning of the heart, stomach, blood vessels, glands, and other internal organs. The hypothalamus is in a particularly good position to regulate the internal environment because, in addition to its connections with other parts of the brain, it monitors the chemical contents of the blood vessels that pass near it, and it can influence the pituitary gland—which in turn controls the other endocrine glands of the body—as well as the autonomic nervous system, which is the branch of the nervous system that serves the internal organs. We shall mention, in particular, the role of the hypothalamus in relation to biological drives, reward-punishment, and emotion.

Controls Biological Drives   In the first place, *the hypothalamus controls several biological drives, such as hunger (eating), thirst (drinking), and sex.* Normally the female cat is sexually receptive about twice a year, due to sex hormones its body secretes. At those times it makes a characteristic low, throaty, purring sound, seeks male cats and human beings, and rubs against them. If sexually stimulated, it will crouch by bending its front legs, and tread in place with its hind legs by bending first one, then the other. When not in heat, however, the normal cat reacts to sexual stimulation by moving away or showing anger. One researcher found that a cat whose spinal cord had been cut *below* the hypothalamus—so that the hypothalamus was no longer influencing its behavior—reacted positively to sexual stimulation all the time, regardless of the amount of sex hormones in its system. Only if the cut were made *above* the hypothalamus, so that that region remained attached to the spinal cord, did the cat's behavior show the normal dependence on sex hormones.

> **QUESTION 15.**   Which of the following behaviors do you think could be produced by electrical stimulation of the hypothalamus? (Check these behaviors in the following list.)
>
> _____   A dog trying frantically to get its master to throw a stick.
>
> _____   A rat overeating.
>
> _____   A monkey climbing up and down trees for hours on end.
>
> _____   A goat drinking an enormous amount of water.

Acts as a Reward Center   Secondly, *one part of the hypothalamus, together with nearby regions, seems to be a reward center. Another area of the hypothalamus is part of a larger punishment region.* Electrical stimulation in the reward region causes the animal to repeat what it was doing just before the stimulation.

> **QUESTION 16.**   What effect should electrical stimulation in the punishment region have on behavior that occurred just before the stimulation?

The reward region in the brain was discovered in 1953 by a postdoctoral student named James Olds (Olds, 1955). He tried to implant some electrodes in the reticular formation of rats, and he then sent current through these electrodes, expecting that this might have some effect on learning. One rat reacted differently from the rest. If this rat received brain stimulation when he was at a particular spot in the training apparatus, he soon returned to that spot. When the same animal was placed in a T-maze and given brain stimulation each time it turned right, it was soon turning right on every trial. And, when the rat was starved for twenty-four hours and food then placed at the end of the right alley, it turned right as before and continued up the alley. However, as soon as it received the brain stimulation it stopped and did not go on to the food at the end of the alley. Later, when this unusual rat was sacrificed, it was found that the electrode had accidentally been placed, not in the reticular formation at all, but in another region nearby that came to be considered the reward region.

QUESTION 17.   A rat with an electrode implanted in a reward area of the brain is placed in an unfamiliar box containing a lever that, when pressed, causes a small electric current to be delivered to the brain electrode. What kind of change would you expect to occur in this rat's behavior as it remains in the box?

Affects Emotional Behavior   Finally, the hypothalamus, together with several other regions in the center of the brain, is involved in emotional behavior. Philip Bard's classic study of rage behavior in the cat (Bard, 1934) demonstrates its role. Rage involves the autonomic nervous system, whose sympathetic and parasympathetic divisions have largely opposite effects on the internal organs and other nonskeletal muscles. *The sympathetic division of the autonomic nervous system is dominant in moments of stress and prepares the organism to deal with the stress.* The enraged Halloween black cat, poised to attack or flee, with its spitting, its dilated pupils, its hair standing on end, and so forth, is the picture of sympathetic dominance. *The parasympathetic division is dominant in calm, nonstressful moments, and has, for the most part, the opposite effects.*

QUESTION 18.   Which division of the autonomic nervous system has each of the following effects? (Write "sympathetic" or "parasympathetic" before each effect.)

_____ A drop in blood pressure.

_____ An increase in heart rate.

_____ An increase in perspiration due to fear.

_____ A release of adrenalin into the blood system.

What Bard did was to sever the brains of cats at different locations and observe the effects on their rage behavior. In brief, here are the results of his research:

1.   When the cut was made just above the hypothalamus so that this area remained attached to the spinal cord but the cerebral cortex and the higher regions of the brain were disconnected from it, the cat still showed an organized rage reaction.

2.   When the cut was made just *below* the hypothalamus, the various parts of the rage reaction still occurred, but they were not as well organized as

they normally are. For example, the cat would often show signs of contentment, such as purring, at the same time it was hissing in rage. Bard concluded from this study that the hypothalamus plays a part in the organization of emotion.

What Regions of the Cerebral Cortex Do

The human cerebral cortex is like a helmet several inches thick that covers the top and sides of the brain center. The surface of the cortex is uneven and appears to be covered with hills and valleys. Two of these valleys or fissures are important landmarks for locating the various lobes of the cortex. These two fissures and *the four lobes of the cortex are shown in Figure 5-7.*

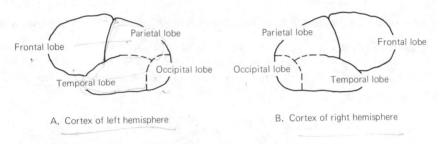

Parietal lobe

Frontal lobe

Occipital lobe

Temporal lobe

Parietal lobe

Frontal lobe

Occipital lobe

Temporal lobe

A. Cortex of left hemisphere

B. Cortex of right hemisphere

FIGURE 5-7. The lobes of the cerebral cortex.

QUESTION 19. Without looking at Figure 5-7, label the four lobes in the following drawing of the right cerebral cortex.

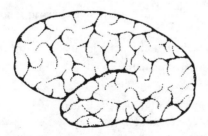

Several areas of the cortex receive information from various sense organs. *The main cortical areas for vision, hearing, and the body senses* (touch, pain, etc.) *are shown in Figure 5.8. Electrical stimulation applied directly to these areas of the cortex in a conscious human patient causes him to report fragmentary, unorganized sensations of the appropriate kind.* For instance, if the visual area is stimulated, the person may report seeing such visual fragments as a color, a long white mark, stars, or flashing lights. Patients stimulated in the visual area never report meaningful, organized objects such as a friend, a building, or a car.

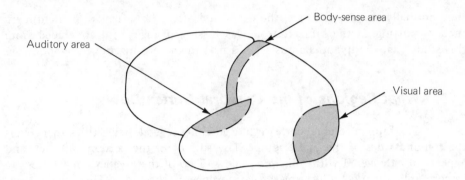

FIGURE 5-8. **Sensory regions of the cortex. These occur in both left and right hemispheres.**

QUESTION 20.   Persons suffering brain damage at the numbered locations on the cortex of the hemisphere illustrated below would be expected to show what effects? (Write the number of the location beside the matching effect.)

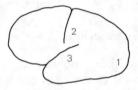

_____ Has no feeling in a particular location on the right side of his body.

_____ Has no feeling in a particular location on the left side of his body.

_____ Has difficulty hearing.

QUESTION 21.   When electrical stimulation is applied directly to the location on the cortex that is marked X below, what is the most likely result? (Check one.)

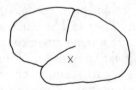

_____ The person will see a flash.

_____ He will see an automobile.

_____ He will hear a rumbling sound.

_____ He will hear a song.

_____ He will feel a tingling in his hand.

_____ He will feel a steering wheel in his hand.

In other regions of the cortex, direct electrical stimulation causes movement of a finger, a foot, or some other part of the body. The principal motor region is located just across the fissure from the body-sense area.

QUESTION 22. In which of the areas shown in the following diagram is direct electrical stimulation most likely to produce movement on the *right* side of the body? (Circle A, B, C, or D.)

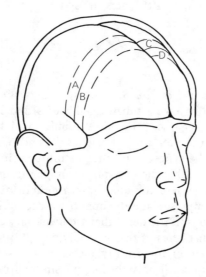

All the sensory and motor areas take up only about one-fourth of the surface of the cortex. The remaining areas have long been called "association areas," on the assumption that in these areas information from the various sense receptors are brought together and used in higher mental processes such as learning, memory, and thinking. And, in fact, there is some evidence to support this general idea. At least the higher mental processes of speech and complex problem-solving seem to be carried out in some of the association areas.

BRAIN CHANGES DUE TO ENVIRONMENT

The basic structure of the nervous system is determined primarily by heredity. But the fact that organisms can learn indicates that experience with the environment must be capable of changing the nervous system in more or less permanent ways. In recent years researchers have begun to look for such changes.

Research on this topic has been conducted at the University of California at Berkeley since the 1950's (Rosenzweig, Bennett, and Diamond, 1972). The general method used by the Berkeley research group is to place some rats in a standard laboratory environment, some in an impoverished environment, and some in an enriched environment (see Chapter 2, page 32)). After the rats have been in these environments for a month or more, they are sacrificed and their brains analyzed in a number of ways. Some of the findings to date are that the brains of the rats with the enriched experience have a thicker and heavier cerebral cortex, contain more of certain chemicals involved in synaptic transmission, and have larger synaptic areas. Although scientists are a long way from understanding exactly what is happening here, even these initial findings show that experience definitely does influence the structure of the nervous system.

SUMMARY

The basic element of the nervous system is the neuron. All neurons, whether sensory or motor, have dendrites, cell bodies, and axons, and are separated from other neurons by synapses. The nerve impulse, which follows an all-or-none principle, travels along the axon until it reaches the end. There it releases a chemical that moves across the synapse and fires or inhibits firing of the next neuron in the chain. A nerve is a bundle of axons belonging to many different neurons.

In the nervous system the quality of a neural message depends only on the destination of the impulses, and the quantity aspect of the message is signalled by the number of neurons in the nerve that are firing, as well as by their frequency of firing. The two hemispheres of the brain divide up different tasks in different ways: for the tasks of receiving sensory messages and sending motor messages, each hemisphere is connected only to the opposite half of the body. For speech, the left hemisphere is dominant in most people.

Beginning with the lower levels of the nervous system, we first mentioned the spinal cord: while most messages travel up the spinal cord to the brain for processing, in the case of reflexes the sensory-motor connections are made right in the spinal cord. A little higher up is the cerebellum; it is responsible for coordination. Some important regions in the center of the brain are the reticular formation and the hypothalamus, which controls biological drives, reward-punishment, and —in part through its influence on the sympathetic and parasympathetic divisions of the autonomic nervous system—emotion.

Sitting on top of the brain center like a helmet is the cerebral cortex, with its frontal, temporal, parietal, and occipital lobes. Some areas of the surface of the cortex are sensory areas, others are motor areas, and the remaining regions are thought to be association areas.

BEHAVIOR TO EXPLAIN

In one study (Melzack and Scott, 1957), each of ten Scottish terriers was raised from birth to eight months of age alone in a cage that prevented the dog from seeing out. Then they were taken out of the isolation cages and put into a normal environment; about a month later they were brought into the laboratory for tests. A surprising finding was that these dogs seemed incapable of feeling pain. When, due to the dogs' unpredictable movements, the researchers stepped on their paws or tails, the animals did not howl or show any of the other normal signs of pain. Furthermore, they did not withdraw from the place where the injury was received. How do you explain this strange behavior?

1.   Think of all the principles you can that might help to explain this behavior.

2.   State an hypothesis involving a physiological explanation of this behavior.

3.   Describe a study that could be done to test your hypothesis, including both the design and the measuring instruments you would use.

chapter six

Perceptual Explanations

Take a moment to inspect the inkblot in Figure 6-1. What do you think it looks like? Two kings sharing a crown, a charging bison, a hooded monk?

Theoretically speaking, an individual's perceptions are what things look like to him. But this definition of perception is only theoretical, because no outside observer can look inside the individual's "mind" to observe directly what things look like to him. How can outside observers get information relevant to the individual's perceptions, then? For one thing, they can observe the words he uses to describe his perceptions. For another, they can observe various nonverbal behaviors of his that suggest strongly what his perceptions must be. Thus, *in observable terms, the observer must infer what the subject's perceptions are, on the basis of that subject's verbal reports or other relevant behavior.*

QUESTION 1.   Select a perception that you are experiencing right now. Now, from a scientific point of view:

A. Describe this perception in theoretical terms:

B. Describe this perception in observable terms:

FIGURE 6-1. **Inkblot.**

Research has produced a wealth of information about perception, much of it fascinating. Although more is known about perception than about most other topics in psychology, we will have to be content with sketching the main outlines of the topic.

The question of how perception occurs may be divided into two subquestions. The first is, How do the sense receptors pick up stimuli? We shall show that some error occurs at this step. The second subquestion is, How is the information that is gathered by the receptors interpreted? Considering the fact that sensory information contains error, perceptual interpretations of this information turn out to be surprisingly accurate.

THE RECEPTION OF STIMULI

The five classic senses are seeing, hearing, tasting, smelling, and touching. Each involves a particular type of sense receptor, an organ that is especially constructed to pick up information about a particular kind of stimulation. Thus the eye picks up information about light waves; the ear, about sound waves; the tastebuds and smell receptors react to certain chemicals in foods and gases; and the touch receptors in the skin and muscles detect pressure on the body.

Scientists now know that there are several additional senses. For example, although most people do not realize it, they have a kinesthetic sense that provides information about the positions and movements of the various parts of the body. The kinesthetic receptors are located in the joints, tendons, and muscles, and react to muscle movements and steady positions of the body. This is the sense that makes it possible for you to touch your forefinger to your nose when your eyes are closed. Without the information about the position of your head and the position of your forefinger that is provided by the kinesthetic sense, you would not be able to accomplish this feat or many other behaviors that most of us take for granted.

In the rest of this chapter, we will limit our discussion to the visual sense, because more is known about the eye than about any other sense receptor, and because vision is the sense that we are most aware of.

The Parts of the Eye

As shown in Figure 6-2, the eye is a fluid-filled ball with a transparent lens in front. This lens adjusts so as to focus the image of the object being looked at onto the back of the eye. There is a diaphragm (the iris) that dilates or contracts so as to let the proper amount of light into the eye. Lining most of the inside of the eye is the retina, a light-sensitive surface.

As a visual receptor, the eye has several imperfections, one of which is the blind spot. This is where the optic nerve leaves the retina, carrying visual information to the brain. *You cannot see images that fall on the blind spot, for the optic nerve does not react to light striking it; however, you are not aware of this gap in your picture of the world.* You can demonstrate this to yourself by closing your left eye and looking at the X in Figure 6-3 with your right eye. Then adjust your distance from the page until the circle at the right disappears. It will probably take you a few moments to find the appropriate distance; about a foot is right for most people. At that point the circle is focused exactly on the blind spot of your right eye. But do you notice any interruption of the pattern of squares when the white circle disappears?

The blind spot does not usually produce errors in vision because, for one reason, when we use both eyes at once, objects that fall at the blind spot of one

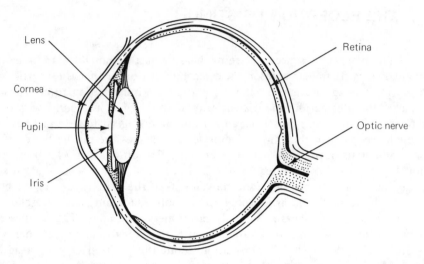

FIGURE 6-2. **The human eye.**

FIGURE 6-3. **Demonstration of the blind spot.**

eye can be seen by the other eye. Nevertheless, the blind spot is a good.example of the main theme of this chapter: we get information from our sense organs that is incomplete in some ways, but our interpretive processes manage to compensate for these deficiencies.

QUESTION 2.   Suppose that a psychologist asked a lifeguard to close his right eye and look at a screen. Then he flashed on the screen for a split second a picture of a beach with six people swimming in the water. One of these swimmers was exactly at the blind spot of the lifeguard's open eye. Then the experimenter asked the subject how many swimmers he had seen. Which of the following replies would the subject be most likely to make? (Circle 1, 2, or 3.)

1.   "I saw six swimmers."
2.   "I saw five swimmers."

3. "I saw five swimmers, but there was one spot where I couldn't see, and there may have been other swimmers at that spot."

Another small imperfection in the eye is the fact that the retina is not one continuous light-sensitive sheet. *The only parts of the retina that react to light are the small receptor cells called rods and cones that are packed together throughout it. The cones pick up images in color (or black and white, if that is the color of the object), and are more numerous in the center of the retina. The rods, like black-and-white film, pick up images only in black and white, and they are more numerous in the outer regions of the retina.*

QUESTION 3.   We can see, to some extent, both objects that are directly in front of our eyes and objects that are to the side.

A.   Which kind of visual receptor cell mainly picks up the images of objects that are directly in front of the eyes? (Circle one.)
1. Rods
2. Cones

B.   Which kind of visual receptor cell mainly picks up the images of objects that are somewhat to the sides of the line of vision? (Circle one.)
1. Rods
2. Cones

C.   A person should be able to better see the color of which objects? (Circle one.)
1. Those he is looking directly at.
2. Those he is looking somewhat to the side of.

Thresholds and Sensory Adaptation

Having described some of the parts of the visual system and how they operate, we now turn to the question of the effectiveness of sensory systems. One of the most widely used measures of sensory effectiveness is the threshold. *Roughly speaking, a threshold is the faintest stimulus the sense receptor can pick up. If that stimulus is very faint, the threshold is said to be low; if it is not very faint, the threshold is said to be high.* This terminology can be confusing because in most contexts "high" is good and "low" is bad. It is just the reverse with thresholds, however, because a low threshold indicates better sensory performance than a high one.

For example, the detail-vision threshold is often measured with the familiar eye-chart, which consists of rows of letters that become smaller and smaller. A subject who is able to read only a few of the upper (larger-letter) rows has a higher detail-vision threshold than a person who can read the lower rows also. This is illustrated in Figure 6-4.

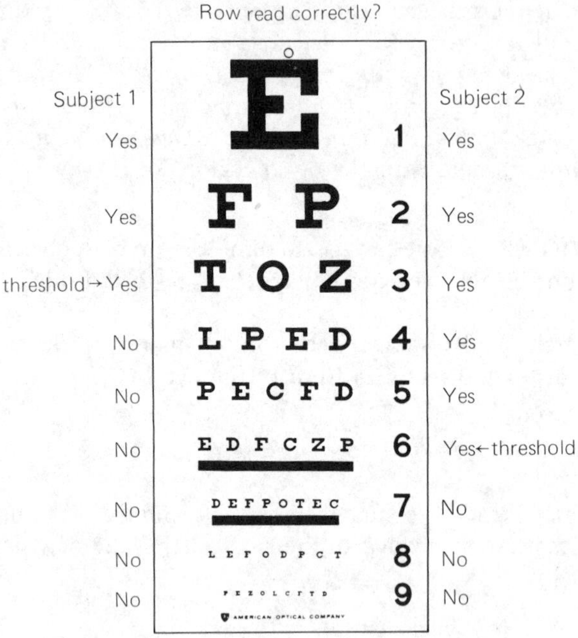

Row read correctly?

Subject 1			Subject 2
Yes	E	1	Yes
Yes	F P	2	Yes
threshold→Yes	T O Z	3	Yes
No	L P E D	4	Yes
No	P E C F D	5	Yes
No	E D F C Z P	6	Yes←threshold
No	D E F P O T E C	7	No
No	L E F O D P C T	8	No
No	P E Z O L C F T D	9	No

AMERICAN OPTICAL COMPANY

FIGURE 6-4.

Another method of measuring a threshold is used by doctors who want to test a patient's hearing. The doctor asks the patient to close his eyes, then holds a wristwatch close to the patient's ear. If the patient hears the ticking, the watch is moved farther and farther away until he no longer hears it. A patient who stops hearing the watch when it is two feet away has a higher hearing threshold than one who continues hearing it until it is five feet away.

QUESTION 4.   U.S. fighter pilots stationed on carriers in the Mediterranean often have to go up to check out blips on the ship's radar. If pilot A can tell whether an object is a Russian plane when he gets within eight miles of it and pilot B cannot tell until he gets within five miles of it, which pilot has the *higher* threshold for identifying Russian planes? (Circle one.)

1. A
2. B

It would be useful if the psychologist could assume the threshold he has measured was that subject's threshold under all conditions. However, thresholds are influenced by many factors. One of the most important of them is adaptation. *Adaptation refers to the influence of the level of recent stimulation on a threshold. For all senses, the threshold is increased when the sense organ has just been subjected to a high level of stimulation and is decreased when the sense organ has just been subjected to a low level of stimulation.* For example, when you first put a lemon drop into your mouth, the sour taste seems strong. This is because the threshold for sour stimuli is low due to a low level of prior stimulation. However, the longer the candy stays in your mouth, the weaker the sour taste seems. Your threshold is rising because of the high level of sour stimulation produced by the lemon drop in your mouth. In other words, you are adapting to the sour stimulus.

> **QUESTION 5.** Mr. A works in a quiet office, while Mr. B works in a noisy factory. If, during working hours, you took them both into a laboratory and measured their auditory thresholds, which would you expect to have the *higher* threshold? (Circle one.)
>
> 1. A
> 2. B

Another example of sensory adaptation is the fact that a person can see better and better the longer he is in a relatively dark place, such as a movie theatre. When this kind of adaptation is measured carefully, the threshold is found to decrease in two distinct drops, as shown in Figure 6-5.

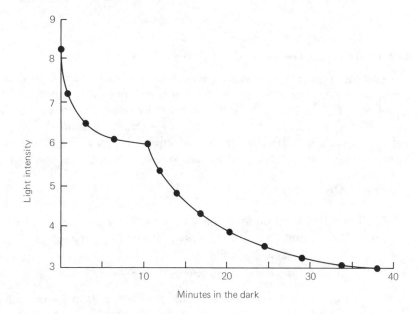

FIGURE 6-5. **Dark adaptation.**

Why are there two drops in this kind of visual adaptation? The answer seems to be that the first drop is the adaptation of the cones, while the second drop is that of the rods. That is, *at the beginning of visual adaptation the cones adapt more quickly than the rods, and thus have the lower threshold. After a few minutes, however, the cones reach their maximum adaptation; the rods then overtake them, and eventually reach a much lower threshold than the cones.* This is shown in Figure 6-6.

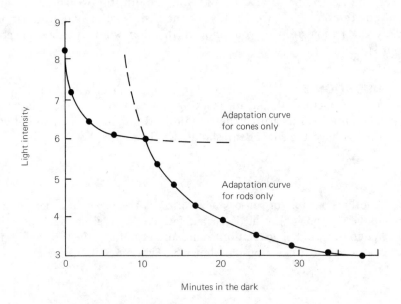

FIGURE 6-6. **The rods and cones in dark adaptation.**

Applying this principle to the person who has just entered the darkened movie theatre, we can predict that his vision will improve for the first 10 minutes or so, and that during this time he will see best by using his cones, which will give him color vision. From that point on, his vision will improve even more, but only for objects that are slightly on the side of his line of vision and thus stimulate the rods. Such objects will be seen only in black and white.

QUESTION 6.

A. If you had been outdoors on a dark night for one minute, in which case would you be more likely to see a dim star? (Circle one.)

1. If you looked directly at it.
2. If you looked a little to the side of it.

B. If you had been outdoors on a dark night for 20 minutes, in which case would you be more likely to see a dim star? (Circle one.)

1. If you looked directly at it.
2. If you looked a little to the side of it.

THE INTERPRETATION OF STIMULI

People partly make up for deficiencies in the information provided by their sensory systems by automatically organizing and interpreting that information—a process of which we are unaware.

Perceptual organization has been the primary interest of Gestalt (Gesh-*talt*) psychology, an influential "school" of psychology that began in Germany. The battlecry of Gestalt psychology has been, "The whole is greater than the sum of its parts." This means that the whole objects we perceive (for example, a melody) are not just a sum of their parts (the separate notes of the melody). Instead, these whole perceptions arise spontaneously out of certain *relationships* among the parts. Thus when a melody is transposed into a different key, it is still perceived as the same melody because the relationships among the notes have remained the same, even though the notes themselves are now different than before.

In this section we will describe some of the kinds of perceptual wholes —and the relationships that give rise to them—that the Gestalt psychologists have studied. We hope that these examples will help to convince you that you do organize and interpret everything you observe.

Perceptual Grouping

Your sensory systems present the world as a collection of separate elements—such as leaves, bricks, and people—and you, in your perceptions, rather accurately group those elements together into larger, more meaningful units. You group the leaves of one tree together and distinguish them from the leaves of another tree; you group together the bricks of one building, as opposed to those of other nearby buildings; and you perceive people as organized into such groups as families, clubs, and friendships.

What laws determine which elements you perceptually group together, and which you do not? The laws that have been suggested by the Gestalt psychologists can be described most clearly in terms of a concrete example. As one of the authors was looking out the window, trying to think of a good example for this purpose, he saw one right in front of his eyes. Four men with shovels were working beside a classroom building that was under construction. Then along came three inspectors, dressed in suits and ties, who walked together through the cluster of workmen. Needless to say, the author perceived the three inspectors as a group distinct from the four workers. The fact that he grouped the seven men in just this way can be explained by the following "laws of perceptual grouping."

1. *Principle of nearness: stimulus elements that are close together tend to be perceived as a group.* The three inspectors were closer to each other than they were to any of the four workers, and that is probably one reason they were perceived as a group. This principle, like most perceptual principles, has traditionally been illustrated with abstract, geometrical shapes, such as the circles in Figure 6-7. Notice how nearness almost forces you to group 1 and 2 together, 3 and 4 together, and 5 and 6 together, in Figure 6-7. You probably can't see 2 and 3 as a group, no matter how hard you try.

FIGURE 6-7. The principle of nearness.

FIGURE 6-8.   Photoreproduction as an example of the principle of nearness. When a photograph is to be printed, it is transformed into tiny black dots that are closer together or further apart. When the dots are close together they tend to be perceptually grouped together.

QUESTION 7.   Suppose you were the teacher of a third-grade class, and wanted to organize the floor space of the classroom so that there was one special area for remedial work with the slower students and another for advanced work with students who were ahead of the class. So that some of the favorable reputation of the advanced area would rub off on the remedial area, you wanted to encourage students to perceive these two areas as grouped together. According to the above point, which of the following floor plans would probably be the better way of doing this? (Circle one.)

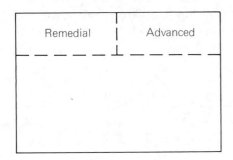 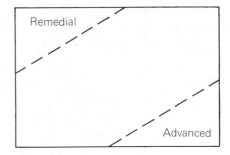

2.   *Principle of similarity: stimulus elements that are similar tend to be perceived as a group.* The three inspectors who were walking through the construction site were more similar in appearance to each other than they were to the workers, and this is probably another reason the observer grouped them together. All three were well-dressed, had their left hands in their pockets, were strolling at a leisurely pace, and were looking at the new building. The workers, in contrast, carried shovels, were dressed in work clothes, and were looking at the inspectors.

A more abstract example of the same principle is shown in Figure 6-9, where the pair of X's is usually perceived as one group, and the pair of circles as another. Nearness is not responsible for this perceptual grouping, because all the elements are the same distance apart.

$$X \qquad X \qquad 0 \qquad 0$$

FIGURE 6-9. **The principle of similarity.**

QUESTION 8.   Assume you have already set up the remedial and advanced areas in your third-grade classroom, and now you want to decorate them. Your main goal is still to make the positive connotations of the advanced area spread to the remedial area. Which of the following decorating plans would probably better achieve this goal? (Circle 1 or 2.)

1. Decorate both areas with color posters.
2. Decorate one area with color posters, and the other with hanging mobiles.

3. *Principle of continuity: stimulus elements that are part of a smooth, continuous sequence tend to be perceived as a group.* The three inspectors were walking in a straight row, three abreast. Even if nearness and similarity had not caused the author to perceptually group them together, the fact that they formed a smooth, continuous sequence—in this case, a straight line—would have. Another, more abstract example of the same principle is shown in Figure 6-10. According to the principle of continuity, the dots shown in Figure 6-10 are more likely to be perceptually grouped as shown in B, not as shown in C.

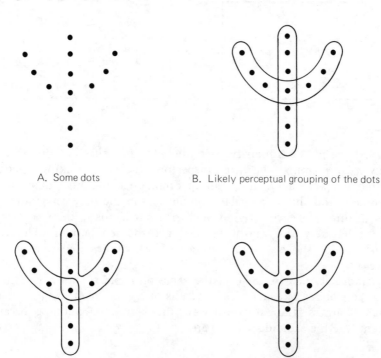

A. Some dots   B. Likely perceptual grouping of the dots

C. Unlikely perceptual groupings of the dots

FIGURE 6-10. **The principle of continuity.**

QUESTION 9.   The figure 4 that you see in drawing A below is also present in drawing B. Can you see it there? Use the above principle to explain why it is more difficult to pick out the 4 in B than in A, even though there are more extraneous lines in A to confuse you.

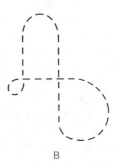

A   B

Figure-Ground Perception

Another way in which people unconsciously organize or interpret what they observe is to make a sharp perceptual distinction between objects or groups of objects upon which they are focusing their attention (figure) and those which are in the background (ground).

When the author looked out at the construction site, he saw the three inspectors as figure and the building behind them as ground. This is shown in Figure 6-11, where the "figure" is shaded while the "ground" is not. Although it is obvious that the retina could not have made any sharp distinction between the inspectors, on the one hand, and the building, on the other, they were nevertheless perceived quite differently.

FIGURE 6-11. **Figure (shaded areas) and ground.**

Three differences between the perception of figure and the perception of ground are: (1) the boundary between the figure and the ground is perceived to give shape to the figure, but not to the ground; (2) figure is perceived as nearer, while ground is perceived as more distant; and (3) ground is perceived as extending behind the figure.

These three differences can be seen in the example of the inspectors and the building. Let's begin with the perception of shape. Look at the line that forms the boundary between the three men and the background. From the information provided by your retina, this line could indicate the shape of the figure, or the shape of the ground (the shape that would be left if the three inspectors were cut out of the drawing), or both. However, you undoubtedly perceive this boundary in only one of these ways: you perceive it as indicating the shape of the figure and not of the ground. In the same way, we perceive a doughnut as having shape rather than the hole in the middle.

Second, the three inspectors in Figure 6-11 appear to be closer to the viewer, while the ground appears to be farther away.

Third, although the viewer cannot see that part of the ground which is behind the inspectors, he nevertheless thinks of it—perceives it—as continuing behind them.

There is a very simple explanation for all three aspects of figure-ground perception in this example. Namely, we perceive the illustration this way because it actually is this way. The boundary line actually does indicate the shape of the inspectors, not the shape of the wall behind them, and the ground is perceived as more distant than the figure—and extending behind them—because that actually is the case. However, this is not a complete explanation of figure-ground perception because these same perceptual phenomena occur even in flat, two-dimensional drawings. The characteristics of figure-ground perception can be seen especially clearly in "reversible figures," such as Figure 6-12.

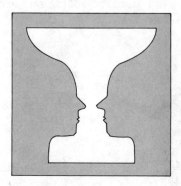

FIGURE 6-12. Reversible figure.

Look at this drawing for a minute or so. Sometimes you will perceive the white area (vase) as figure, and at other times you will see the dark area (two faces) as figure. When you are seeing the vase as figure, the shaded area becomes ground and, in accord with the principle governing figure-ground perception, loses its shape, looks farther away, and appears to extend behind the vase. When this perception is reversed, so that the shaded area now becomes the figure, it takes on very different properties. Suddenly it has shape and looks nearer than the white area, and the white appears to extend behind it.

QUESTION 10.   Suppose that on the wall of your room you have hung a poster of the Beatles. Because you want only Paul McCartney's face to show, you have taken a large piece of black paper, cut out a hole exactly the shape of McCartney's face, and taped it on top of the poster. What are people likely to perceive when they first see your poster with the black paper over it? (Check one of each pair.)

A.

_____ The black paper is one complete, uncut sheet.

_____ The black paper has a hole cut out for Paul McCartney's face.

B.

_____ McCartney's face is in front and the black paper is in back.

_____ The black paper is in front and McCartney's face is in back.

Distance Perception

Another characteristic of the objects you perceive is distance. You see the world as having depth and, if called upon to do so, you can usually make a fairly accurate estimate of how far away a given object is. Yet your eyes do not give you direct information about distance. Because the retina is a two-dimensional surface, it can give only a flat, two-dimensional picture of the world. Then how is it that the world appears to have depth? Apparently what happens is that you perceive distance by using various kinds of nondistance information that the eye does provide to make inferences about distance. These kinds of information are called distance cues. Changes in distance cues produce changes in your perception of distance, and if distance cues are lacking, you cannot judge distance accurately.

One distance cue is interposition, or apparent blocking. If one object partially blocks the view of another object, the observer perceives the object that is blocking as less distant than the object being blocked.

FIGURE 6-13. **An example of the distance cue of interposition.**

QUESTION 11.   Circle A, below, which has a piece cut away, is closer to the viewer than circle B. If the viewer looks through a peephole that allows him to see only the circles (not the bases of the stands) and if the peephole is situated so that circle B fits exactly into the cut-out curve of circle A, which circle will he perceive as closer to him? (Underline A or B.)

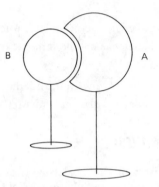

Another distance cue is retinal disparity, a term that refers to the degree of disparity, or difference, between the views our two retinas give us of an object. Because our eyes are located in different positions in the head, they do give us two slightly different pictures of anything we look at. You can demonstrate this for yourself by holding up a forefinger a few inches in front of your face. First close your right eye and notice the left eye's picture of that finger. Then close the left eye and notice how different is the right eye's picture of the same finger. When both eyes are open at once, of course, you do not see two separate pictures but one unified picture that appears to have depth. *The greater the retinal disparity, the less the perceived distance of the object.* When you hold your forefinger close to your face, the pictures given by the two eyes are more different than when you hold it farther from your face.

QUESTION 12.   You are trying to swat a mosquito that is humming around you. Which mosquito below is closer to you? (Circle A or B.)

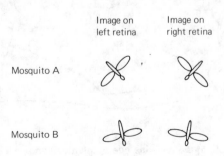

The Perceptual Constancies of Size and Shape

Constancies of size and shape are still another example of perceptual inferences being more accurate than the information provided by the sensory systems.

Size constancy refers to the fact that we perceive or judge the sizes of objects quite accurately, and our judgment is not affected by the distances of those objects. This is puzzling because it would seem that the perception of the size of an object must be based upon the size of the image that object casts on the retina. Yet retinal size is determined not only by the true size of the object, but also by its distance from the eye. (See Figures 6-14 and 6-15.)

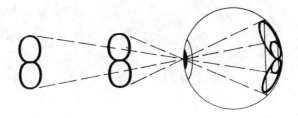

A. Side view

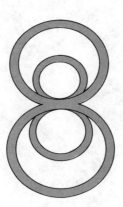

B. Observer's view

FIGURE 6-14. Size of retinal image as influenced by the size and distance of the object.

Shape constancy refers to the fact that we perceive or judge the shapes of objects relatively accurately, regardless of the angles from which we view those objects. Yet the shape of the retinal image of an object is influenced not only by the true shape of the object, but also by the viewing angle. This is shown in Figure 6-16, where the viewer perceives all of the shapes to be rectangular doors, even though some of these retinal images are far from rectangular.

FIGURE 6-15.   **Which car would you rather own? Photos by Ben Rose.**

Just how do people manage these feats of perceptual constancy? One possible explanation has probably already occurred to you: perhaps the sizes and shapes of objects are perceived so accurately simply because people are familiar with the objects and remember what they look like at different distances and angles. There is nothing wrong with this explanation. Familiarity probably does account for many cases of perceptual constancy, because many of the objects we perceive are familiar ones.

However, perceptual constancy also occurs for unfamiliar objects, and the familiarity explanation certainly cannot apply there. For example, in a classic experiment (Holway and Boring, 1941) on constancy, subjects had to estimate the true sizes of circles of light. These circles were made by shining a beam of light from a projector onto the back of a screen. Since the entire experiment was run in the early morning hours, the hall in which the screen was located was dark, except for a few reflections here and there produced by the projector light. The true size of the circle was varied, and so was the distance of the circle (and the screen) from the subject. Under these conditions, the subjects' estimates of the true sizes of the circles were very accurate. Since this outcome cannot be due to familiarity, there must be another way of perceiving size.

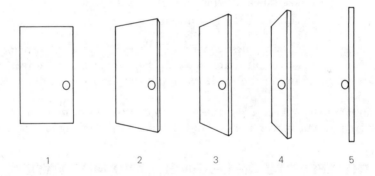

FIGURE 6-16. **Shape constancy.**

Psychologists think that *one way perceptual constancies occur is that organisms unconsciously use what information they have about the variable that is causing the distortion to correct the distorted information provided by the sense organs.*

This would mean, for example, that since distance is the distorting variable in the case of size perception, people need accurate information about the distance of an object in order to perceive its size accurately. If no distance cues are available, accurate perception of size should be impossible. This is illustrated by an experience reported by Francis Gary Powers, the pilot of the American U-2 spy plane that was shot down over Russia in 1960:

As I parachuted down part of the aircraft passed me, twisting and fluttering like a leaf. . . . I had no way to estimate size or distance. It could have been a small piece up close or a large piece some distance away (Powers, 1970).

Powers could not judge size by using information about distance because several miles above the earth there was no interposition and the objects were far enough away that retinal disparity was ineffective.

QUESTION 13.

A. Under which condition would the subjects in the Holway and Boring experiment (page 00) be more accurate in their estimates of the true sizes of the circles? (Circle 1, 2, or 3.)
   1. They could see the hallway in which the circles were located.
   2. Curtains prevented them from seeing the hallway.
   3. It wouldn't make any difference.

B. Under which condition would a student looking at a diagram of the spinal cord for the first time be better able to perceive its true shape? (Circle 1, 2, or 3.)
   1. He, was clearly told that it was a top view.
   2. He was not told what the viewing angle was.
   3. It wouldn't make any difference.

Perceptual grouping, figure-ground perception, distance perception, and perceptual constancy—each illustrates the same fact: Perception is an interpretation that makes up for many of the inadequacies of the information provided by our sense organs.

So far we have been concerned with the effects of immediate stimulation upon perception. But perception is also influenced by learning and motivation.

THE EFFECTS OF LEARNING AND MOTIVATION

An 18-year-old boy who lived in a quiet suburb had an obsession with his car, a light blue Mercury Comet, on which he had spent $3,000 to soup up. One morning he and his father were awakened by a noise about 4 A.M. and, since vandals had broken into the car several times recently, they went outside to investigate. They found nothing and went back to bed. An hour later, the boy thought he heard another suspicious noise outside. He got a shotgun and went to the window. Down below he saw a shadowy figure moving in the early morning light. He aimed and fired, killing a young boy who was doing his morning paper route. This tragedy was due to the teenager's unique perception. Another person hearing the same noise and seeing the same shadowy figure probably would have thought, "It's only the paper boy." Why did the teenager perceive it as a prowler who was after his car? Undoubtedly the explanation lies in his learning and motivations. He was strongly motivated to protect his car, and he had experienced several acts of vandalism against it.

Learning

If a person has had experience perceiving a stimulus in a particular way in the past, he will tend to perceive it in the same way in the future. In an experiment (Toch and Schulte, 1961) whose subjects were policemen and non-policemen, a violent picture was exposed to one eye of the subject at the same time a nonviolent picture was exposed to the other eye. Under these circumstances subjects will often perceive only one of the two pictures. The question in this study was, which picture would they perceive? It turned out that the policemen perceived the violent picture much more often than the other subjects did. Although the explanation of this result is not certain, it seems likely that learning played a part. In their work policemen have considerable experience with violence, and this might make them more likely to perceive violence in other situations.

For another example, a student who in high school had several arbitrary and autocratic teachers may tend to perceive his professors in college as being arbitrary and autocratic also, even if they are not.

QUESTION 14.   Suppose you were about to begin a job working with children. You have already learned that one of the children, Jimmy, has a history of beating and neglect by his parents while another child, Walter, comes from a loving, supportive home. Which of the following predictions would you make about these two children? (Draw a line from each name to a prediction.)

Jimmy   will probably perceive any interest you show in him as an attempt to hurt him.

Walter   will probably perceive any interest you show in him as an attempt to help him.

Motivation

Motivation to obtain a positive reinforcer—the fish you're trying to catch or the trophy you're trying to win—*often leads to perceptual emphasis of stimuli related to that reinforcer.* There are several ways in which this perceptual emphasis may occur. For one thing, the threshold for the reinforcer-related stimuli may be lowered. An example of this is the well-known tendency of athletes and sports fans to see rule violations by the other side especially quickly. A careful study of this kind of influence on perception has been done (Hastorf and Cantril, 1954). A film of a football game that had recently been played between two traditional rivals, Dartmouth and Princeton, was shown to students at both colleges. As they watched the film, the subjects kept count of the rule violations they saw each team make. The average Dartmouth subject perceived 4.3 Dartmouth violations and 4.4 Princeton violations, while the average Princeton subject perceived 9.8 Dartmouth violations and 4.2 Princeton violations. Presumably, these perceptions—particularly those of Dartmouth violations—were influenced by motivation to have their teams look good.

Another kind of perceptual emphasis is perceiving something that is not really there. In one study (McClelland and Atkinson, 1948), men were deprived of food for periods of time ranging from one hour to sixteen hours. Then they were told that pictures would be shown on a screen very, very dimly, and were instructed to write down their descriptions of what they saw. The projector operator went through all the motions of inserting pictures, but actually none were projected. The subjects, however, did not discover this and they all reported meaningful perceptions. The men who had been deprived of food the longest reported the largest number of food-related perceptions.

A third kind of perceptual emphasis is exaggeration of some characteristic of a stimulus, such as its size. One study that showed this used hypnosis to produce "motivation." Each subject was hypnotized and told that he was very poor:

He had been born of poor parents and his childhood had been spent in poverty; his father had never had an adequate income and consequently could not afford many of life's necessities; his clothes had been rags, his diet meager, his allowance negligible; he could not go to high school because he had to help support his family; he was still very poor; he had no regular job; what money he did earn was used to help support his family and to pay some of his many debts (Ashley, Harper, and Runyon, 1951).

At another time the same subjects were told, again under hypnosis, that they were very rich:

He had been born of very wealthy parents; he lived in a large mansion in the best and wealthiest neighborhood; he had attended the very best schools; he had always had a large allowance and never had to wish for anything; his father had given him a car and a large expense account when he had entered high school; his clothes had always been of the best quality and very expensive; he had never had any financial worries; at present he had an extremely large income that was further supplemented by his father (Ashley et al., 1951).

The purpose of these two treatments was to make motivation for money high in the one condition and low in the other. Once this had been done, the next step was to find out how this motivation influenced the subjects' perceptions of coins. A penny, a nickel, a dime, and a quarter were shown to each subject, and he was asked to estimate the size of each by adjusting the size of a spot of light. The results of the study were that subjects overestimated the sizes of the coins when they were "poor," and underestimated them when they were "rich."

In summary, we tend to see what we want to see: we see it even when it isn't there, and when it is there we have an especially low threshold for seeing it, and see it in an exaggerated way.

QUESTION 15.   Suppose that Sue is lonesome for her boyfriend, Bill, who has been away for several months.

A.   Sue watches another girl shuffling through the dorm mail, that actually contains no letter from Bill. How likely is Sue to think she sees a letter from Bill in the stack of mail, compared to someone more objective about Bill, such as her roommate? (Circle one.)
1.   More likely than her roommate.
2.   Just as likely as her roommate.
3.   Less likely than her roommate.

B.   Sue has a color photo of Bill tacked up on her wall. If we measured perception of the brightness of the photo, how bright would it look to Sue and to her roommate? (Circle one.)
1.   Brighter to Sue than to her roommate.
2.   Equally bright to both girls.
3.   Brighter to the roommate than to Sue.

C.   One afternoon Bill is due to arrive for a visit. Sue and her roommate are out in front of the dorm waiting for him to show up. Which of them is likely to recognize his car first in the distance? (Circle one.)
1.   The roommate will recognize it first.
2.   Sue and her roommate will both recognize it equally quickly.
3.   Sue will recognize it first.

While positive reinforcers usually lead to perceptual emphasis, the effects of negative reinforcers are inconsistent. Sometimes they produce perceptual emphasis, and sometimes perceptual de-emphasis. In one study, American subjects were found to overestimate the size of a Nazi swastika, while in another, taboo words such as "raped," "whore," and "Kotex" were found to have higher thresholds than neutral words.

SUMMARY

Theoretically speaking, a person's perceptions are what things look like to him, although in practice they must be inferred from his verbal reports or other relevant behavior.

Although the eye (the only sense receptor we discussed) is well constructed to pick up information about light waves, it is not perfect. For example, it has a blind spot, and the only parts of the retina that react to light are the rods and cones. The threshold of the eye, as well as of other sense organs, shows adaptation. During visual adaptation to the dark, first the cones are more sensitive, then the rods.

We partly make up for the deficiencies in the information provided by the sense organs by perceptually interpreting that information. Examples of such interpretation are perceptual grouping, which is influenced by the nearness, similarity, and continuity of stimulus elements; figure-ground perception; distance perception, which relies on distance cues such as interposition and retinal disparity; and the perceptual constancies, where the organism uses information about the distorting variable to correct for the distortion of the retinal image, allowing him to judge such variables as size and shape accurately.

Perception is influenced not only by current stimuli, but also by learning and motivation. We tend to perceive objects according to our past experience, and if we are motivated to obtain an object, we tend to perceptually emphasize it in several ways.

BEHAVIOR TO EXPLAIN

Some automobile drivers are a menace on the highway; they have accident after accident, "totaling" one car after another. Insurance companies, knowing this, would like to avoid insuring drivers who have had several accidents, even for high premiums. Why do these drivers have so many accidents, while other persons who drive just as much have none?

1.   Think of all the principles you can that might help to explain this difference in behavior.

2.   State an hypothesis involving a perceptual explanation of this behavioral difference.

3.   Describe a study that could be done to test your hypothesis, including both the design and the measuring instruments you would use.

chapter seven

Motivational Explanations

You see a well-dressed young man sprinting along a business street. He weaves in and out of the crowds like a halfback, then cuts across the street, nearly colliding with a car.

You come to a dead stop and watch, and so do several other passersby. Is this man running away from something? Or is he trying to reach his car before he gets a parking ticket? Or what?

The man comes to a bank, slows down, and walks in, just as the clock reaches 2 P.M., and a bank employee comes out to lock the door.

WHAT IS MOTIVATION?

In Theoretical Terms

The usual theory is that behavior is motivated by two kinds of factors: motives and incentives. *The motive is the internal urge or desire,* such as the desire of the man to withdraw money from the bank before it closed. A motive is considered an internal force that pushes the organism to behave in a particular way.

The incentive is the thing the organism wants—in other words, its goal. In the above example the incentive was the money that the man wanted to withdraw. An incentive may be thought of as an external force that pulls the organism to behave in a certain way.

Another example of motive and incentive is shown in Figure 7-1.

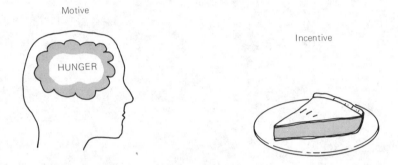

FIGURE 7-1. An example of a motive and an incentive.

QUESTION 1.   A boy who went camping for a week all by himself returned home with a strong desire to be in the company of other people.

A.   What was the motive here?

B.   What was the incentive here?

So far we have been using only theoretical terms—motive, urge, desire, incentive, goal—none of which is directly observable. Now let us look at some of the observable stimuli and responses that are usually linked to these theoretical terms.

In Observable Terms

There are several observable factors that are usually considered to be related to motivation: some are stimulus variables that lead to motivation, and others are response variables that result from motivation.

A stimulus variable that seems to influence most motives is amount of deprivation. This variable may be used to influence a subject's motivation. As you will recall, in the study on the effects of hunger motivation on perception that was described on page 148, the researchers deprived their human subjects of food for periods ranging from one to sixteen hours. Amount of deprivation can also be used as a measure of motivation. That is, an organism's degree of motivation may be defined as the amount of time that he has been deprived of the incentive, whether by the researcher or not.

> **QUESTION 2.**   What is one way you could increase a subject's motivation to be successful?

As for response variables that result from motivation, there are generally considered to be two: activation and direction. As a result of his motivation to withdraw money from the bank before it closed, the behavior of the man described at the beginning of this chapter was highly activated—he was running, instead of walking or standing still, and his feet were directed straight toward the bank, instead of wandering about indecisively.

The following sections will describe some of the specific motives science knows most about. We will describe first some biological motives, such as hunger, then some psychological ones, such as the motive to be active and the achievement motive. The biological motives are usually called drives, and we will follow this practice.

BIOLOGICAL DRIVES

Homeostatic Drives

The concept of homeostasis helps make sense out of many of the biological drives. The concept is this: a complex physiological balance is necessary to the survival of the body. Therefore the body has mechanisms to restore this balance when it is upset—that is, when a bodily need arises.

Some of these homeostatic mechanisms are automatic, not requiring motives or behavior at all. For example, when a man needs water, a hormone is released that allows the kidneys to reabsorb water so that less water will be excreted in the urine. If, on the other hand, a man has an excessive amount of water in his body, less of this hormone is produced and the kidneys put more water into the urine.

Another way of restoring vital physiological balance is through behavior. This is where the homeostatic drives come in. To experience one homeostatic drive, try this: exhale and don't inhale right away. As you sit there not breathing, what is happening inside your body? The vital physiological balance is gradually being lost as your oxygen supply is used up. The result is a drive for air, reflected in a very unpleasant, suffocating sensation in your chest. You can see now why this is called a *drive*; it almost forces you to breathe.

Curiously enough, some crucial physiological needs produce no drives. An example is the need to avoid too much carbon monoxide. If a man sits in his car with the engine running, a leaky exhaust pipe may cause the car to fill up slowly with carbon monoxide. Although a lack of air quickly produces a strong drive, an overconcentration of carbon monoxide produces no drive at all. The man may die without ever suspecting that anything is wrong.

In summary, *a homeostatic drive is a drive that leads the organism to correct a situation that could, if ignored, lead to its injury or death.*

QUESTION 3.   Apply the above definition to each of the following:

A. Freud speculated that there is a "death wish" that leads people to injure or destroy themselves. If this death wish existed, would it be a homeostatic drive? (Circle one.)
  1. Yes
  2. No

B. It has been claimed that sexual abstinence has never physically damaged anyone. If this is true, is sexual motivation homeostatic? (Circle one.)
  1. Yes
  2. No

C. Could pain motivation ever be homeostatic? (Circle one.)
  1. Yes
  2. No

Hunger

Hunger is a homeostatic drive. Most of the research on hunger has been aimed at discovering the mechanisms by which the body's physiological need for food is translated into hunger motivation. Four important mechanisms have been found: stomach stimulation, mouth stimulation, blood chemistry, and brain stimulation.

STOMACH STIMULATION   *While the stimuli produced by stomach contractions are normally related to hunger, they are apparently not essential for hunger.* Studies have shown that reported hunger pangs correspond closely to the periods when stomach contractions are at their maximum. But apparently there are other hunger mechanisms that can carry on in the absence of signals from the stomach, because it has been found that people who have lost their stomachs in surgery still get hungry.

QUESTION 4.   If certain nerves were injured so that you could no longer feel your stomach, would you still experience hunger motivation? (Circle one.)

1. Yes
2. No

MOUTH STIMULATION   *Stimulation of the mouth and throat in the process of chewing and swallowing food helps to reduce hunger motivation.* This was shown by a rather clever experiment on rats (Berkun, Kessen, and Miller, 1952). Before the experiment, each of the animals had been equipped with a plastic tube attached to an incision in its stomach. During the experiment, the rats were first fed a fixed amount of milk in one of two ways: either the milk was injected directly into the stomach through the plastic tube, or else they drank it in the normal way from a dish. In the latter procedure, of course, the rat's mouth and throat were stimulated during feeding, while under the former method they were not. Which method of feeding reduced hunger more? To find out, each rat was next given a large container of milk and allowed to lap up as much as it wanted.

QUESTION 5.   In the last phase of the above experiment, when all the rats ate as much as they wanted, what was the behavior of the rats that had previously been tube-fed? (Check one.)

_____   They ate more than the other group.
_____   They ate the same amount as the other group.
_____   They ate less than the other group.

BLOOD CHEMISTRY   *Another factor that has been found to influence hunger is some unidentified ingredient in the blood.* For example, when dogs that were just hungry enough to begin showing stomach contractions were given transfusions of blood from very hungry dogs, their stomach contractions increased. However, efforts to find out exactly what blood ingredient has this effect have not been very successful.

QUESTION 6.   Suppose you were a doctor transfusing whole blood into a patient who happened to be showing signs of hunger. After the transfusion, the hunger signs stopped much more quickly and completely than they usually do in such cases. What would you conclude about the person who had given this blood?

BRAIN CENTERS   We mentioned in Chapter 5 that the hypothalamus controls eating behavior. *Researchers have found in the hypothalamus a pair of "start" centers and a pair of "stop" centers that dramatically influence eating.* In each of these pairs, one neural center is in the left hemisphere of the brain and the other is opposite it in the right hemisphere.

The "start" centers apparently function to start eating behavior. If these centers are damaged, an experimental animal will refuse to eat, and it will die unless tube fed. The vehemence with which a rat suffering this kind of brain damage rejects food (and water, because centers for thirst lie in the same region of the hypothalamus) is interesting. If food or water gets on its paws or body, the rat immediately shakes or rubs them off. If, despite its resistance, milk is forced into its mouth, the rat lets it all dribble out the side. Curiously enough, this is exactly how a normal rat reacts when its milk is made bitter by adding quinine to it (Teitelbaum and Epstein, 1962).

QUESTION 7.   Another piece of evidence that these areas are indeed "start" centers is that when they are electrically stimulated by electrodes implanted in the rat's brain, the following happens: (Check one.)

_____   The animal starts to eat.

_____   The animal stops eating.

_____   Nothing happens; the animal continues whatever it was doing.

The two "stop" centers, of course, normally act to stop eating. If these two areas are damaged, the rat will eat and eat and eat, as though there were nothing to stop him. Such a rat will soon become obese (see Figure 7-2). There is something unusual about this rat's hunger, however. Unlike the normal hungry rat, the one with the damaged "stop" centers won't work for its food. And it is very choosy about what it eats; it will eat only food that is especially tasty.

There is still a lot to learn about the hunger drive. One major question is, How do the four mechanisms of stomach stimulation, mouth stimulation, blood chemistry, and activity in the hypothalamus fit together in controlling eating behavior?

Thirst

Thirst, too, is a homeostatic drive. Probably your thirst motivation has kept your need for water so well satisfied that you don't know what extreme thirst is like. Here is a glimpse of what it was like for a group of U.S. cavalrymen who got lost while chasing Indians in Texas in the 1870's (King, 1958). Hunger motivation was added to thirst soon after the water gave out, because their mouths and throats got so dry they couldn't swallow their food. What sleep they were able to get on those hot, dry plains was filled with dreams of feasts at which they were drinking and eating to their hearts' content. For some reason, they became partially deaf, and had to repeat questions to each other several times. They began to lose confidence in their comrades and to be suspicious of them. Some of these effects are difficult to understand; but at least it is clear that the effects of thirst were pervasive.

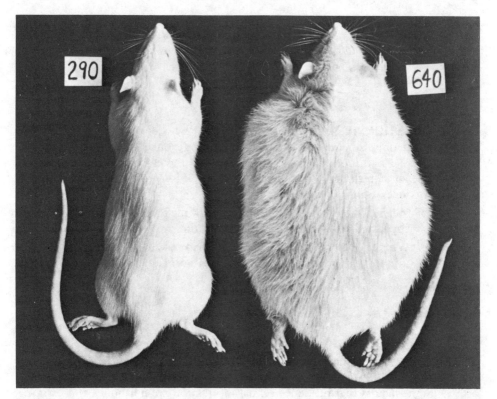

FIGURE 7-2. A normal rat and a rat that is obese due to hypothalamic damage. Courtesy of Philip Teitelbaum.

The major causes of thirst are the same four kinds of factors that are important for hunger: stomach stimulation, mouth stimulation, blood chemistry, and brain stimulation: Stomach stimulation is due to water in the stomach. Scientists have identified at least one blood ingredient that affects thirst—salt. If humans are given injections of a solution that is saltier than the body fluids, they get thirsty. The hypothalamus contains "start" and "stop" centers for drinking, as well as for eating.

QUESTION 8. When the cavalrymen described above finally found a lake, the urge to drink was irresistible. Even after their stomachs were completely filled with water, they still felt thirsty. How do you explain their continued thirst, even when the messages from their stomachs to their brains must have indicated that their stomachs were full?

QUESTION 9.   People stranded in lifeboats on the ocean soon learn that ocean water doesn't quench their thirst. Why doesn't it?

QUESTION 10.   Neurons can be fired by pressure, as well as by electrical impulse. An operation was performed on a 22-year-old woman to remove a tumor that had apparently been pressing on the neurons of one of her thirst "start" centers (Wolf, 1958). What was the effect of this operation? (Circle 1 or 2.)

1.   Whereas before the operation her drinking had been normal, afterward she asked for a drink every five minutes.
2.   Whereas before the operation she had asked for a drink every five minutes, afterward her drinking was normal.

Sex

Sexual motivation, although it falls in the biological category, is not homeostatic. Priests and hermits completely abstain from sexual activity for long periods of time, and they live as long as anyone else.

Some factors that influence sexual motivation are hormones and learning.

HORMONES   Hormones play an important part in sexual motivation and behavior. Take the case of singing in canaries. Although female and male canaries look almost identical, there is one easy way to tell them apart: while the females make individual chirps, only the males make the continuous sound that is called singing. However, if a female is given an injection of male sex hormone, she will, after a week or so, begin to sing like a male, and this singing will continue for several weeks.

It is suspected that some dealers who ship canaries to the United States have capitalized on this fact. Some pet shops have found that their canaries, although they were singing vigorously when they arrived, in a short time mysteriously lost their voices (Herrick and Harris, 1957).

Sex hormones are critical for the development of normal sexual structures and normal sexual behavior in all animals. *Once sexual maturity has been reached, however, sex hormones are less important for sexual behavior in humans than in lower animals.* For example, female rats will mate only when they are in "heat." This is the time of ovulation, when certain sex hormones are released into the blood stream. In contrast, human females report that they have no more sexual desire at ovulation than at other times of the month.

QUESTION 11.   Which would show a greater decrease in frequency of mating? (Check one.)

_____ A female rat whose ovaries (a source of sex hormones) had just been removed.

_____ A human female whose ovaries had just been removed.

LEARNING   While hormones are less important for sexual behavior in man than in lower animals, learning is more important. *There seems to be no limit to the stimuli that man can learn to be sexually motivated by.* Male homosexuals have learned to be sexually aroused by the sight of the male body, instead of the female body. One homosexual wrote how, in his boyhood, his mother had insisted that he take swimming lessons at the "Y." But he always found a way to avoid going, because they swam nude at the Y, and he was afraid he would be bothered by disturbing fantasies (Miller, 1971).

For several centuries, the Chinese male was taught by his culture to be sexually aroused by the sight and touch of a dwarfed, misshaped female foot! During these centuries Chinese parents, to make sure their young daughters would later be able to attract a husband, tightly bound their feet. The little girls suffered terrible pain at first, and it was difficult to walk upon the deadened, twisted feet that resulted (Levy, 1969).

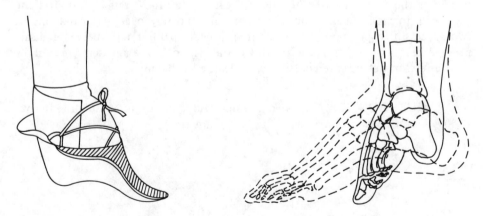

FIGURE 7-3. **The dwarfed foot that Chinese males once found so attractive.**

QUESTION 12.   Which of the following stimuli could humans conceivably learn to be sexually aroused by? (Check all possible answers.)

_____ Nylon stockings

_____ Sailboats

_____ Pillows

_____ Baby carriages

_____ Lawn mowers

BEHAVIORAL RESULTS OF SEXUAL MOTIVATION   *Many of the responses to sexual motivation are learned.* Whereas previously we talked about learning to be sexually motivated by certain stimuli (A in Figure 7-4), now we are talking about learning how to react to that motivation (B in Figure 7-4).

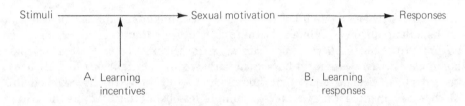

FIGURE 7-4. **Learning and sexual motivation.**

Let's begin with the example of courting behavior. It becomes obvious that this is learned when you look at the Goajiros tribe of South America, where it is the practice for a woman to express her interest in a man by tripping him during a ceremonial dance.

Learning may also be necessary for sexual intercourse. For example, although most male rats don't have to learn to copulate, some apparently do. These rats react the first time to a female in heat by dashing erratically around the cage, dragging the female about the floor, and crawling over her. After one or two successful copulations have occurred, however, this erratic behavior disappears. As for humans, the Sirionos in Central America bite and scratch to show their affection during intercourse, clearly learned behavior.

QUESTION 13.   It is sometimes said that sex is an inborn motive. Describe some ways in which this is not true.

A frequent reaction to sexual motivation is to inhibit sexual behavior and thoughts. Learned social taboos, such as the incest taboo, are often responsible for such kinds of sexual inhibition as impotence and repression. Sigmund Freud was one of the first to realize the importance of sexual inhibition. He discovered that frequently, when he explored the roots of a patient's problems, he stumbled onto important events of a sexual nature that the patient had apparently pushed out of his mind, or "repressed."

Neurotic patients are not the only ones who sometimes inhibit sexual thoughts. An experimenter (Clark, 1952) brought groups of college men into a classroom, and had them look at slides. Some saw slides of nude women, which were intended to arouse their sexual motivation; others saw only slides of landscapes and buildings. Next all the subjects were shown some drawings of situations with sexual connotations, and were instructed to write stories about these situations. The researcher then counted how many times sex and guilt about sex were mentioned in the stories. He found *less* sex and guilt in the stories written by the men who had just looked at the pinup girls. Although they presumably had greater sexual motivation than the other group, they apparently repressed it in the classroom environment.

Surprised by this finding, the experimenter wondered if he would get different results by repeating the study at a fraternity beer party instead of in a classroom. So he got the cooperation of several fraternities by offering to pay for their drinks, and tried out his hunch. In this environment, he got results that were just the opposite of the previous ones. Here he found that the men who had just seen the nude pictures put *more* sex and guilt into the stories they made up, compared to the men who had merely seen the landscapes.

QUESTION 14.   Even if the ethical problem of invasion of privacy can be overcome, it can still be difficult to measure sexual motivation, either by questioning the subject or by observing his behavior. Explain the difficulty, basing your answer on what you learned from the above experiment.

Another kind of behavior that is related to sexual motivation is the physiological responses that occur before and during sexual intercourse. Until recently, the main source of information about these responses was sexual folklore. Then in 1966, a book was published that reported on the sexual responses of nearly 700 volunteers who were closely and carefully observed under laboratory conditions. Several new findings resulted from this study. For example, it was found that some women are capable of having several orgasms in close succession, while men can have only one at a time (Masters and Johnson, 1966).

Fear

Fear is a learned motive. In itself, it is not homeostatic or, for that matter, even biological. We include it among the biological motives because fear learning is often based upon pain, which is biological.

Fear is by no means the only learned motive. We have learned to get hungry when we smell the aroma of broiling steaks and to get thirsty when we hear the tinkle of ice cubes in a drink. Furthermore, many women are addicted to TV soap operas, and their husbands get upset if anyone interrupts them while they are watching pro football on Sunday afternoon; these, too, look like motives and are certainly learned.

Classical conditioning seems to be the main way fear is learned. One example of classical fear conditioning was described in Chapter 3—the woman who was conditioned to feel uneasy whenever she looked at or wore the dress that she had been wearing at the time of a frightening near-accident. Another example is the study (Watson and Rayner, 1920) carried out many years ago by John Watson, the founder of behaviorism. Watson used as his only subject an infant known to posterity as "Little Albert." Like many other psychologists, we do not completely approve of the way Watson treated Albert in this study, but we cannot deny that the study was an informative one.

Watson's first step was to look for an unconditioned stimulus, one that nine-month-old Albert was afraid of. Although the infant turned out to be relatively fearless, there was one thing that would make him cry—a loud noise. Starting with this fear, Watson set out to condition Albert to be afraid of something else—a lovable, furry white rabbit. This, of course, was the conditioned stimulus.

Next Watson stood in front of Albert, hiding the rabbit, while his co-worker stood close behind the little boy, a steel rod suspended from one hand and a hammer poised in the other. Then Watson uncovered the rabbit, and just as Albert reached out to pet it, the hammer struck the steel rod a resounding blow. Albert was upset by the noise, to say the least.

A few minutes later, rabbit and loud noise were presented together once again. After only seven such pairings, the rabbit was shown to Albert without any noise, and he beat such a hasty retreat on his hands and knees that the experimenters were barely able to catch him before he fell off the table.

This study is diagrammed in Figure 7-5.

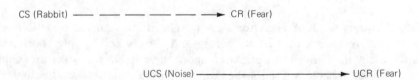

FIGURE 7-5. Diagram of Watson's classical conditioning of a fear response in Little Albert.

QUESTION 15.

A. Describe how you could teach a dog to be afraid of the sight of cars, and thus to stay away from them.

B. In the training procedure you just described, what is the
CS:
UCS:
CR:
UCR:

PSYCHOLOGICAL MOTIVES

Not so many years ago, psychologists knew little about motives other than the biological ones. Many psychologists thought that all motives were either biological or else, like fear, learned as the result of biological motives. In recent years, however, more has been learned about psychological motives. A few of the many psychological motives are the motives to be active, to investigate novel stimuli, and to achieve.

ACTIVITY   *There seems to be a motive to be active.* Consider the college student who has been cooped up in his room for several days, writing a term paper. Doesn't this deprivation of activity have effects similar to those of food deprivation? That is, doesn't it increase motivation? Doesn't the student begin to have trouble sitting still at his desk, and to talk about going "stir-crazy?"

QUESTION 16.   Woman A has a desk job; woman B is a high school teacher. Considering only the above point, which woman would you expect to have which of the hobbies listed below? (Write A or B before each hobby.)
_____ This woman's favorite hobby is square-dancing.
_____ This woman's favorite hobby is reading novels.

NOVEL STIMULI   *There seems to be a motive to investigate novel stimuli.* One investigator (Butler, 1957) demonstrated this motive in a study of Rhesus monkeys. The subjects were put into an isolation box, and were trained to press a switch that opened a small window, providing a glimpse of the activities in the laboratory monkey colony outside (see Figure 7-6). Viewing these activities presumably provided more novelty than did simply looking at the bare interior of the isolation box.

Next there was a period during which some of the monkeys were deprived of looking outside by being kept in the box for eight hours with the window locked shut, while another group of monkeys was not confined in the closed box at all.

Finally the window was unlocked, so that pressing the switch would open it once again, and each monkey was tested in the box for one hour. The results support the above point: the monkeys that had been deprived of the novel stimulation for eight hours pressed the switch more frequently than those that had not experienced this deprivation.

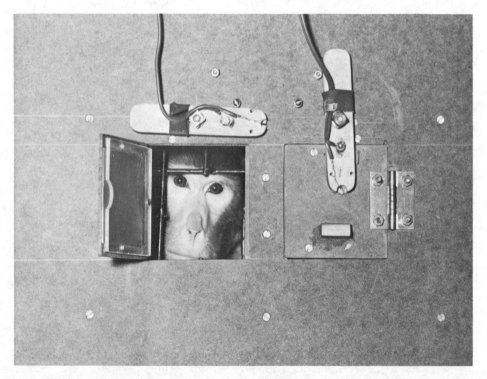

FIGURE 7-6. A monkey who has pressed a switch looking out at interesting activities. This apparatus was used to measure motivation to investigate novel stimuli. Harry F. Harlow, University of Wisconsin Primate Laboratory.

QUESTION 17. Human experiments have been done in which the experimenter shows drawings to the subject, and measures how much time he spends looking at each drawing. On the basis of the above principle, which drawing in each of the following pairs do you think subjects typically spend more time looking at? (Circle one drawing in each pair.)

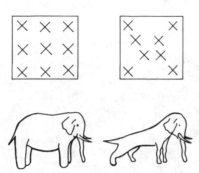

ACHIEVEMENT   Probably the best understood psychological motive is the "need for achievement," which has been studied for more than twenty years by psychologist David McClelland.

One of McClelland's most important contributions was to develop a method of measuring the need for achievement, or "n Ach," as he abbreviates it. He decided to use a projective test, in which subjects would be asked to write stories about pictures such as the one shown in Figure 7-7. McClelland was sure that if two people—one high and one low in n Ach—were shown such a picture, the stories they wrote would reveal their achievement motivation. *In their stories, people with high n Ach would say that the characters were striving to achieve some difficult goal, while those with low n Ach would not see any such striving.* For example, a high n Ach individual might say that the boy in Figure 7-7 was determined to become the president of the chain of stores for which he worked, while a person with low n Ach might say that the boy had an after-school job only because his parents made him take it, and that he would quit as soon as he was allowed to.

Although McClelland was confident that these general kinds of differences would occur, he did not know *exactly* what kinds of stories high and low n Ach subjects would make up. To find this out, McClelland decided to take two equivalent groups of subjects and make the n Ach of one group higher than that of the other, then show both of them the drawings and see what the differences were in the stories they wrote. But how could he make the n Ach of one group higher than that of the other? McClelland did it by depriving one group of achievement—that is, he led them to believe they had done very poorly on an intelligence test—while giving the other group no such failure experience. As expected, the stories written by the two groups were quite different, and McClelland derived from those differences a set of rules about what kinds of story features should be counted toward the n Ach score.

QUESTION 18.   Which of the following stories, written about a drawing of a boy seated at a desk with an open book in front of him, shows higher n Ach? (Circle 1 or 2.)

1. "He is daydreaming about his girl friend, and having trouble keeping his mind on the dull textbook. He has been hating school for several

FIGURE 7-7. The type of picture used in McClelland's test for N Ach.

years, just waiting until he reaches 16 so he can drop out and get married. On the day he reaches 16, he will leave school, get married to his girl friend, and never read another textbook."

2. "This boy is studying physics, because he wants to learn all there is to know about electricity. He told his teacher that he was interested in electricity, so the teacher loaned him this book to read. When he grows up, he will become a famous physicist, and will invent a new way of getting electricity directly from the sun's rays, which will be a boon to mankind."

MASLOW'S THEORY OF MOTIVATION

How are the various motives organized? We will discuss in this section the well-known theory (e.g., Maslow, 1970) of psychologist Abraham Maslow, who tried to put what he considered the major human motives into a meaningful system. At many points Maslow's theory goes beyond available evidence. Hypotheses, however, have their value.

Maslow suggests that the five main kinds of human motives, arranged from lowest to highest, are (1) physiological, (2) safety, (3) social, (4) self-esteem, and (5) self-actualization.

PHYSIOLOGICAL MOTIVES   These are the motives that were presented in the beginning of this chapter—hunger, thirst, and so on. They are the motives psychologists have studied most.

SAFETY MOTIVES   These motives arise from people's need to have the world be safe and stable.

SOCIAL MOTIVES   People need warm and friendly human relationships and they need to belong to groups.

SELF-ESTEEM MOTIVES   People want to achieve, and they want others to respect them for their achievements. McClelland's n Ach would seem to belong in this category.

SELF-ACTUALIZATION MOTIVES   The individual needs to strive to attain the fullest possible development of his own unique potentialities.

QUESTION 19.   Below are Maslow's five kinds of motives, listed in order:

_____ 1. Physiological   _____ 4. Self-esteem
_____ 2. Safety   _____ 5. Self-actualization
_____ 3. Social

Indicate which of these motives is the primary one involved in each case below by writing the letter of each case beside the appropriate motive in the above list.

a. Three-year-old Sally never knows what to expect from her father, who is an alcoholic.

b. Eight-year-old Jim is always telling his classmates big stories about how well he can shoot a bow and arrow and how many frogs he has caught.

c. During Stalin's rule in Russia, the secret police would knock on a person's door late at night, and take him away from his family, never to be seen again. In many cases, there was no apparent reason why that person should have been singled out for arrest. When the news of these arrests got around, people began to think: "They might arrest anyone. I may be next."

d. Suppose there were a drastic shortage of heating fuel in the U.S., so that most people could not heat their houses above 40 degrees Fahrenheit during the winter.

e. Advertisers often try to sell their products by hinting that a person will be shunned by others if his hair is greasy, if he has body odor, or if his teeth are yellow.

Now let's talk about the meaning of the order of Maslow's five motives. *Maslow says that a particular motive comes into play only when all the lower motives have been satisfied.* Thus the five groups of motives are like five rungs of a ladder; to get to a particular rung, you first have to climb all the lower rungs (i.e., satisfy all the lower motives). For instance, if a person is hungry, he will not be able to pay much attention to safety, social needs, and so on, until he has found food. And, even if he has reached the level of self-actualization,

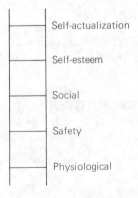

FIGURE 7-8.   Maslow's hierarchy of motives compared to a ladder.

whenever any lower motive goes unsatisfied—for example, if he misses a meal—then that lower motive will dominate his behavior once again.

QUESTION 20.   A girl in the first few weeks of her freshman year in college is most concerned with making new friends.

A.   Applying Maslow's theory strictly, which of the motive categories would you predict are currently well-satisfied for this girl? (List them.)

B.   According to Maslow's theory, what motive categories are currently not satisfied for the same girl? (List them.)

C.   After a few months at college, this girl succeeds in making lots of friends, and becomes a member of several groups. According to Maslow's theory, what new kinds of behavior would you now expect her to show? (List them.)

One study (Aronoff, 1971) that seems to support Maslow's theory was done on the men who cut sugar cane on the West Indies island of St. Kitts. The study was conducted in 1962 and again in 1966. For some reason, most of the 1962 cane-cutters had grown up in families that were torn by death or desertion. As we would expect from such childhoods, these men showed, on a test of Maslow's five motives, a strong concern with safety and little concern with social or esteem motives. Even the nature of their work groups seemed to reflect their need for safety. They worked in groups of about a dozen men under a dictatorial head cutter. The head cutter often abused his power by giving the men credit for less work than they had done or by making them work through the noon hour while he sat nearby eating his lunch. Despite this mistreatment, they never complained. They seemed to need the security of having someone to make all the decisions; without him, they would say, they might never do any work at all.

By 1966, as it happened, there had been an almost complete turnover in cane-cutters. Most of the new men, in contrast with the previous group, had grown up in families that were not struck by desertion or death.

QUESTION 21. According to Maslow's theory, how much concern would this 1966 group of cane-cutters have with the following needs? (Circle appropriate term.)

1. Safety: low concern   high concern
2. Social and self-esteem: low concern   high concern

QUESTION 22. In 1966, a work group of cane-cutters still consisted of a dozen men and a head cutter. But there were changes that were consistent with the changes in the kinds of men in these groups. Circle one of each pair of statements below that indicates the direction you think these changes took.

A. 1. The men were *more* cooperative and friendly with each other than before.

  2. The men were *less* cooperative and friendly with each other than before.

B. 1. The head cutter made more of the decisions than before and the men made fewer.

  2. The head cutter made fewer of the decisions than before and the men made more.

CONFLICTS BETWEEN MOTIVES

So far, we have been talking mostly about situations in which only a single motive is present. Here it is easy to predict the direction of a subject's behavior: if the motive is to approach an object, he will move toward it, and if the motive is to avoid the object, he will move away from it.

Unfortunately for the organism's peace of mind, things are usually not that simple. Usually the organism has two or more motives which are active at the same time, and often these motives conflict in one way or another. *Three basic kinds of motivational conflict have been distinguished: (1) approach-approach conflict, (2) avoidance-avoidance conflict, and (3) approach-avoidance conflict.*

Approach-approach conflict occurs when the organism is motivated to approach two different goals, and can't have both at once. For example, Steve wants to marry Suzanne, and at the same time wants to continue dating Paula. Or a student wants to go to a rock concert one Sunday evening, but also wants to spend that evening studying for a Monday morning exam.

Avoidance-avoidance conflict occurs when the subject wants to avoid one outcome, and at the same time wants to avoid its alternative. For instance, a man may wish to avoid going to a PTA meeting one evening, but also want to avoid staying home to baby-sit with the children. The same type of conflict faces the child who has just been told that he must eat his spinach or get a good spanking.

In approach-avoidance conflict, the organism simultaneously wants to approach and to avoid the same object. Conflict of this type frequently occurs with regard to sexual behavior: the person wants to engage in sexual behavior, but at the same time—because of fears or social taboos—he wants to avoid it. Approach-avoidance conflict is also common in aggression. We sometimes would like to attack someone verbally or physically, but are afraid to do it.

These three kinds of motivational conflict are diagrammed in Figure 7-9.

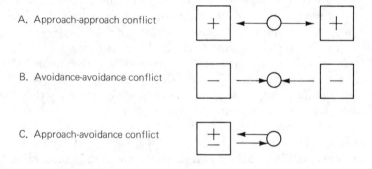

A. Approach-approach conflict

B. Avoidance-avoidance conflict

C. Approach-avoidance conflict

FIGURE 7-9.   Three types of motivational conflict.

QUESTION 23.   Identify the following examples of conflict by writing "approach-approach," "avoidance-avoidance," or "approach-avoidance" in front of each one.

_____   A woman wants to apply for a position of great responsibility, but is afraid to do so because it would be so painful if she were turned down.

_____   A teacher doesn't want to sign a required loyalty oath because he thinks it violates his rights, yet he doesn't want to lose his job for refusing to sign it.

_____   A student would like to go into pre-med and eventually become an M.D., but he is also strongly tempted to major in English.

Conflict, because it can be extremely unpleasant, may lead to the use of defense mechanisms, as well as to various kinds of abnormal behavior. Some of these effects of conflict will be described in Chapter 9.

SUMMARY

In theoretical terms, behavior is motivated by motives and incentives. In observable terms, one stimulus variable that influences most motives is amount of deprivation, and the main response variables that are influenced by motivation are the activation and direction of behavior.

Biological drives include the homeostatic drives, such as hunger and thirst. Both hunger and thirst are influenced by stomach stimulation, mouth stimulation, blood chemistry, and activity in "stop" and "start" centers in the hypothalamus. A nonhomeostatic biological drive is the sex drive. Sexual motivation in humans, as compared to lower animals, is influenced less by hormones and more by learning. Learning also strongly influences the responses to human sexual motivation, including the response of inhibiting sexual behavior and thoughts. Fear is a biological drive that is learned, typically through classical conditioning.

Psychological motives include the motives to be active, to investigate novel stimuli, and to achieve. "N Ach" is measured by asking subjects to write stories about certain pictures, and scoring the extent to which they say that the person in the picture is striving to achieve some difficult goal.

Maslow has tried to organize the main kinds of human motives, which he believes to be (1) physiological, (2) safety, (3) social, (4) self-esteem, and (5) self-actualization needs. According to Maslow's theory, each of these motives comes into play only when all the lower ones have been satisfied.

When the same individual has several motives at once, it is possible for motivational conflicts to occur. The three basic kinds of motivational conflicts that have been distinguished are (1) approach-approach, (2) avoidance-avoidance, and (3) approach-avoidance.

BEHAVIOR TO EXPLAIN

Americans eat a lot. Even with the help of Weight-Watchers, Inc., Diet Pepsi, and Sucaryl, we are in danger of becoming a nation of fatties. Why do people in this country eat so much?

1.   Think of all the principles you can that might help to explain this behavior.

2.   State an hypothesis involving a motivational explanation of this behavior.

3.   Describe a study that could be done to test the hypothesis you stated above, including the design and the measuring instruments you would use.

chapter eight

Personality Explanations

WHAT IS PERSONALITY?

Let's look at the case of two freshmen who have tried out for the college football team. Frank and Mike played football in high school for the same length of time and were considered to be above average in skill. Both students worked very hard each day of the preseason practices. However, in the final week before the season begins, they are both cut from the squad. The coach tells both of them that he does not think that they are ready for the team this year.

Frank reacts to this news by staying in the locker room long after the practice session, not talking to the members of the team, just sitting in front of his locker in idle thought. He finally goes back to his dorm, misses dinner, stays in his room alone that night, cuts classes the next day, and generally withdraws from his day-to-day campus activities. Although he resumes eating and going to classes the next day, his general level of activity remains low for weeks.

Mike, on the other hand, dresses quickly, leaves the practice field and returns to his dorm. There he finds a group of his friends and talks at great length with them about his experiences with the football team. The main reason he was cut, he suggests, is that the coach is a poor teacher. He says that with a coach like that the team probably won't do very well this season and he is glad not to be a part of it. Later that night he goes downtown and catches up on the activities that were ruled out during training. A few weeks later when basketball tryouts start, Mike is among the first to go out on the court, trying his best to make that team.

In this somewhat exaggerated example we see two people who are very similar in many respects. They are both males, approximately the same age, bright enough to be entering college, physically active enough to be interested in athletics, and strong enough to be good high school football players. Despite these similarities, there is a marked difference in the way the two of them reacted to a similar situation. Frank became depressed and withdrew from his friends and activities, while Mike engaged himself with many people and many activities. It is such differences in individual response to similar situations that are the basis of our judgments about personality. People react differently and we attribute these differences to personality.

Personality is not another separate and distinct area of psychology. The theories and research in personality are closely related to the other areas of psychology, such as development, learning, and motivation. All play a role in the development of those characteristics that we call personality.

Most people feel that they know something about psychology, and it is usually in the area of personality that they feel most knowledgeable. People are quick to attribute an individual's behavior to the type of personality he has. Given this overwhelming interest in the area of personality, you might expect that there would be many definitions of the word. This is true. However, we will use a composite definition which is relatively general and therefore probably acceptable to most people. *We will define personality characteristics as those enduring attributes of the person which affect his interpersonal behavior.*

This definition contains several key points that deserve explanation. First of all, the word enduring. This means that the observed attributes occur repeatedly over time. If we observed Frank over a period of time, we would probably notice that he usually greets bad news by withdrawal, and that Mike usually reacts to the same sort of event with increased activity.

The word attributes means that personality characteristics are theoretical inferences that are based on observed behavior. If we observed a man who works extra hours on his job, spends much of his free time making improvements on his house, and also involves himself in some volunteer community activities, we might describe this man as "industrious." We have all probably known at least one woman who would be described as a "socialite" type. She can be observed hostessing tea groups, organizing charitable balls, and lunching at the town's exclusive country club.

It is important to understand this point, since the mistake is often made of viewing such attributes as intrinsic to the person. If we view attributes as intrinsic, we fail to see the events which may have led to these personality patterns or to realize that there may be situations in which these patterns do not operate. In our example of the industrious man, we might assume that he was born to be industrious and therefore be blind to the sequence of events that has resulted in this behavior pattern and to the fact that this pattern may change in the future. In summary, the psychologist looks at the specific activities of a person, and on the basis of this information describes his personality attributes.

> **QUESTION 1.** In each of the following pairs check the phrase that describes a specific observable behavior (not an attribute).
>
> 1. a. _____ Aggressiveness
>   b. _____ Frequently hits playmates
> 2. a. _____ Greets new people in a group
>   b. _____ Extravert
> 3. a. _____ Studies three hours per day
>   b. _____ Studious

Another important phrase in the definition is interpersonal behavior. We are most interested in those characteristics which affect how the person deals with other people. A person's behavior toward members of his family (and their behavior toward him) is important interpersonal behavior. The expression "mama's boy" and "black sheep of the family" refer to attributes based on certain patterns of behavior in the family. Many behaviors, of course, are not interpersonal. For example, you might always read the newspaper starting at the back and going toward the front. Assuming that there was no one waiting for the front section of the paper, this would not be part of your personality according to the above definition.

This does not mean that we are concerned only with the things a person does while in the presence of others. If a person spends most of his time alone, this has a bearing on interpersonal behavior because the more time he spends by himself the less time he can be interacting with others.

> **QUESTION 2.** Listed below are various kinds of information that we might have about an individual. Put a check mark in front of each phrase that describes a personality characteristic.
>
> _____ The person is usually among the first to speak in a group situation.
> _____ The person has a beautiful tan after a vacation.
> _____ The person eats with his left hand.
> _____ The person is always late for appointments and meetings.
> _____ The person smokes two cigars a year, on New Year's Day and on his birthday.
> _____ The person's mood changes greatly from week to week.
> _____ The person always drives a convertible.

_____ The person walks slowly because of his sprained ankle.

_____ The person has no ashtrays in his house.

_____ The person speaks in a loud, booming voice, dresses in wild colored clothes and associates with a reckless group of people.

_____ The person always writes with a pencil.

METHODS OF STUDYING PERSONALITY

There are several approaches to the study of personality. *One of these is called the nomothetic approach. This approach seeks to study particular personality traits in a selected group of people and then to make generalizations about how these traits determine the behavior of a wider range of people.* For example, a psychology department might discover that almost all of its majors had had experiences helping dependent people, and that this experience had led them to choose psychology as a major. The department might design a study to find out if this same factor was important for psychology majors at other schools.

FIGURE 8-1. The nomothetic approach to the study of personality involves the study of one particular characteristic in many individuals, while the idiographic approach involves the study of many characteristics in one individual.

The other approach is called idiographic and stresses the intensive study of a single individual in order to make generalizations about how that person reacts in a wide range of environments. If we had continued our exploration of the activities of Mike or Frank, we would have been pursuing an idiographic approach to personality description. For another example, all of us do some informal idiographic investigation during the early stages of a friendship. We want to know how a friend will respond in certain situations, so we carefully observe his reactions to many situations to be able to predict his future behavior.

Each of these approaches aims at generalizations about personality. While the goal of the nomothetic study is to make generalizations about groups, the goal of the idiographic study is to make generalizations about one individual.

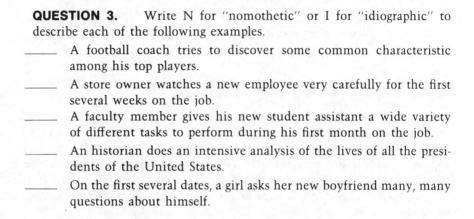

QUESTION 3.   Write N for "nomothetic" or I for "idiographic" to describe each of the following examples.

_____ A football coach tries to discover some common characteristic among his top players.

_____ A store owner watches a new employee very carefully for the first several weeks on the job.

_____ A faculty member gives his new student assistant a wide variety of different tasks to perform during his first month on the job.

_____ An historian does an intensive analysis of the lives of all the presidents of the United States.

_____ On the first several dates, a girl asks her new boyfriend many, many questions about himself.

There is considerable discussion among psychologists as to which approach to the study of personality better serves the purposes of psychology. Proponents of the nomothetic approach argue that it is very important to be able to make statements about specific kinds of traits that apply to groups of people. On the other hand, advocates of the idiographic approach contend that one never sees the whole personality of an individual unless he makes an extensive examination of that individual, and further, that looking only at selected traits can lead to a biased picture of personality. It is probably safe to say that neither position will fall by the wayside in the near future. Researchers trained in both traditions will continue their explorations of personality and find that their procedures complement each other on obtaining critical information.

The greatest barrier to advances in personality study is that many investigators fail to follow some of the basic methodological rules discussed in Chapter 1. Many see the study of personality as the "human" side of psychology, a perception that is usually accompanied by the attitude that scientific principles need not be applied to it. *The most common faults are that investigators do not (1) carefully define their variables, or (2) establish accurate procedures for measuring these variables.* In the section on theories of personality you will meet several terms that have no commonly accepted definition or method of measurement. Some examples are Freud's "libido" and "super-ego" and Rogers' concept of "self." If a commonly acceptable procedure for defining or quantifying such terms was developed, further progress in explaining personality development would be attained.

QUESTION 4.   You wish to formulate a statement about an individual's personality. Arrange the following steps in correct sequential order to arrive at an adequate explanation of personality by placing number 1, 2, 3, or 4 in front of each.

_____ Observe the behaviors in a number of situations.

_____ Pinpoint some specific behaviors to be examined.

_____ Make some hypotheses about the occurrence of the behaviors.

_____ Have other investigators observe the behaviors.

MEASUREMENT OF PERSONALITY

Collecting information about personality is a critical concern of psychologists. The two major sources of evidence about the operations of personality are clinical situation and experimental research. In the former situation, the major focus is on helping a client while data collection is a secondary concern. In research programs, a direct attempt is made to answer some of the puzzling questions about personality.

Suppose you were thinking about taking a course from a particular instructor next semester. How might you get information about the instructor to help you decide whether you want to take his course?

Observation

One of the techniques psychologists use to gather information about personality is to observe the actions of the person or persons being studied. For instance, you might go to the class to watch the instructor yourself. The psychologist will usually look at two aspects of an act: why it is done and how it is done. The question of why concerns the motivation of the person. Accurate observational information about motivation is obtained only when we have the opportunity to observe a person over extended periods of time. It is important to be able to see patterns of behavior over time. The question of how refers to what is called the sylistic component of the action—the way in which the act is carried out. Obviously an act with a specific goal can be carried out in many different ways. The instructor may set a deadline for a term paper and present it to his class by saying that it will allow time for careful grading and will also avoid a last-minute rush. On the other hand, he could set the same deadline and spend many minutes threatening the students about what will happen if the papers are late. It is usually the stylistic component of an act that allows us to identify the actor. This is what an entertainer emphasizes when doing an impersonation. We have all seen Ed Sullivan impersonated many times. The hand-wrenching, facial contortions and voice inflections are all stylistic components of his behavior. And it is the stylistic component of a crime that allows the police to deduce who did it.

Verbal Reports

Verbal reports are a second source of information from which we make inferences about personality. Verbal reports may be obtained from the subject himself or from other persons who have had opportunity to observe him. For example, you might speak with the instructor of the course you are considering taking and ask him about his attitudes toward teaching, his methods of operating in the classroom, and his expectations about student participation. You could also talk with some of the students who have had the instructor in the past and find out such information as how much reading he requires, how he behaves in class, and how he grades. You might also find out how this instructor makes them feel—at ease, happy, anxious, or angry. Of course whenever verbal reports are used, the problem of objectivity arises. *Verbal reports are likely to be inaccurate, due not only to the passage of time, but also to the personal involvement of the one relating the information.* That is, if you talked with a student who took this instructor's course some previous semester, the information he gives you may be inaccurate because he has forgotten exactly what his experience with the instructor was like. Furthermore, either the students or the instructor himself are likely to have feelings that will bias the information they give you.

Psychologists realize that people do not create all of these distortions intentionally. If you had an argument with a fellow student or roommate, you would probably give a biased account of that argument to an interviewer no matter how hard you tried to be objective about it. People are sometimes reluctant to talk about themselves for fear of how others might evaluate them. Suppose you were being asked personal questions about your feelings and philosophy of life. Assuming that you did not know the interviewer very well, you might answer quite cautiously at first. The psychologist realizes the importance of overcoming this reluctance. If you noticed that the questioner never criticized your answers, you would probably begin to speak more freely about your feelings and thoughts. Psychologists have found that such an atmosphere of acceptance does encourage more complete responses during interviews.

There is another kind of verbal report called the empathetic verbal report. Here the person giving the report puts himself in the position of another to whom some event is happening, and gives an account of the reactions and feelings of that person to the event. The assumption is that the person reporting will actually be giving some of his own personal reactions and feelings and attributing them to the other person. This type of verbal report is very useful when a person is hesitant or reluctant to talk about his own feelings, as when he is being asked about a past event which brings on painful memories or feelings of guilt. The empathetic verbal report is probably not as threatening as a personal verbal report. As you can see, the empathetic verbal report is related to projective testing.

QUESTION 5.   Read the following description carefully, looking for the various kinds of information-gathering techniques that occur.

A five-year-old boy is very aggressive around the house, frequently hitting his mother and his two-year-old sister. The situation has become so bad that the mother seeks the help of a psychologist. The mother speaks with the psychologist in his office and gives detailed information about the boy's activities at home. The psychologist then suggests that they go to the boy's nursery school and speak with him. He thinks this would be easier for the child than bringing him into a strange office.

Upon arriving at the school the mother and the psychologist speak with the boy's teacher who describes the boy's actions at school. Afterwards the three adults watch the boy for about twenty minutes while he is on the playground. Then the boy is called into the school and the psychologist asks him questions about his feelings toward his parents and younger sister. While they are talking they notice two boys start to fight on the playground. The psychologist asks the boy what he thinks started the argument and fight. At the end of their conversation the psychologist thanks the boy for his cooperation.

After each of the following information-gathering techniques, list all the appropriate examples that you found in the preceding account.

Observation of actions:

Self verbal report:

Verbal report of others:

Empathetic verbal report:

Observation and verbal report form the basis for other procedures of personality assessment. Measures such as inventories, projective tests, rating scales, and interviews are nothing more than a series of observations and verbal reports carried out in carefully designed settings.

THEORIES OF PERSONALITY

A great deal of effort has been devoted to the task of describing and explaining personality. Some psychologists have developed extensive theories to account for the development of personality; others have conducted research programs to investigate some of the critical variables in the dynamics of personality. In all cases of personality theory and research, the underlying concern is to understand man's activities and experiences including both the behavioral and the emotional components. There has been considerable speculation and controversy about

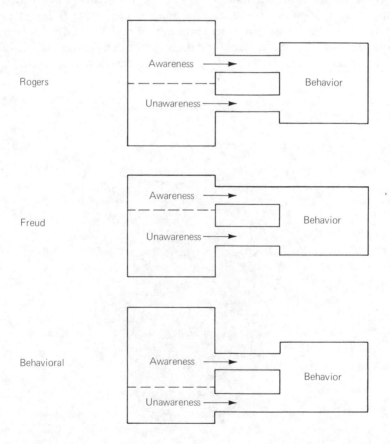

FIGURE 8-2. The different theories of personality vary to the degree that they emphasize the role of awareness/unawareness in determining behavior.

the importance of various factors in personality. For example, the role of unconscious events—events about which we are not aware—has long been a key issue. Some investigators suggest that we are strongly influenced by such events, while others contend that only events of which we are aware have an effect upon personality.

Although theories of personality differ in many respects, nearly all of them agree that personality is a developmental process. Beyond this, personality theories vary on such matters as the importance of biological, motivational, social, and environmental factors. Theories also vary in their degree of completeness, that is, how much of the developmental process is accounted for by the theory.

Freud's Theory

Probably the most elaborate and widely known theory of personality development is that of Sigmund Freud. Freud's thory is motivational and stresses the role of drives, the most basic drive being the sexual one. Freud divides personality into three systems. *The id consists of the individual's basic drives.* Its sole function is to satisfy these drives without any concern for practical considerations. This

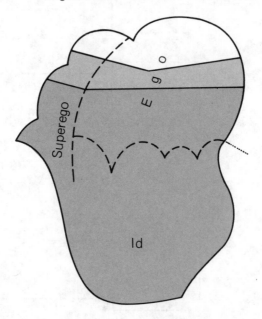

Region of contact with outer world

FIGURE 8-3. The structure of personality according to psychoanalytic theory. The large dark-shaded area represents unconscious activity in personality functioning. The lightly shaded and white areas represent preconscious and conscious activity respectively.

is man's most primitive level of functioning. *The ego consists of the individual's learned skills for overcoming barriers and thus more effectively satisfying his drives.* For example, if a student wanted a date for his fraternity dance, he would be using his ego skills if he went to some spot on campus where he knew he would probably meet some coeds rather than simply remaining in his room dreaming about meeting Miss America. *The superego is, in part at least, the same thing as conscience. It is responsible for seeing to it that behavior measures up to society's norms.* Freud viewed these three personality systems as being in a state of conflict: the id's demand for immediate satisfaction of drives and the ego's schemes to provide that satisfaction are not always acceptable to the moralistic superego.

> **QUESTION 6.** Write id, ego, superego, or any combination thereof before each of the following sentences to indicate which seem to predominate in that example. A person is hungry and engages in the following behavior:
>
> _____ He gets three dollars and heads for a restaurant.
> _____ He fantasizes about gourmet meals being served him in an elegant restaurant.
> _____ He steals a steak from the local supermarket.

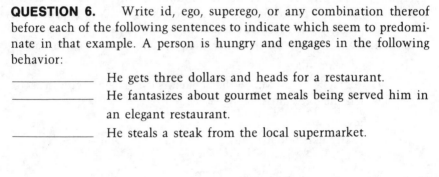
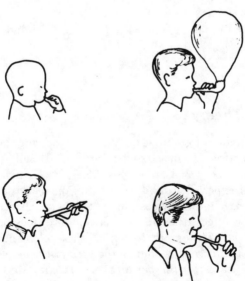

FIGURE 8-4. Behaviors of the oral stage reflected in man. It is thought that man continues to manifest throughout his life behaviors which can be interpreted as expressions of the various stages of development. These expressions are sometimes seen in behavioral traits, such as, stubbornness and aggressiveness, as well as in specific behavior.

Freud also said that every child passes through a series of developmental "psychosexual" stages. In order, these are the oral, anal, and genital stages. Freud's idea was that in the course of development the sexual drive is focused successively on these zones of the body. For example, according to Freud, during the oral stage the infant's mouth is the area that is most sensitive to pleasurable stimulation. The infant's main activity during this period is sucking on a nipple. Furthermore, the person's experiences at each of these early stages leave a lasting imprint on his behavior. This means that the early experiences of a child have a powerful effect on his later life.

Although many laymen seem to think that Freud's theory is the most important one in all of psychology, that is not true by any means. Although psychologists pay homage to Freud as a founding father, many of them are very critical of his theory of personality because of the scarcity of supporting evidence. The major problem with Freud's supporting evidence is that it is based on clinical information and interpretation rather than on empirical research data.

QUESTION 7.   Match the behaviors listed below with the stages during which they are most likely to occur.

Behaviors	*Stages*
A. Early dependent feeding _____	1. Oral
B. Interest in groups, and members of opposite sex _____	2. Anal
C. Toilet training _____	3. Genital

Rogers' Theory

Another important group of theories of personality are those which focus on a person's perception of himself. These are called "self" theories and are best exemplified by the theory of Carl Rogers. *The key elements of Rogers' theory are an individual's experiences and his perception of those experiences.* Rogers discovered during psychotherapy sessions with clients that a person's perception of his experiences is affected by his self-concept and does not always agree with reality. *He found that the extent to which these elements agree is related to the person's level of adjustment—that is, the greater the agreement between reality and perception, the better the person's adjustment.* Among clients just beginning psychotherapy, Rogers found, the level of agreement between these two elements is quite low.

When a person has an experience that is contrary to his current self-concept he can do one of two things. First, he can perceive this new experience objectively and integrate it into his present self-concept without distortion. Or

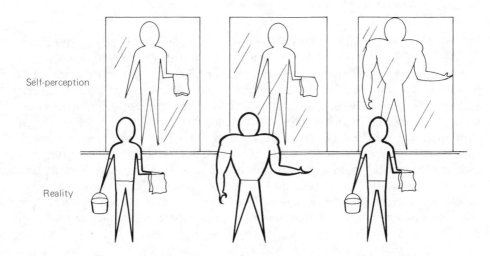

FIGURE 8-5. Rogers' theory emphasizes the development of a person's self-perception. In comparison to reality, our self-perception can be accurate (left), underestimated (center) or overestimated (right).

second, he can deny the perception or distort his interpretation of it. This second road, Rogers believes, leads to poor adjustment. To return to the example of the two football players, a "healthy" interpretation of being cut from the squad might be that competition at the college level is stiffer than in high school, and therefore requires some physical attributes or skills that Frank and Mike do not have. This does not require a change in the concept that they were good high school players. A less healthy interpretation might be to insist that they are among the best players trying out for the team, and that the coach cut them from the squad only because he did not like them.

QUESTION 8.   Bob and Jean have been dating steadily for eight months. Their last several dates together have not been as enjoyable as earlier ones; they haven't agreed on what to do, they haven't had much to say to each other, and so forth. Lately Jean has said no whenever Bob has asked her for a date. Make a check mark beside the reaction that, according to Rogers' theory, seems most healthy.

_____   Bob tells himself that he was never really interested in Jean and was only dating her while waiting for someone better to come along.

_____   Bob feels that he and Jean had a good relationship, enjoyed each other's company, learned a lot about each other and themselves and that now it's appropriate for each of them to explore other interests.

_____   Bob feels that Jean will realize she is making a terrible mistake and will soon come running back to him.

Sheldon's Theory

While nearly all theories of personality are concerned to some extent with the effects of physiological factors on behavior, the theory of William Sheldon is primarily concerned with this kind of factor. *Sheldon's general hypothesis is that there is a relationship between an individual's physique and his personality.* For example, persons with a soft, fatty physique are frequently found to enjoy comfort and sociability and to have slow reactions, while those with a lean, fragile physique are often found to be self-conscious, fearful of people, and inhibited. *Sheldon described the male physique in terms of three body types: mesomorph, endomorph, and ectomorph.* These body types refer to tissue development that starts at a very early age and remains essentially unchanged throughout a person's development. Next *Sheldon developed a list of personality traits and found that there were significant correlations between body type and personality traits.*

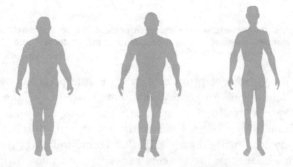

FIGURE 8-6. Sheldon's body types. The endomorph (left) tends to be round in build with well-developed visceral organs and relatively weak bones and muscles. The mesomorph (center), the athletic type, has strong bones and muscles. The ectomorph (right), the stringbean type, has long, slender arms and legs and light muscles.

QUESTION 9.   In his studies Sheldon, himself, was the main person responsible for making both the judgments about body type and personality traits. This being the case, what criticism would you make about Sheldon's work?

A final point should be made about Sheldon's theory. The fact that he found a relationship between body type and personality traits does not necessarily mean that a particular body type *causes* a particular personality trait. An alternative possibility, for example, is that society expects individuals with certain body types

to behave in certain ways, and that these expectations lead them to behave accordingly.

Trait Theory

Up to this point we have been reviewing theories that attempt to explain
personality as a whole. *Some psychologists feel that it might be more useful to
break the concept of personality down into smaller elements—to study specific
personality traits. A trait is a general trend in behavior.* For example, an individual
who helps his neighbor with small jobs and who participates on committees in
his community might be described as "cooperative." The word cooperative summarizes a group of consistent habits. The same individual probably has other habits
that could be grouped together and described by other trait names. Describing
an individual's personality as a cluster of traits has the advantage of facilitating
measurement, since the behaviors underlying traits can be fairly readily observed.

According to some theorists, there are several levels of personality traits.
These levels and their relationship to the broader notion of personality types are
shown in Figure 8.7. For example, introversion—a type—refers to a broad range
of specific traits. You might test your understanding of this concept by writing
into Figure 8-7 some other behaviors that would be examples of the habitual
response level and the specific response level.

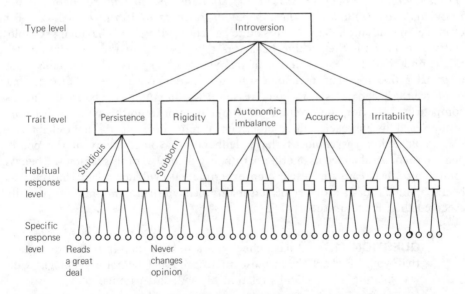

FIGURE 8-7. This diagram shows the relationship between specific responses of a person and
trait level of behavior and type level of description. It can be seen that the description becomes
broader and encompasses a wide range of activities with the movement from specific response
to type description.

QUESTION 10.   Extraversion is a personality type. Write in below descriptions of behaviors that exemplify various levels of traits that are related to extraversion.

Trait level:

Habitual response level:

Specific response level:

Behavioral Theory

Another approach to the study of personality that, like the trait theories, stresses specific behaviors, is the behavioral approach. While the trait theory is more concerned with description, the behavioral approach puts more emphasis on understanding how the individual's behaviors originated. Most simply stated, *the behavioral approach consists of (1) studying the current behaviors of the individual and (2) relating these behavior patterns to learning processes.* For example, in studying a man who is said to be "competitive," a behavioral psychologist would look for the specific behaviors that resulted in this description. He might find that the man is active in many kinds of sports and also talks a lot at social gatherings. The psychologist would then look for the conditions that reinforce these behaviors. If for some reason it was important to change this man's competitive behavior, the psychologist would attempt to do this by using learning principles. This approach will be described in more detail in the next chapter.

Behavioral psychologists have deliberately avoided many of the poorly defined theoretical concepts of other personality theories. For this reason the behavioral approach is easier to test. Much experimental evidence about learning has been obtained, but as a theory of personality behaviorism is no more universally accepted than Freudian theory.

QUESTION 11.   Place a check mark next to the kinds of information that would probably be of most interest to a behavioral psychologist who was looking into a client's relationship with his parents.

_____   The client's discussion of his feelings about his parents.

_____   The number of times per week the client has had conversations with his parents.

_____ A recurring dream of the client.

_____ The amount of time the client spends at home with his parents.

_____ The client's feelings about himself in relation to his brothers and sisters.

QUESTION 12. Before each of the terms below write "Sheldon," "Rogers," "Freud," "behavioral theory," or "trait theory" to indicate which of these it is most closely associated with.

_____ Extravert

_____ Fat and jolly

_____ Reinforcement

_____ Pleasure vs. reality

_____ Collection of habits

_____ Conditioning

_____ Perception of self

HEREDITY AND ENVIRONMENT IN PERSONALITY THEORY

The question of how heredity and environment influence personality development is of basic importance for personality theory. Attempts to isolate the influence of heredity upon personality have focused on two specific areas—intelligence and personality traits. There is a long-standing controversy among scientists whether races differ in native intelligence. Of particular concern have been the alleged differences between the white and black races. Obviously this question is of critical concern in contemporary America. Of equal concern is the role that hereditary factors might play in the transmission and development of normal and abnormal personality traits. The impact of such a relationship on the understanding of criminal behavior, for example, could be overwhelming.

The difficulty of separating the effects of heredity and environment are well known. Consider, for example, the fact that every measurement of the influence of heredity must be carried out in some environment. This leaves open the possibility that the results are influenced by that environment. The results of nearly every heredity-environment study done on these topics are open to criticism on this account.

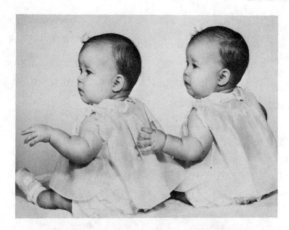

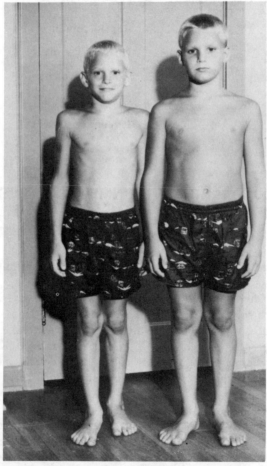

FIGURE 8-8. Identical twins (top) have the same heredity. Fraternal twins (bottom) do not have the same heredity; they are simply siblings born at the same time. (From Sanford and Wrightsman, *Psychology: A Scientific Study of Man.*)

Studies of Identical Twins

Many researchers studying the impact of heredity on intelligence and personality have used identical twins as subjects. At first glance this group seems to be ideal for such studies. Identical twins are the only humans who are known to have identical heredity since both developed from a single fertilized egg. In twin studies it is assumed that if the twins react in the same way when placed in different environments, these similarities must be due to heredity.

There are, however, several difficulties in twin research. One is that the number of identical twins who have been reared apart is small. Another is that it is harder than most people think to determine whether twins are actually identical. The third difficulty is that when twins are separated, it usually occurs very late in childhood. As a result it will never be possible to decide with certainty whether similarities in their behavior are due to identical heredity or early shared environment. This is a problem that can probably never be solved because the welfare of the children is obviously more important than the requirements of research.

Twin Studies and Intelligence

Now we will look at some results of twin studies. In general the intelligence scores of identical twins—even those raised in different environments—are similar. However, many studies have shown that these similarities tend to decrease as the environments become more dissimilar (Newman, Freeman and Holzinger, 1937). For example, there have been cases in which one twin was placed in a foster home where there was great stress upon education, while the other twin was placed in a foster home in which there was little emphasis upon academic pursuits. After a number of years in these two very different environments, the identical twins were found to differ considerably in IQ.

Because of the problems in using identical twins, researchers have also used nontwin children in some of their investigations. For example, several studies have shown that the intelligence of adopted children is more closely related to that of their natural parents than to that of their adopted parents—(Skodak and Skeels, 1949) even after ten or more years with their adopted parents.

In an attempt to integrate the variety of findings, some researchers have concluded that hereditary factors set limits within which intellectual capacity can develop. The degree to which the capacity develops within these limits is dependent on the specific environmental factors the child encounters during development.

Obviously it is difficult to determine the effects of heredity upon intelligence, even in the relatively well-controlled twin studies. If this is so, you can imagine how speculative our conclusions must be about the determinants of the intellectual differences that exist between races.

QUESTION 13.   Read the situations described below and rank them according to the amount of similarity that you would expect to find on intelligence scores. Give a rank of 1 to the most similar and the rank of 5 to the most dissimilar:

_____ Two identical twins are born and raised by their natural parents until age 12. Then their parents are killed in an accident and the twins are placed in separate private schools. After that they go to different colleges.

_____ Two brothers aged 18 months and 4 months have to live with an aunt because of family circumstances. They continue to live with her until they go to college.

_____ Two identical twins are separated from their parents at birth and raised in separate foster homes in two different parts of the country.

_____ Two sisters aged 7 and 11 years have been raised by their natural parents since birth.

_____ Identical twins are separated from their parents at 6 months of age and placed in the same foster home where they stay through their school years.

Twin Studies and Personality Traits

With regard to the effect of heredity on personality traits, Gottesman (1963) found identical twins to be more similar than fraternal twins in their responses to several scales of the MMPI. In another study, Shields (1962) found similar test scores among identical twins and even marked similarities in some behavior patterns, such as smoking. This second study included groups of identical twins that had been reared apart as well as identical twins reared together. The similarities for those raised apart were as strong as for the ones raised together.

QUESTION 14.   In twin studies of the type just described, what is the key independent variable, and what are some of the important dependent variables?

Using a slightly different approach, a researcher named Kallmann studied the contribution of heredity to schizophrenia and other psychotic reactions. Briefly, his procedure was as follows: When he found a case of a hospitalized psychotic patient, he would check the hospital records to see if this patient had an identical twin, a fraternal twin, or other siblings. If so, Kallmann would then try to find out whether the relative had ever been diagnosed as psychotic. He found that the probability of the relative having a mental illness was higher, the closer his relationship was to the psychotic patient. That is, the incidence of mental illness was greatest for the identical twins, next greatest for the fraternal twins, and least for the nontwin siblings. Kallmann did not believe that mental illness is directly inherited. Rather he theorized that there are genetic factors that predispose the person to mental illness, but that he does not actually become ill unless environmental conditions also are conductive to its development. This is very similar to the conclusions of many researchers in the area of intelligence.

QUESTION 15.   In carrying out his research, Kallmann personally selected hospital patients that he judged to be undergoing a psychotic reaction. He also personally checked the hospital files and made the judgment about the mental health of the relatives of the patient. In other words, he was responsible for both sides of the judgment. From your readings in previous chapters, name some possible sources of error in this research.

Social Variables and Personality

Suppose that John is sitting around a table with five buddies in a bar downtown. They went there after class to celebrate the end of another long week, and have been drinking for a couple of hours. Someone suggests having another round and this idea is met with great enthusiasm all the way around the table. Now it is John's turn to react. He is driving and knows that he has had as much as he should. However, everyone else has reacted so positively that he is reluctant not to go along with the group. So he conforms to the majority and sits back, uncomfortable with his decision.

This scene demonstrates a current social influence on behavior. *A current influence on behavior refers to the effects of the immediate social situation on a person's reactions.* The experiments done by Solomon Asch (see Chapter 4) typify this kind of effect. Asch demonstrated that people can be made to give what they know is a wrong answer if enough other people give that wrong answer before them.

A young boy changes schools when his family moves to a new neighborhood. Very quickly he finds out that he has difficulty keeping up with the other boys and girls in his class. They seem to be able to read and write much faster than he can. He has never seen anything like it; at his former school most of the children spent their free time playing ball and riding bikes and gave very little attention to schoolwork. This difference in focus of activity is causing him difficulty in adapting to his new environment.

This example describes the effect of a developmental determinant of behavior. *A developmental determinant is a past event that influences present behavior.* We see that the boy's previous history of spending most of his free time playing is now causing him difficulty in his new academic setting. *Two of the main developmental social factors that influence personality are culture and social class.* The finding that Jewish Americans are more concerned about and more responsive to pain and illness than Irish Americans is an example of cultural influence. An example of the influence of social class is the differing child-rearing practices characteristic of different socioeconomic groups.

QUESTION 16.   Identify each of the following determinants of behavior by writing "current" or "developmental" in the space before it.

_____   A boy was raised in a family that spent most vacations camping. As a teenager this boy now finds that he enjoys active outdoor sports.

_____   A girl was recently in an auto accident and suffered cuts on her face. Now she prefers to spend much of her time alone.

_____   A football player has scored three touchdowns in each of his last three games. His coach is now having problems getting him to practice seriously.

_____   A young boy raised in a predominantly Italian neighborhood in a large city is experiencing many problems in an elementary school that is several miles away from his home.

SUMMARY

Personality characteristics are defined as those enduring attributes of the person which are significant for his interpersonal behavior. Studying personality characteristics in groups of people is known as nomothetic investigation, while extensive study of a single individual is called the idiographic approach. Techniques such as observation and verbal report are used to collect information about personality. These techniques are sometimes used in testing situations along with such instruments as inventories, projective tests, and rating scales.

Many theories of personality have been formulated and they rest heavily on principles from other areas of psychology. Freud's theory emphasizes motivation, particularly sexual and aggressive drives. Rogers' theory is concerned with a person's perception of self and how this is developed. Sheldon's theory is heavily physiological and states a relationship between a person's physique and his personality. Some theorists have stated that a person is best known by specific traits which characterize his behavior. A trait is seen as a general trend in behavior. The principles of learning play an important role in the explanation of personality according to the behavioral model. This model emphasizes the effects of social and environmental factors on behavior. The current habits of a person are important in describing his personality and these habits are determined by the conditioning process through which the person has passed since his earliest years.

In understanding personality, it is important to assess the influence of heredity and environment. Psychologists continue to do considerable research on this question. Cultural and social class factors are also investigated to understand their impact on the development of personality.

BEHAVIOR TO EXPLAIN

Individual differences in intelligence affect many aspects of our lives. We have seen special programs developed by the government to facilitate the intellectual growth of selected groups; many of us have been exposed to some type of academic tracking system in elementary or high school.

1.   Think of all the principles you can that might help to explain individual differences in intelligence.

2.   State an hypothesis involving an environmental explanation of these differences.

3.   Design a study that could be done to test your hypothesis, including both the design and the measuring instruments you would use.

chapter nine

Clinical
Explanations

In the previous chapter, we explored personality and the factors that influence its functioning. There are occasions, however, when an individual's functioning is impaired. This results in abnormal behavior, which often requires clinical intervention. The occurrence and treatment of abnormal behavior is the subject of clinical psychology. In this chapter, we shall look first at the development of abnormal behavior and then at some of the methods of therapy that have been used to deal with it.

WHAT IS ABNORMAL BEHAVIOR?

Although it is no easier to define abnormal behavior than to define personality, one point of agreement is that abnormality cannot be defined in absolute terms. Instead, it must be defined in a relative way. A quick review of any anthropology textbook, or even a review of the history of the United States shows that abnormal behavior is not an absolute standard that remains unaltered by time or place. For example, there exist cultures in which human sacrifice is a highly valued, and therefore could hardly be considered abnormal behavior.

The Statistical Model of Abnormality

The point that seems to be emerging is that *abnormality must be statistically defined; that is, it must be defined as a deviation from a norm or average.* This concept is attractively simple, but there are some difficulties with it. The first problem is to define the norm or average. There are very few behavior patterns in any culture that are so universally shared that deviations are readily identifiable. Beyond the fact that we all eat and most of us wear clothes in public, behavior ranges widely. Finding an average within this range is difficult and often must be done quite arbitrarily. Many psychologists are concerned about who establishes what behaviors are to be considered the norm. Many believe that too much of this decision-making rests in the hands of too few people. Often, standards that discriminate against large groups of people result, for example, standards of legal processes that have been developed with a lack of sensitivity for the lower socioeconomic class citizen.

A second difficulty with the statistical model of abnormality is the fact that it does not distinguish between favorable and unfavorable deviations from the norm. All unusual behaviors, whether good, bad, or indifferent, are considered abnormal.

QUESTION 1.   According to the statistical definition of abnormality, which of the following would have to be considered abnormal? (Check all appropriate answers.)

_____   A person with an *IQ* of 100.

_____   A person with an *IQ* of 57.

_____   A person with an *IQ* of 142.

_____   A person who risks his life to protect a stranger from an assailant.

_____   A person who walks to work.

_____   A person who gives $75,000 a year to charity.

In the preceding question, you probably found yourself checking items that you never had considered abnormal before, but that certainly fit the statistical definition. Unless we modify this definition, we will have to consider behaviors that are better than average to be abnormal. Then normal behavior would be that which is common and mediocre.

One way of solving this problem has been to limit the concept of statistical abnormality to those deviations from the norm that are in a negative direction.

For example, drinking alcoholic beverages is common in our society. There are, however, those who completely abstain and those who overindulge. While both of these behavior patterns are deviations from the average, our society does not view abstinence as abnormal, while it does consider excessive drinking as a problem.

The Individual Model of Abnormality

Another possible solution to the problem of defining abnormal behavior is first to determine key ingredients of a normally-functioning individual, then assume that an individual who deviates from these criteria is functioning inadequately. Some of the criteria that have been used are:

1. Awareness, acceptance, and correctness of self-concept.
2. Continued growth and self-actualization.
3. Integration and unity of personality.
4. Autonomy and self-reliance.
5. Accurate perception of reality, and social sensitivity.
6. Mastery of the environment and adequacy in meeting the demands of life.

These very general criteria seem to describe an individual who functions consistently in his social milieu and who does not draw excessive amounts of negative attention to himself. They leave room for a wide range of behaviors, all of which have in common the fact that they are predictable, and that they probably will not be seriously harmful to the individual himself or to those about him.

QUESTION 2. Check the following items that would be abnormal, according to the preceding definition.

_____ An individual with an *IQ* of 57.

_____ An individual who exercises vigorously.

_____ An individual who is so concerned about neatness and cleanliness that it interferes with some of his daily commitments.

_____ A person who saves mementos and souvenirs from every event in his life.

_____ A person who is regularly receiving therapy from a psychologist.

Now that we have formulated a workable definition of abnormal behavior, we will look at some statistics on its occurrence. In studying these statistics, we should understand that no record is made of a case of abnormal behavior until it comes to the attention of some professional. Furthermore, researchers studying abnormal behavior obtain most of their information from the files of public service facilities such as hospitals and clinics. Such information is not as easy to obtain from psychiatrists or psychologists in private practice.

QUESTION 3. Which of the following is most likely to appear in statistical summaries of abnormal behavior? (Check one.)

_____ A behavior that bothers the friends and relatives of an individual.

_____ A behavior that is bothersome to the individual himself, but which he does nothing about.

_____ A behavior of an individual that is so disturbing it leads him to seek help at the local mental health clinic.

_____ A behavior of an individual that bothers him so much he speaks to a close friend about it.

INCIDENCE OF ABNORMAL BEHAVIOR

Urban—Rural Incidence

Many studies have shown a higher rate of mental illness in urban than in rural areas. It is probably true that life in cities, especially large ones, is more complex, more rapidly paced, and generally more demanding than life in rural areas. These factors may result in a higher rate of mental illness.

Before we accept this explanation, however, we should look at some other factors that might be responsible for these findings. For one thing, since many urban activities are carried out in the company of other people, abnormal behavior may be more easily detected there. By comparison, in many of the rural jobs and life styles—such as farming—the person behaves in relative isolation, so that any abnormal behaviors are not as likely to be noticed.

Also, rural families are usually better equipped to deal with a relative who is experiencing adjustment problems. There is usually more room both inside and outside of the house for the mentally ill individual to move about without interfering with the normal routines of the household.

A third factor that may contribute to the higher recorded rates of mental illness in cities is the greater availability in urban areas of professional assistance such as hospitals, clinics, clinical psychologists, and psychiatrists, and the likelihood that city dwellers will make use of such services when experiencing adjustment difficulties.

In conclusion, while the demands of city life may contribute to a higher incidence of abnormal behavior, it is not the only possible causal factor.

Socioeconomic Incidence

Mental illness is also related to socioeconomic status. In general, *surveys have shown a higher incidence of mental illness among lower socioeconomic classes.* While it may be that the strains of lower-class life result in a higher rate of mental illness, other explanations are also possible.

One alternative explanation is that mental illness leads to a decline in the individual's social status. Although a case of mental illness is not recorded until the individual has contacted a source of help, before this time the individual may have been struggling with his problem by himself. As a result, he may have lost time at work or even lost his job, which would influence his social class, as usually defined. In such a case, then, the abnormal behavior has resulted in a lower social class, instead of the reverse. This undoubtedly occurs sometimes, but it is impossible to say how often.

Another possible explanation is that the incidence of mental illness appears greater in the lower class because the definitions of acceptable (i.e. normal) behavior are based on middle-class behavior.

A third explanation is that lower-class individuals have to rely more heavily on public hospitals and clinics for assistance, and consequently, their cases are more likely to be included in surveys of mental illness. People in higher-income brackets more often consult private practitioners and therefore are not as often represented in statistics. (It might be noted that when surveys of this nature are carried out on the files of public institutions, the patient is not identified.)

Age and Sex Incidence

There is also a relationship between age and rate of mental illness. Figure 9-1 shows the incidence of mental illness at various age levels. This figure indicates that the incidence is lowest at the ages up to 15 years. This might be due to the fact that most children live in relatively protected home environments until this age. After that, they typically have to face more demanding social environments.

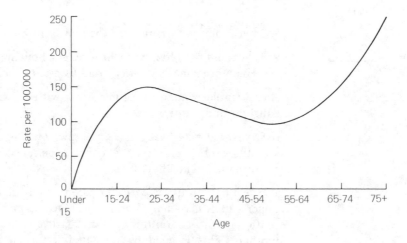

FIGURE 9-1. **Incidence rate of mental disorder by age at first admission to a public or private mental hospital in the United States in 1965.**

From the late twenties there is a fairly steady increase which reaches a peak in the early forties. This is the time in a person's life when he is concentrating on the growth of his family as well as on his occupational growth and development. Mental illness during this period is conspicuous and most damaging to the person's goals. For these reasons, help is probably sought very quickly during this age range.

From the early forties to about age 65, there is a leveling off and even a slight decline in incidence. Generally speaking, a person's life style is fairly stable by this time and if things have gone smoothly until now, they probably will continue that way.

Figure 9-1 shows a steady increase in the proportion of hospital admissions after age 65. This marked increase is due to disorders that are specific to elderly people, and also to the lack of home care available to elderly people who experience adjustment problems.

Finally, we might mention the relationship between sex and rate of mental illness. Recent studies indicate that there is no significant difference between sexes in the overall rate of mental illness. However, each sex seems to have specific types of disorders more frequently associated with it.

You will recall from our discussion in Chapter 8 about the influence of heredity and environment on abnormal behavior that one investigator found a greater incidence in families that already had a history of mental illness. It was unclear, however, to what extent this effect was due to genetic factors or to environmental factors.

QUESTION 4.   Which of the following persons is most likely to be experiencing some adjustment difficulty currently or in the near future; which is least likely? (Write "most likely" and "least likely" in front of them.)

_____ A 14-year-old boy living with his family in a city.

_____ A 32-year-old twin living in a low-income housing project. His brother has a history of adjustment problems.

_____ A 67-year-old woman living on a farm with her granddaughter and family.

_____ A 52-year-old man living in a small town with his wife and three children. He has never experienced any major adjustment difficulties.

_____ A 6-year-old girl living with her parents in a suburban upper-middle-class neighborhood. There are many activities in the community for the girl and her two brothers. This is good because their father is away several nights each week because of his extremely demanding job in the nearby city.

DEFENSE MECHANISMS

How does abnormal behavior develop? Many psychologists think that anxiety plays a key role. *Anxiety is a state of apprehension that is often related to the anticipation of some future danger, such as punishment or threat to self-esteem.* Probably all of us have experienced anxiety. One need only recall his feelings when anticipating a new social situation such as a blind date or when preparing for a tough exam.

Anxiety seems to be most pronounced when there is some uncertainty about the future. There are many factors in our society that almost guarantee that a young person will experience uncertainty and therefore anxiety. In trying to make career plans, for example, there is always the question mark about what vocation to choose.

The techniques for dealing with anxiety are called defense mechanisms. *A defense mechanism is a learned way of dealing with anxiety by reducing conflict and by enhancing self-esteem.* For example, we all have had the experience of performing poorly on an exam. A common reaction is to blame the instructor for asking poor questions or for covering only unimportant material. This is the defense mechanism of rationalization. *In rationalization the individual explains his behavior in socially acceptable ways* ("I failed the test because the teacher did a poor job") *and attempts to conceal the real basis for his behavior* ("I failed because I've been partying too much and haven't studied for three weeks"). Rationalization is one of the most common ways of reducing anxiety.

In the preceding example, although the student places the blame on the instructor, he cannot express his anger directly toward him for fear of reprisal. So, when he returns to his room, he might become angry at his roommate for some little thing he did wrong. This is the defense mechanism of displacement. *Displacement occurs when the individual's feelings toward the real object of anxiety (teacher) are blocked, so he expresses them instead toward a safer and more available target (roommate).*

QUESTION 5.   Write "rationalization" or "displacement" before each of the following defense mechanisms.

_____ A man whose boss has required him to work late the last three nights is becoming very critical of his wife.

_____ A student who fails an exam defends his failure by saying that 80% of the class failed.

You may have recognized your own occasional use of the above defense mechanisms. Everyone uses defense mechanisms and, in moderation, they can be a harmless and effective way of disposing of minor conflicts and thereby reducing anxiety and threats to self-esteem.

It should be noted that defense mechanisms are not deliberate efforts to deceive ourselves or others. For the most part, we are not aware we are using these devices.

NEUROTIC REACTIONS

There are two distinct kinds of situations in which defense mechanisms do not work to our advantage. One is where the anxiety-producing conflict lasts a long time. The second is where a new type of anxiety-provoking situation arises for which we have no established defense mechanism. In either case, the usual result is an overwhelming flood of anxiety. The anxiety is so severe that it blocks our learned processes of adjustment. The result is a psychoneurotic or neurotic reaction.

The Anxiety Reaction

There are several types of neurotic reactions but the common element in each of them is overwhelming anxiety. Anxiety shows up in different ways in the various neurotic reactions. One of the most common neurotic reactions is the anxiety reaction, characterized by general nervousness and a high degree of tension. The anxiety is not associated with any particular stimulus, but occurs in a wide variety of situations. Most often the individual cannot pinpoint why he is anxious. This chronic state of anxiety, sometimes called "free-floating" anxiety, is occasionally punctuated by acute anxiety attacks that may last from several hours to several days. The attacks are usually accompanied by physical symptoms such as headache or backache. The individual sometimes becomes excessively concerned about these minor symptoms, and is then called a "hypochondriac." His exaggerated complaints seem to serve the purpose of distracting his attention from the severe anxiety he is experiencing.

A look at a case report might be helpful in understanding the anxiety reaction. A successful business executive experienced an acute anxiety attack every two or three months. The man's wife was eight years older than he, and he was no longer physically attracted to her. He had become increasingly interested in younger women, and had begun to think how much more enjoyable it would be to have a younger, more companionable wife. During this period, he met a girl with whom he was sure he had fallen in love. The anxiety attacks began shortly afterward. They were always preceded by several days of increased tension and anxiety; the attacks themselves came on suddenly and were very intense.

This man was at a complete loss to explain his attacks. But the explanation was not difficult for an objective observer to find. The patient had had a poverty-stricken and insecure childhood and felt basically inferior, insecure, and threatened by a hard world. These feelings had been intensified when he had failed college courses in his second year, even though his failure had resulted primarily from excessive outside work. He had been able to achieve some security, however, by marrying an older and very strong woman who instilled considerable self-confidence and initiative in him. The marriage had proved financially rewarding and the patient was living in a style that, as a youth, "I hadn't dared to imagine in my wildest dreams!" His persistent thoughts about divorcing his wife, on whom he felt dependent for his security and style of life, thus represented a severe threat to the moderate adjustment he had achieved. The anxiety attacks resulted.

This case shows us some of the *key characteristics of neurotic reactions in general:*

1. *The person is experiencing a conflict that generates anxiety.*

2. *The person usually cannot specify the exact nature of the anxiety-provoking conflict.*

3 *The anxiety becomes manifest either as "free-floating" anxiety or as some other symptom.*

In different kinds of neurotic reactions, anxiety is expressed in different ways. A brief overview of some of the other types of neurotic reactions will clarify this point.

Other Neurotic Reactions

A depressive reaction is usually precipitated by a recent severe loss that the person has experienced. It is frequently hypothesized that persons showing this kind of reaction have feelings of guilt about some aspect of the loss. For example, the person may have had some negative feelings about a relative or friend who died, which created in him a sense of guilt. The anxiety associated with the guilt is partly relieved by depression and acts of self-depreciation; apparently feeling bad allows the person to better handle his guilt.

A phobic reaction is an intense, irrational fear of a specific object or situation. Phobia is irrational because there is no objective reason for the person's fear. Many psychologists think that phobias, although uncomfortable themselves, serve to keep the person away from situations that might produce even more anxiety.

An obsessive-compulsive reaction is characterized by frequently recurring, unavoidable thoughts (obsessions) or actions (compulsions). The person seems to have no control over these thoughts or actions. It is generally believed that they have some relationship to a situation that is anxiety-provoking for the person. For example, in some cases, compulsive handwashing has been found to be related to unacceptable sexual urges.

Finally, *conversion reactions are characterized by incapacitating bodily ailments, such as blindness or paralysis, that have no apparent physical basis.* It is thought that such reactions serve the purpose of removing the person from anxiety-inducing situations. For example, a traveling salesman who was doing very poorly in his business became blind. There was no physical impairment associated with the blindness, and after therapy his full vision was restored. The therapist indicated that the man was anxious about his poor sales performance and that

FIGURE 9-2. Two common types of phobias are fear of heights and fear of small places. .

FIGURE 9-3. Compulsive behavior. Compulsive behavior is a repetitive, ritualistic activity that a person performs to relieve anxiety. The well-known children's chant, ''Step on a crack and you'll break your mother's back,'' while stepping carefully from one pavement square to another, has its source in an irrational anxiety.

being blind provided a legitimate means of avoiding the situation in which he was failing.

QUESTION 6.   Match the appropriate neurotic reaction with each description by drawing a line connecting them.

1.	Anxiety reaction	a. A person who has achieved some success in his profession claims he really didn't have much to do with it.
2.	Depressive reaction	b. A soldier is unable to support a gun in his rifle arm when in combat.
3.	Phobic reaction	c. A man habitually calls the school his children attend to check on their safety.
4.	Obsessive-compulsive reaction	d. A young girl fears crowded places.
5.	Conversion Reaction	

Despite the variety of symptoms that a person may employ to deal with his anxiety, *several characteristics are fairly common among those persons who can be called neurotics:*
   1.   *They feel basically inadequate and inferior in dealing with life.*
   2.   *They are tense and overly sensitive.*
   3.   *They are egocentric—that is, very concerned about themselves.*
   4.   *They are easily fatigued and often have bodily complaints.*
   5.   *Their interpersonal relationships are frequently poor.*
Many people show some of the above characteristics for brief periods of time. The neurotic shows these characteristics for long periods of time, and he usually cannot solve his problems without professional assistance.

PSYCHOTIC REACTIONS

Some mental or personality disorders are far more severe than neurotic reactions. These are called psychotic reactions. *A psychotic reaction or psychosis usually affects the entire personality of the individual and results in such profound disturbance that the person is usually incapable of participating in everyday activities.* In a psychotic reaction, all of the defense mechanisms that the person has been using to deal with his world break down completely. Hospitalization is usually required.

Psychologists are uncertain whether psychotic reactions are related to neurotic reactions or are totally different. On the one hand, both kinds of reactions affect the individual's ability to function. On the other, some of the characteristics found in psychotic reactions are not found in neurosis, and because of this some psychologists insist that they are separate kinds of disorders.

Characteristics of Psychosis

There are three main characteristics that differentiate psychosis from neurosis. One is that psychosis involves a *loss of contact with reality. Frequently the behavior of the psychotic individual has no understandable relationship to his environment.* This is most easily noticed in the patient's verbal behavior, which is often nonsensical.

FIGURE 9-4.   An example of the disturbed thought process of a severely psychotic individual. Although it appears meaningless to most people, the information and thought behind it may have significance for the psychotic patient who drew it. Ciba Pharmaceutical Co. Used with permission.

The second and third distinguishing characteristics are that *psychotic persons experience hallucinations and delusions,* while neurotic individuals do not. *An hallucination is an experience for which there is no known sensory input*—for example, hearing voices when no one is around, or seeing things that aren't there. *A delusion is a persistent thought which has no basis in reality.* For example, a psychotic person may report that he has been appointed to a special mission by the president of the United States. Delusions often fall into two categories, delusions of grandeur and delusions of persecution. As the names indicate, in these kinds of delusions the individual exaggerates his own importance, and believes that others are plotting against him.

QUESTION 7.   Check the cases below that show evidence of a psychotic reaction.

_____ A man complains of dizzy spells while at work.

_____ A person loses sleep because of vivid nightmares, and then has unpleasant social interactions the next day.

_____ A person is very tense about a problem and withdraws from his friends for a week.

_____ A person does not recognize people he has known for years.

Types of Psychotic Reactions

There are three major types of psychotic reactions: schizophrenic, affective or manic-depressive, and paranoid. While these three reactions have characteristics in common, each also involves behaviors that are distinctive to it. We will briefly describe each type of psychotic reaction.

The schizophrenic reaction is by far the most-often-diagnosed psychotic reaction and the most frequent reason for admission to psychiatric hospitals. *The person experiencing a schizophrenic reaction usually becomes very apathetic, shows no emotional response or inappropriate emotional response, and tends to withdraw from social contact.* As this condition progresses, the person becomes almost totally immobilized and experiences hallucinations and delusions. At the present time little is known about the causes of schizophrenia. There is still considerable controversy about the roles of heredity and environment in this disorder (see Chapter 8).

The affective or manic-depressive reaction is characterized by exaggerated swings in the person's moods. Some manic-depressives vary between extreme elation and extreme depression, others between a relatively calm state and extreme excitement, while still others vacillate between the calm state and extreme depression. When a person is in an highly excited state, he appears to have endless amounts of energy and may harm people and destroy property. On the other hand, the person in extreme depression is sometimes in a stuporous state in which he will not even tend to his basic bodily needs. Sometimes patients in this state have to be fed through a tube to be kept alive. Frequently, the patient will not remember these extreme episodes after they are over.

The paranoid reaction is the rarest psychotic reaction. In this type of reaction, *the person experiences a whole system of delusions, usually delusions of persecution.* For example, if a letter is delivered open to his house, he may interpret this to mean that someone is reading his mail and monitoring all of his activities. The notable thing about these delusions is that they fit into a logical system.

A brief case study may help isolate some of the kinds of symptoms we have been discussing:

During high school John began taking long walks alone, missing meals, staring out his window for hours on end, and in general withdrawing. His family did not become worried for they interpreted his behavior as the blossoming of a scholarly way of life. As time went by his mother heard him talking to someone in his room when there was no one else there. One day he stated that he had been given special intellectual abilities and that he was a genius. He spoke of having a study companion who would appear through the walls of his room and who would give him secret instructions while he was taking tests. His family had him hospitalized when he revealed that he was being subjected to irradiation and that the pigeons in the neighborhood were attempting to talk to him.

FIGURE 9-5. A patient in a severe psychotic depression. Ciba Pharmaceutical Co. Used with permission.

QUESTION 8.   List the various psychotic symptoms detailed in the above case study. Where appropriate, tell what kind of symptom it is.

QUESTION 9.   What kind of psychotic reaction is described in the preceding case study? Explain your choice.

A summary of the differences between the neuroses and psychoses is given in Table 9-1.

TABLE 9-1   A COMPARISON OF NEUROTIC AND PSYCHOTIC REACTIONS

FACTOR	PSYCHONEUROSES	PSYCHOSES
OVERALL BEHAVIOR PATTERN	Some loss of reality contact but continued social functioning.	Reality contact and social functioning severely impaired.
NATURE OF SYMPTOMS	Wide range of psychosomatic complaints but no hallucinations or other markedly deviate behavior.	Wide range of psychosomatic symptoms and delusions, hallucinations, and other severely deviate behavior.
SOCIAL BEHAVIOR	Behavior rarely injurious to the patient or to society.	Behavior frequently injurious to patient or to society.
TREATMENT	Outpatient psychotherapy is usually adequate.	Usually requires hospitalization, during which various kinds of therapy are used.

OTHER REACTIONS

Sometimes a person is confronted with a disturbing situation so unfamiliar to him that he has no learned way of dealing with it. None of his patterns of behavior or defense mechanisms seem to work in this situation and there is not sufficient opportunity to learn any new adaptive responses. The result is a tempo-

rary breakdown of normal behavior, called a transient situational personality disturbance. An example is combat fatigue, which usually results from long exposure
to extremely demanding battle conditions. For most people, this is an unfamiliar
situation for which established responses are inappropriate. As a result, the person
might engage in random and apparently disorganized behavior.

It is important to note that this temporary breakdown in behavior does
not indicate an underlying personality dysfunction, as do neurotic and psychotic
reactions. Most often this is a temporary condition and the person resumes normal
functioning once the crisis is past.

There is a kind of abnormal behavior in which—in contrast to the disorders
described up to this point—anxiety is not thought to play a key role. This is the
*sociopathic personality disturbance. The sociopathic personality is generally
viewed as a person who does not learn from experience and who is not aware
of the consequences of his behavior.*

One of the most interesting kinds of reaction within this general category
is the *antisocial reaction, which describes a person who is unable to live by
the norms of society.* His behavior is usually impulsive and directed toward immediate gratification of his needs. At first appearance, such a person may be affable,
socially enjoyable, and fun to be with. But this is just part of the routine he
uses to get what he wants. This reaction is a problem primarily for the people
this individual attempts to exploit, and for the police and courts.

*Addiction to drugs or alcoholic beverages is usually considered another
type of sociopathic personality disturbance.* Although anxiety often plays an important part in addiction, this kind of behavior is nevertheless placed in the sociopathic category because addicts do not seem to learn very readily from experience.

QUESTION 10.   Before each of the following descriptions, write in
what type of reaction it is.

_____   A 42-year-old man has recently been jailed for the
                    fourth time for the same kind of offense.

_____   Following an auto accident, a young girl shows severe
                    behavior deterioration.

_____   A young boy recently lost his entire family in a fire.
                    Since then his behavior has been very disorganized.

_____   A promising young law student loses many excellent
                    opportunities for advancement because he is not ready
                    for court appearances due to intoxication.

All the types of mental illness considered so far are known as functional
disorders. In functional disorders, there is no known physiological or organic basis
for the disturbance. For this reason, they are assumed to result from some personal-

ity dysfunction. In organic disorders, in contrast, there is known brain damage which is assumed to cause the disturbance.

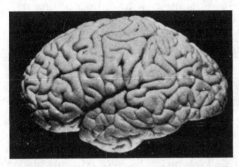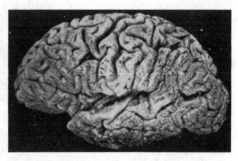

FIGURE 9-6. Normal and diseased brains. The normal brain at the left can readily be distin-guished from the diseased brain at the right. All organic disorders show some deterioration of the brain.

There are two subcategories of organic disorders: acute and chronic. Acute brain disorders usually occur as the result of a specific, known trauma such as an accident or serious illness. Chronic brain disorders, on the other hand, develop slowly over time and are the result of gradual deterioration. The most common example of a chronic organic disorder is senile psychosis, which affects older people. In aging, there is a gradual breakdown of brain cells and when this reaches an advanced stage, it affects behavior. Since there is organic involvement in this disorder, the effects cannot be reversed. Treatment is usually focused on helping the person function as effectively as possible.

> **QUESTION 11.**   Write in "acute" or "chronic" to identify each of the following organic disorders.
>
> _____   A person shows disturbed behavior patterns after an auto accident.
>
> _____   An elderly person gradually displays new and unusual types of behavior.
>
> _____   A young boy has some memory loss after being hit by a bat during a baseball game.

EXCEPTIONAL INDIVIDUALS

While the problems of the neurotic or psychotic individual seem to stem largely from his inner conflicts and frustrations, the difficulties of the so-called "exceptional" person arise from his unusual ability—either unusually low or unu-sually high. While we will confine our discussion to the problems that arise from exceptionally low and high intelligence, persons with defects of speech, eyesight, and so on share many of the same problems.

One of the major concerns of workers in this field is to deal with the negative attitudes that others may take toward the exceptional individual just because he is different. The retarded child is taunted with "idiot," "dummy," and "retard." And it is not always pleasant for the exceptionally gifted child to be called a "brain" or a "know-it-all." One step taken to alleviate this problem has been to choose very carefully the terms used to categorize retarded individuals. Today we hear such terms as custodial, trainable, and educable, which refer to the learning ability of the retarded person. They are an improvement over the older terms idiot, imbecile, and moron because they have fewer negative connotations.

The custodial retarded individual is one with an IQ between 0 and 24. At maturity, he may attain the intelligence of the average 3-year-old, which means that he may learn to say a few words and walk clumsily, but will probably always require custodial care in such things as washing and dressing.

The trainable retarded person is one with an IQ between 25 and 49. He may eventually reach the intelligence of the average 7-year-old. He may be trained to perform simple tasks, such as to carry out a job in a sheltered workshop. He probably will not, however, be able to compete for a job on the open labor market.

The educable retarded person has an IQ up to 75. Since he may reach the intelligence of the average 12-year-old, it may be possible for him to hold a fairly good job, marry and raise a family, and buy a home. Although he may have a good oral vocabulary, he typically has difficulty in dealing with the abstract—as in learning to read or to do mathematics.

To make matters worse for the retarded individual, he typically has more physical defects and poorer health than the average person.

At the other end of the IQ scale is the intellectually gifted person, with an IQ above 140 or so. Just as the retarded tend to be less physically fit than average, the gifted tend to be more physically fit than the norm, as well as better adjusted in general.

A second goal of those who work with exceptional individuals is to provide them with opportunities to develop their potential. The retarded child can be placed in special classes where he will not be discouraged by work that is too difficult for him. The intellectually gifted child may be advanced a grade in school or provided with especially challenging work in his present grade.

QUESTION 12.   Three levels of retardation have been described. List one behavior you would expect to be within the capacity of an individual at each level, and one that would probably be beyond his capacity. Try to name different behaviors for each level.

	Within capacity	*Beyond capacity*
1. Custodial		
2. Trainable		
3. Educable		

METHODS OF TREATMENT

Over the years, clinical psychologists and psychiatrists have developed several techniques to deal with the types of abnormal behavior that we have discussed. Before we describe some of these techniques, let us take a moment to distinguish between the clinical psychologist and the psychiatrist. A clinical psychologist is trained in psychology with special emphasis on the areas of personality development, abnormal behavior, and the treatment of abnormal behavior. He typically believes that research is an important key to the understanding of abnormal behavior.

In contrast, a psychiatrist is a medical doctor who has gone through the regular medical training and then has specialized in the treatment of abnormal behavior. Because the psychiatrist is trained in medicine, he may use whatever drugs or other medications he deems necessary in the treatment of his patients.

There is an ongoing controversy between many clinical psychologists and psychiatrists. The basis of this controversy is that most psychiatrists believe that causes of abnormal behavior or mental illness, as they prefer to call it, should be treated in the same way as any physical illness. That is, the therapist should look for the underlying cause—just as a physician might look for the cause of pneumonia—and then use medical techniques to combat this cause. Many clinical psychologists—especially those trained under the supervision of psychiatrists—share this point of view. But another large group of clinical psychologists argue that there is no clear evidence that abnormal behavior is like physical illness. Instead of assuming underlying causes, they claim, the therapist should directly attack the abnormal behavior itself.

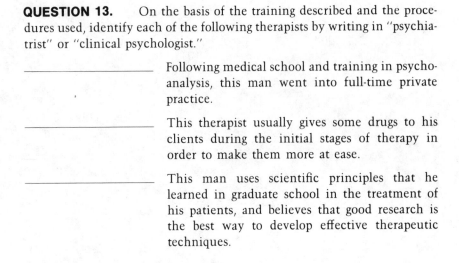

QUESTION 13.   On the basis of the training described and the procedures used, identify each of the following therapists by writing in "psychiatrist" or "clinical psychologist."

_____   Following medical school and training in psychoanalysis, this man went into full-time private practice.

_____   This therapist usually gives some drugs to his clients during the initial stages of therapy in order to make them more at ease.

_____   This man uses scientific principles that he learned in graduate school in the treatment of his patients, and believes that good research is the best way to develop effective therapeutic techniques.

Individual Therapy Methods

If a person experiencing an adjustment problem decides to seek help, several options are available. His choice will depend on his personal preferences and the severity of his disorder. If the disturbance is mild, as in the case of a neurosis or a transitional situational personality disorder, the person might seek individual or group psychotherapy on an out-patient basis. This means that the only change in his activities is that he begins to visit a clinical psychologist or psychiatrist each week. In individual psychotherapy, the professional sees one client at a time. Usually the therapeutic sessions are about one hour long and occur from one to several times a week.

PSYCHOANALYSIS   There are several different types of individual psychotherapy, some based on particular personality theories. The model that is probably the oldest and that is used most frequently by psychiatrists is called psychoanalysis. This is a method introduced by Sigmund Freud that attempts to make a person aware of his repressed conflicts and motives on the assumption that this will help the person to behave in a more healthy way. During development, Freud claimed, we experience desires and motives that are unacceptable and therefore are pushed out of our thinking. Although we are not aware of them, these repressed motives have an undesirable influence on our behavior, and must be recognized by the individual before he can begin to behave in a healthy manner.

Because repressed motives are unacceptable to us, they are relatively difficult to recall and to think about. Psychoanalysis includes specific procedures designed to help people think about this troublesome material. One such method, called free association, requires the client to say aloud everything that comes to his mind without attempting to edit the content, no matter how foolish, absurd, or irrelevant it may seem. The assumption is that if the person does not use his defenses to edit the content of his thought, revealing information about his conflicts and motives may be obtained.

Another method is dream interpretation, which requires the patient to recall his dreams. The psychoanalyst interprets these dreams in order to discover the patient's conflicts and repressed motives.

FIGURE 9-7. **Drawing of a child's dream.** **After the drawing was completed by the child, a psychologist would ask the child to tell the story behind the picture and would ask questions about the characters in the drawing and story. Some speculative interpretations would be made about the dream.**

Psychoanalysis is a very intense type of psychotherapy and usually requires the close association of therapist and client over several years. Analytic sessions are usually scheduled for three or more times per week. Because it is so time-consuming, this is a very costly type of treatment and is therefore restricted to a very select clientele.

QUESTION 14.   Circle the following procedures that are likely to occur in the psychoanalytic type of individual therapy:

1. Have the client maintain a record of his dreams.
2. Have the client come in for a session whenever he feels he needs help.
3. Have the client discuss his relationship with, and his feelings about, his parents.
4. Have the client suppress any thoughts that are disturbing to him.

CLIENT-CENTERED THERAPY   Another form of individual psychotherapy is called client-centered or nondirective therapy, developed by Carl Rogers. In this model, the client is seen as basically oriented toward good, positive, and purposive behaviors. However, as a result of faulty learning or development the person sometimes becomes ineffective, hateful, and self-centered, and therefore incapable of making appropriate responses. The goal of this kind of therapy is to enable the person to function in a constructive way once again.

The role of the client-centered therapist is to provide an atmosphere that is permissive and open, so that the client may freely explore his thoughts and feelings. In this kind of therapy, the therapist provides very little direction. His main aim is to empathize with the patient's feelings and provide an atmosphere in which the client may discover and solve his own problems.

In contrast to Freudian therapy, most of the attention in client-centered therapy is on the present, not the past. The therapist carefully listens to what the client says and attempts to paraphrase his feelings accurately. At no point does he make a value judgment about anything that the client says.

DIRECTIVE PSYCHOTHERAPY   A third model of individual psychotherapy is the directive approach. This is actually a composite of several specific techniques. In the directive model of psychotherapy, the therapist takes an active role, in contrast to the passive role assumed by the client-centered therapist. This includes helping the client to decide on the problems that should be dealt with, the intermediate and long-term goals of therapy, and the overall plan of treatment. In other words, the therapist uses a variety of techniques to get the client active in dealing with his problems.

The directive approach, like the client-centered one, focuses mainly on the current behavior patterns of the client. Many directive therapists believe that the basic problem of the client rests upon his faulty perceptions of the environment. The goal of directive therapy is to explore the origins of these faulty perceptions, to clearly point out to the client how they are irrational, and to show him how they are maintaining his disturbed behavior. It is assumed that an analysis of the faulty perceptions will allow the client to rethink his problems and to develop more realistic and healthy perceptions of his environment, and thus more appropriate behavior.

QUESTION 15.   Write "directive" or "nondirective" before each of the following situations to indicate in which kind of therapy it would be more likely to occur:

_____   If a client arrives late for a therapy session, the therapist discusses possible reasons for the lateness and what it means for therapy.

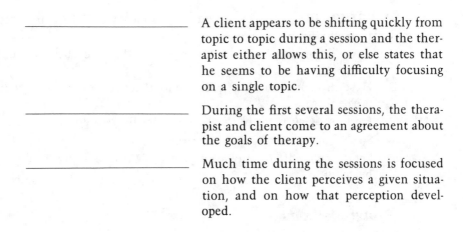

_____ A client appears to be shifting quickly from topic to topic during a session and the therapist either allows this, or else states that he seems to be having difficulty focusing on a single topic.

_____ During the first several sessions, the therapist and client come to an agreement about the goals of therapy.

_____ Much time during the sessions is focused on how the client perceives a given situation, and on how that perception developed.

A particular type of directive psychotherapy that is being used with increasing frequency is _behavior modification_. The behavior modification approach is based on the principles of learning reviewed in Chapter 3. _The basic assumption of this approach is that all behaviors—abnormal as well as normal—are learned through reinforcement._

The first step in behavior modification is to specify the problem behavior in observable terms. Next there must be a careful analysis of the stimuli that may be reinforcing this behavior. A third step is for the client to decide what changes in behavior he wants. Finally, attention is focused on rearranging the environmental conditions that affect the behavior. If, for example, the goal of therapy is to reduce the frequency of a particular behavior, the extinction procedure might be used.

Behavior modification was first applied in institutional settings, such as psychiatric hospitals, where the environment is fairly limited, routine, and staff-controlled. After many dramatic demonstrations of its effectiveness, attempts were made to use it in more normal, everyday situations. However, behavior modification is more difficult to apply in non-institutional situations, because it is more difficult to control reinforcers. Suppose, for example, that a teacher is trying to stop the temper tantrums of one of her students by using extinction—that is, by not giving the child any attention when he is having a tantrum. At home, however, the parents do give the child attention when he has a tantrum because this stops his crying. This teacher's efforts to help the child will probably fail because of the inconsistency between her behavior and that of the parents. To correct this situation, the teacher and the parents must get together and agree on a single procedure to be used both at home and at school.

The behavior modification approach has several attractive features. First, it gives results that can be readily measured. Second, the same basic principles apply in all cases. It should be noted, however, that the way in which these principles are applied varies from case to case.

QUESTION 16.   Circle the procedures that would be appropriate in behavior modification therapy.

1. Carefully analyze the conditions under which the behavior usually occurs.
2. Have the client think of past events that are related to the current problem.
3. Find out what types of things the client likes to do.
4. Specify a target or objective for the therapy.
5. Let the client discuss any feelings that might account for the disruptive behavior.

Group Methods

Group therapy differs from individual psychotherapy in a number of ways, some of which are obvious. The number of clients in a therapy group usually ranges between five and eight. There is a therapist—just as in individual psychotherapy—and sometimes a co-therapist. The co-therapist sometimes is actively involved in the group process and sometimes assumes the role of passive observer. The ideal in group therapy is that the group members talk with each other, rather than directing their comments only to the therapist. This sharing of experiences has been found to facilitate helping the group members reorganize troubled aspects of their lives.

RATIONALE FOR GROUP THERAPY   There are a number of practical and therapeutic reasons for using group therapy. Among the practical reasons are:

1. By allowing a therapist to see a group of patients at once, it relieves the serious problem of lack of professional time.
2. The cost per client is less and therefore group therapy is available to a wider range of clients.

Among the therapeutic reasons are:

1. There are occasions when an individual is having problems but is not disturbed enough to need individual psychotherapy. Group therapy may be appropriate in these cases.
2. Many patients find it easier to speak in a group setting than in an individual one.
3. Clients often find it reassuring to find that other people are experiencing difficulties similar to their own. As a result, they are often more optimistic and more motivated to change themselves.

GOALS OF GROUP THERAPY   The goals of a therapy group usually fall into one of three categories: supportive, re-educative and reconstructive. The supportive type of group is the least involving and is usually geared toward assisting the group members through some current crisis. The re-educative group is more involving and usually focuses on the development of new, more effective ways of handling certain situations. The reconstructive group is the most involving and is geared toward bringing about major changes in the personality structures of the members.

QUESTION 17.   Identify each of the following examples of therapy groups by writing "supportive," "re-educative," or "reconstructive" before it.

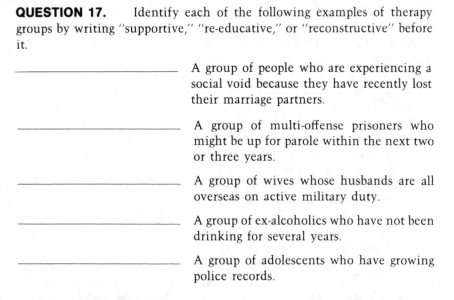

_____   A group of people who are experiencing a social void because they have recently lost their marriage partners.

_____   A group of multi-offense prisoners who might be up for parole within the next two or three years.

_____   A group of wives whose husbands are all overseas on active military duty.

_____   A group of ex-alcoholics who have not been drinking for several years.

_____   A group of adolescents who have growing police records.

CLIENT CHARACTERISTICS   There are certain key variables that should be considered when selecting clients for a group. Each client should have at least the following characteristics: (1) good contact with reality; (2) a reasonably effective level of interpersonal skills so that he can effectively operate in a group; and (3) sufficient personal flexibility so that he can both contribute to the group and serve as an observer of other group members.

On the other hand, there are certain types of clients who should not be admitted to a therapy group: (1) the person who is severely disturbed; (2) the person who is acutely anxious or depressed (he probably won't be able to communicate effectively); and (3) the person who is overtly destructive (he might harm other group members).

QUESTION 18.   According to the above criteria, which of the following clients would be good candidates for therapy groups. (Circle each.)

1. A drug addict who is still going through withdrawal symptoms.
2. A college student who is experiencing some minor adjustment difficulties during his first year at college.
3. A group of psychotic patients who have been hospitalized for many years with little more than custodial care.
4. A group of soldiers about to face their first combat mission.

THE PROCESS OF GROUP THERAPY   Many things may happen in a group therapy session. Most of the time is spent discussing problems and expressing feelings about these problems. Sometimes, members express how they are feeling toward another group member when he is speaking about a problem. It is the role of the therapist to carefully monitor all of this activity and to provide feedback to the group and the individual members concerning their reactions and feelings. At the end of a group session, a summary statement is usually given. If there is a co-therapist acting as an observer, he is usually the one to give the summary.

Groups usually meet once or twice a week for an hour to an hour and a half. The total number of sessions varies considerably, depending partly upon whether the group is open or closed. An open group is one in which members move in and out of the group over time. When a member feels that he has reached his goals he may leave the group and be replaced by a new member. A closed group, on the other hand, is one that remains intact until the entire membership feels that it is time to terminate the group.

While discussing group methods, we should mention the emerging interest in group processes among normally functioning individuals. You may have read articles about sensitivity groups, encounter groups, T-groups, or marathon groups. Generally the goals of these kinds of groups are: (1) to increase one's awareness of his environment; (2) to increase one's awareness of his own attitudes and feelings; and (3) to improve one's ability to communicate by increasing his sensitivity to others. Such groups are quite popular with people who feel that the routine of daily life has begun to dull their sensitivity to others and their appreciation of their surroundings.

Other Methods

Sometimes a person's behavior becomes so disturbed that he is not able to function adequately in his normal environment. In these cases hospitalization is required.

There are two types of admission to a mental hospital. Voluntary admission occurs when a person himself decides that he needs care and voluntarily admits himself to a hospital for treatment. The other type of admission is through legal commitment. In these cases the patient does not recognize his need for treatment, and it is therefore necessary for his family, his friends, or his physician to recommend his admission to the hospital. The patient is then examined by a team of psychiatrists and psychologists. If they agree that he needs treatment, he is admitted to the hospital. He stays at the hospital under the direction of a physician for as long as the physician feels it is necessary. Recently, the procedures for legal commitment have come under careful review to make sure that they do not discriminate against particular socioeconomic or racial groups. This is related to the question, discussed earlier, of who has the power to define abnormality.

Statistics show that one out of every two hospital beds in the United States is occupied by a mentally ill patient. This large proportion is probably due in part to the fact that many mental patients have been hospitalized for fifteen or more years and will probably remain hospitalized for the rest of their lives. Until recently, the prevailing philosophy of treatment was that mental patients will probably never be cured, so the best that can be done is to give them custodial care for the rest of their lives.

Fortunately, a new philosophy of treatment is rapidly emerging. The basic idea is that the hospitalized patient first needs a period of intensive treatment to reconstruct his life style, and then should be quickly returned to his home community so that he may try out his newly learned adaptive behaviors. This philosophy has resulted in a much more active treatment process and a much higher rate of turnover among hospitalized mental patients.

While in the hospital, the patient may be exposed to a number of different kinds of therapy including individual therapy, group therapy, and drug therapy. The goal of drug therapy is to make the patient's behavior more manageable and acceptable. There are also recreational and vocational activities in the mental hospital that allow the person to develop or maintain his social skills and also to develop occupational skills that he may need upon discharge.

When a patient has shown significant signs of improvement, his case is reviewed by a team of psychiatrists and clinical psychologists. Sometimes when a person is scheduled for release there is an intermediary step before he is returned home. This is the "halfway house"—a residence in which a group of former patients live together and support each other during the initial stages of readapting to society. This intermediary step usually facilitates the transition to the home environment, and reduces the chances that the patient will have to return to the hospital again.

SUMMARY

Abnormal behavior is sometimes defined statistically, that is, as behavior that deviates from a norm. Another procedure is to focus on the key ingredients of a normally functioning individual and view deviations from these criteria as cases of abnormal behavior. Data on the incidence of mental illness shows a general trend for the frequency to be greater in urban areas and among lower socioeconomic groups.

Anxiety, a state of apprehension, plays a key role in the occurrence of abnormal behavior. People usually develop a variety of defense mechanisms to protect themselves from anxiety. When a person's defense mechanisms are inadequate to handle a certain situation, a neurotic or psychotic reaction results. There are several different types of neurotic reactions, such as depressive reaction, phobic reaction and obsessive-compulsive reaction. Each of these disorders shares the characteristic that the person cannot specify the cause of the anxiety he is experiencing.

The psychotic reactions are a more severe type of disturbance which usually affects the entire functioning of the individual. Loss of contact with reality, hallucinations, and delusions are characteristics of the psychotic reactions, such as schizophrenia and manic-depressive reactions.

Another class of disorders are those that involve some injury to the brain. The injury can be a sudden, traumatic event (acute brain disorder) or a gradual deterioration over time (chronic brain disorder).

Treatment for the various kinds of abnormal behavior is provided by several kinds of professionals in a number of different settings. A psychiatrist is a medical doctor with special training in the area of behavior disorders. A clinical psychologist is a person trained in psychology with special emphasis in the areas of personality development, abnormal behavior, and the treatment of abnormal behavior.

Psychiatrists and clinical psychologists use a variety of treatment methods dealing with individual clients and groups of clients. Many of the treatment models used are developed from particular theories of personality (see Chapter 8). The individual treatment methods involve an intense treatment relationship between the client and therapist, while group methods rely on the interaction among a group of clients as well as the intervention of the therapist.

If a person's behavior disorder is very serious, hospitalization is sometimes required. Such hospitalization is frequently followed by some continued treatment in the person's community to facilitate his readjustment.

BEHAVIOR TO EXPLAIN

In clinical treatment methods, there is a recent trend to try to keep even seriously disturbed patients in their own community as long as possible. This trend has resulted in the development of community crisis center programs to deal with acute problems without having to send a person to a state hospital which might be far away. It has also led to the development of halfway houses to facilitate a speedy release of patients who have been hospitalized.

1. Think of all the principles you can that might help explain the presumed positive effect of this approach.

2. State an hypothesis involving a clinical explanation for this treatment approach.

3. Describe a study that could be done to test your hypothesis, including both the design and the measuring instruments you would use.

Appendix

Crowd Noise and Conformity[1]

David S. Dustin

According to LeBon (1952) and others, individuals pattern their behavior after that of others more when they are in a crowd than when they are not. One possible explanation is that the milling, shouting people in a crowd may distract the individual, making it more difficult for him to arrive at his own independent conclusions about what is appropriate behavior in the situation, thus increasing the likelihood that he will conform to the behavior of others. The present study tested the hypothesis that crowd distraction influences conformity.

Due to the difficulty of using live crowds in the laboratory, the only aspect of a crowd used in the present study was its noise. It was expected that the recorded noise of a basketball crowd (CN) would produce more conformity in a problem-solving situation than would no noise (NN).

METHOD

Subjects

Sixty introductory psychology students volunteered to take part in the experiment in return for class credit. Fifteen men and 15 women were assigned to each condition, CN and NN.

Procedure

At each experimental session, two or three Ss[2] of the same sex were seated in adjacent stalls that were open at Ss' backs, and were first given one minute of habituation to the assigned noise treatment. Then booklets containing the 13 matrix problems from the IPAT Culture Free Intelligence Test, Scale 3, Form A, were distributed. In an attempt to minimize Ss' motivation, E[3] stated that his interest was in evaluating the test (not the Ss). One of the six alternative answers to each problem was marked with a red check. This, Ss were told, was the answer most often chosen by the students who had previously worked the problems.

Then Ss were given five minutes to work the problems under the assigned noise condition. CN was delivered from a loudspeaker hung on the wall behind Ss. As measured by a General Radio Company sound-level meter, Type 1551-B, the CN varied from about 93 to 78 db[4] at all seats. Ss were told that this noise was not related to the experiment but was being produced by a lab technician who needed to test equipment.

RESULTS

Although analysis of variance[5] showed no significant differences in number of problems completed in the two noise conditions, it seemed desirable to eliminate this source of variation in conformity scores. Since the first six problems were the only ones completed by all Ss, they were the only ones considered in the analyses.

The response measure was the number of agreements with the checked answers, which were correct for three of the first six items and incorrect for the other three.

As shown in Table A-1, both men and women showed more conformity in the CN condition than in the NN condition. However, this difference was not statistically significant (t[6] $= 1.84$, $p = .07$) for men and women combined. When this difference was analyzed for men and women separately, it was significant for the men ($t = 2.12$, $p < .05$), but not for the women ($t < 1.00$).

TABLE A-1   MEAN CONFORMITY SCORES

	MEN	WOMEN
CROWD NOISE	4.33	4.27
NO NOISE	3.67	4.13

DISCUSSION

The significant increase in the men's conformity from the NN to the CN condition supports the hypothesis that crowd distraction influences conformity, at least for men. It seems likely that distraction affects conformity in the same way an increase in problem difficulty does (Blake, Helson, & Mouton, 1957). That is, both distraction and problem difficulty may have the effect of making it more difficult for the individual to solve the problem that confronts him on his own, therefore making it more likely that he will adopt solutions of others if they are available.

The finding that women showed somewhat more conformity in the NN condition than did the men is in accord with previous findings that, under ordinary noise conditions, women conform more than men (cf. Krech, Crutchfield, & Ballachey, 1962, p. 524). This finding may explain why the women did not show a significant increase in conformity from the NN to the CN condition. That is, perhaps it was simply because there was less room for the women to go up from their already-high conformity scores in the NN condition.

NOTES TO APPENDIX

[1] This is a modified version of an article that appeared in *Psychological Reports*, 1968, 23, 425–426.
[2] *S* stands for subject.
[3] *E* stands for experimenter.
[4] *db* stands for decibels, a measure of sound intensity.
[5] Analysis of variance is one particular test of statistical significance.
[6] The *t*-test is one particular test of statistical significance.

REFERENCES

Blake, R. R., Helson, H., & Mouton, J. S. The generality of conformity behavior as a function of factual anchorage, difficulty of task, and amount of social pressure. *Journal of Personality*, 1957 25, 294-305.

Krech, D., Crutchfield, R. S., & Ballachey, E. L. *Individual in society.* New York: McGraw-Hill, 1962.

LeBon, G. *The crowd.* London: Ernest Benn, 1952. (Reprint)

References

Abernethy, E M. The effect of changed environmental conditions upon the results of college examinations. *Journal of Psychology*, 1940, *10*, 293-301.

Adorno, T. W., Frenkel-Brunswik, E., Levinson, D. J., & Sanford, R. N. *The authoritarian personality*. New York: Harper & Row, Publishers, Inc., 1950. Used by permission.

Aronoff, J. The cane-cutters of St. Kitts. *Psychology Today*, January 1971, 53-55.

Aronson, E., & Carlsmith, J. M. Effect of the severity of threat on the devaluation of forbidden behavior. *Journal of Abnormal and Social Psychology*, 1963, *66*, 584-588.

Asch, S. E. Studies of independence and conformity: I. A minority of one against a unanimous majority. *Psychological Monographs*, 1956, *70*, Whole #416.

Ashley, W. R., Harper, R. S., & Runyon, D. L. The perceived size of coins in normal and hypnotically induced economic status. *American Journal of Psychology*, 1951, *64*, 564-572. Used by permission.

Bard, P. On emotional expression after decortication with some remarks on certain theoretical views. Parts I & II. *Psychological Review*, 1934, *41*, 309-329 & 424-449.

Berkun, M. M., Kessen, M. L., & Miller, N. E. Hunger-reducing effects of food by stomach fistula versus food by mouth measured by a consummatory process. *Journal of Comparative and Physiological Psychology*, 1952, *45*, 550-554.

Bridges, K. M. B. Emotional development in early infancy. *Child Development*, 1932, *3*, 324-341.

Butler, R. A. The effect of deprivation of visual incentives on visual exploration motivation in monkeys. *Journal of Comparative and Physiological Psychology*, 1957, *50*, 177-179.

Clark, R. A. The projective measurement of experimentally induced levels of sexual motivation. *Journal of Experimental Psychology*, 1952, *44*, 391-399.

Cooper, R. M., & Zubek, J. P. Effects of enriched and restricted early environments on the learning ability of bright and dull rats. *Canadian Journal of Psychology*, 1958, *12*, 159-164.

Delgado, J. M. R. *Physical control of the mind*. New York: Harper & Row, Publishers, 1969. Used by permission.

Dustin, D. S. Crowd noise and conformity. *Psychological Reports*, 1968, *23*, 425-426.

Emlen, S. T. Birds. *Psychology Today*, April 1972, 55ff.

Fellows, L. The Duka-Wallas are outcasts in Africa. *New York Times Magazine*, June 25, 1967, 20ff.

Franklin, B. *Benjamin Franklin: His Life*. Boston: Ginn & Co., 1906.

Freud, S. Analysis of a phobia in a five-year-old boy. In *Collected papers of Sigmund Freud*, III. New York: Basic Books, Inc., 1959..

Gesell, A., & Thompson, H. Twins T and C from infancy to adolescence: A biogenetic study of individual differences by the method of co-twin control. *Genetic Psychology Monographs*, 1941, *24*, 3-122.

Gottesman, I. I. Heritability of personality: A demonstration. *Psychological Monographs*, 1963, *77*, Whole No. 572.

Greene, W., The militants who play with dynamite. *New York Times Magazine*, October 25, 1970, 20ff. © 1970 by the New York Times Company. Reprinted by permission.

Harlow, H. F., & Harlow, M. Social deprivation in monkeys. *Scientific American*, 1962 *207*, 136-146.

Hastorf, A. H., & Cantril, H. They saw a game: A case study. *Journal of Abnormal and Social Psychology*, 1954, *49*, 129-134.

Herrick, E. H., & Harris, J. O. Singing female canaries. *Science*, 1957, *125*, 1299-1300.

Hess, E. H. Imprinting. *Science*, 1959, *130*, 133-141.

Holway, A. H., & Boring, E. G. Determinants of apparent visual size with distance variant. *American Journal of Psychology*, 1941, *54*, 21-37.

Hovland, C. I. The generalization of conditioned responses. *Journal of General Psychology*, 1937, *17*, 125-148.

Hovland, C. I., & Weiss, W. The influence of source credibility on communication effectiveness. *Public Opinion Quarterly*, 1951, *15*, 635-650.

Isaacs, W., Thomas, J., & Goldiamond, I. Application of operant conditioning to reinstate verbal behavior in psychotics. *Journal of Speech and Hearing Disorders*, 1960, *25*, 8-12.

Itard, J.-M.-G. *Wild boy of Aveyron*. New York: Appleton-Century Crofts, 1962. (Translated from *Rapports et memoires sur le sauvage de l'Aveyron*, Paris, 1894.)

Jenkins, J. G., & Dallenback, K. M. Oblivescence during sleep and waking. *American Journal of Psychology*, 1924, *35*, 605-612.

Kallman, F. J. The genetic theory of schizophrenia. *American Journal of Psychiatry*, 1946, *103*, 309-322.

King, J. H. Brief account of the sufferings of a detachment of United States Cavalry, from deprivation of water, during a period of 86 hours, while scouting on the "Llano Estacado" or "Staked Plains," Texas. In A. V. Wolf, *Thirst*. Springfield, Ill.: Charles C. Thomas, 1958. Pp. 375-380.

Lazarus, R. S. *Personality*. Englewood Cliffs, New Jersey: Prentice-Hall, Inc., 1971.

Lesieur, F. (Ed.) *The Scanlon Plan*. New York: Wiley, 1958.

Levy, H. S. Culturally imposed "clubfoot." In N. H. Pronko (Ed.), *Panorama of psychology*. Belmont, Cal.: Brooks/Cole, 1969. Pp. 252-253.

Lukas, J. A. 'Whitey hasn't got the message.' *New York Times Magazine*, August 27, 1967, 22ff. © 1967 by the New York Times Company. Reprinted by permission.

Maslow, A. H. *Motivation and personality*. (2nd ed.) New York: Harper & Row, 1970.

Masters, W. J., & Johnson, V. E. *Human sexual response*. Boston: Little, Brown, 1966.

McClelland, D. C., & Atkinson, J. W. The projective expression of needs: I. The effects of different intensities of the hunger drive on perception. *Journal of Psychology*, 1948, *25*, 205-222.

Melzack, R., & Scott, T. H. The effect of early experience on the response to pain. *Journal of Comparative and Physiological Psychology*, 1957, *50*, 155-161.

Miller, M. What it means to be a homosexual. *New York Times Magazine*, January 17, 1971, 9ff.

Morphett, M. V., & Washburn, C. When should children begin to read? *Elementary School Journal*, 1931, *31*, 496-503.

Newcomb, T. M. *Personality and social change*. New York: Dryden, 1943.

Newman, H. H., Freeman, F., & Holzinger, K. J. *Twins, a study of heredity and environment*. Chicago: University of Chicago Press, 1937.

Olds, J. Physiological mechanisms of reward. In M. Jones (Ed.), *Nebraska symposium on motivation*. Lincoln, Neb.: University of Nebraska Press, 1955, Pp. 73-138.

Powers, F. G., with Gentry, C. *Operation Overflight*. New York: Holt, Rinehart, & Winston, Inc., 1970. Used by permission.

Press-Republican (Plattsburgh, N. Y.), March 2, 1968, 3. Used by permission of the Press-Republican and Fr. Paul Walsh.

Rosenzweig, M. R., Bennett, E. L., & Diamond, M. C. Brain changes in response to experience. *Scientific American*, Feb. 1972, *226*, 22-29.

Schachter, S. *The psychology of affiliation*. Stanford: Stanford University Press, 1959. Used by permission.

Schachter, S., & Singer, J. E. Cognitive, social, and physiological determinants of emotional state. *Psychological Review*, 1962, *69*, 379-399.

Scott, J. P. Social behavior, organization, and leadership in a small flock of domestic sheep. *Comparative Psychology Monographs*, 1945, *18* (Whole No. 4). Originally published by the University of California Press; reprinted by permission of The Regents of the University of California.

Segalman, R. The conflict of cultures between social work and the underclass *Rocky Mountain Social Science Journal*, 1965, *2*, 161-173.

Sherif, M., Harvey, O. J., White, B. J., Hood, W. R., & Sherif, C. W. *Intergroup conflict and cooperation: The Cave experiment.* Norman Okla.: University Book Exchange, 1961.

Shields, J. *Monozygotic Twins Brought Up Apart and Brought Up Together: An Investigation Into the Genetic and Environmental Causes of Variation in Personality.* London: Oxford. 1962.

Skodak, M., & Skeels, H. M. A final follow-up study of one hundred adopted children. *Journal of Genetic Psychology,* 1949, 75, 85-125.

Sperry. R. W. Brain bisection and mechanisms of consciousness. In J. C. Eccles (Ed.) *Brain and conscious experience.* New York: Springer-Verlag, 1966. Pp 298-313.

Teitelbaum, P., & Epstein, A. N. The lateral hypothalamic syndrome: Recovery of feeding and drinking after lateral hypothalmic lesions. *Psychological Review,* 1962, 69, 74-90.

Toch, H., & Schulte, R. Readiness to perceive violence as a result of police training. *British Journal of Psychology,* 1961, 52, 389-393.

Verhave, T. The pigeon as a quality control inspector. *American Psychologist,* 1966, 21, 109-115.

Veroff, J., Atkinson, J. W., Feld, S., & Gurin, G. The use of thematic apperception to assess motivation in a nationwide interview survey. *Psychological Monographs,* 1960, 74, Whole No. 449).

Watson, J., & Rayner, R. Conditioned emotional reactions. *Journal of Experimental Psychology,* 1920, 3, 1-14.

Whaley, D., Sibley, S. & Risley, T. Conditioning of appropriate verbal durations in a young boy. Unpublished research cited in D. L. Whaley & R. W. Malott, *Elementary principles of behavior.* New York: Appleton-Century-Crofts, 1971. Pp. 110-113.

White, R. K., & Lippitt, R. *Autocracy and democracy.* New York: Harper, 1960.

Wolf, A. V. *Thirst.* Springfield, Ill.: Charles C. Thomas, 1958.

Suggested Readings

Chapter One

Anthony, D. S. Is graphology valid? *Psychology Today*, August 1967, 30-35. The author presents evidence for the validity of handwriting analysis and describes some of the methods of measurement he has applied to it.

Barber, T. X. Who believes in hypnosis? *Psychology Today*, July 1970, 20ff. Claims that hypnotic induction ("You are becoming drowsy") produces superhuman strength, insensitivity to pain, hallucinations, etc., are based on poorly-controlled studies, Barber's evidence indicates.

McMahon, F. B., Jr. Psychological testing—a smoke screen against logic. *Psychology Today*, January 1969, 54ff. Instead of looking for hidden meanings in a person's responses to the Rorschach Test or the MMPI, why not simply ask him directly about himself?

Rosenthal, R. Self-fulfilling prophecy. *Psychology Today*, September 1968, 44-51. Rosenthal has found that, in very subtle ways, the expectations of experimenters influence the performances of their subjects, and the expectations of teachers influence the performances of their students.

Whyte, W. H. How to cheat on personality tests. In W. H. Whyte, *The organization man*. New York: Simon & Schuster, 1956. Believing that personality tests given by organizations violate the rights of their employees or job applicants, Whyte advises us to cheat on such tests, and gives some practical tips on how to do it.

Chapter Two

Bronfenbrenner, U. The split-level American family. *Saturday Review*, October 7, 1967, 60-66. The author suggests that some developmental problems of modern youngsters might be solved by returning to child-rearing practices of the past.

Carrighar, S. War is not in our genes. *New York Times Magazine*, September 10, 1967, 74ff. The author argues against the recent claims of Lorenz and Ardrey that aggressiveness is inherited.

Elkind, D. Giant in the nursery—Jean Piaget. *New York Times Magazine*, May 26, 1968, 25ff. A personal introduction to Piaget and his theories of intellectual development.

Pines, M. Why some 3-year-olds get A's—and some get C's. *New York Times Magazine*, July 6, 1969, 4ff. Describes recent research on the mental development of young children.

Chapter Three

Deutsch, J. A. Neural basis of memory. *Psychology Today*, May 1968, 56-61. Describes a series of experiments in which the author injected various drugs into rats in order to find out what happens in the nervous system during learning and remembering. A good example of scientific reasoning.

Kamiya, J. Conscious control of brain waves. *Psychology Today*, April 1968, 56-60. Describes studies in which people are taught to produce alpha waves, which correspond to a pleasant, tranquil state of mind.

Lang, P. J. Autonomic control. *Psychology Today*, October 1970, 37ff. Beginning about 1960, psychologists have been discovering that it is possible to learn to control one's heart-rate, blood pressure, sweating, brain waves, and other "involuntary" responses. This article summarizes some of the findings, as well as some attempts to put them to practical use.

Lichtenstein, E. How to quit smoking. *Psychology Today*, January 1971, 42ff. A summary of ways in which psychologists have tried to remove the tenacious habit of smoking. Although most of these techniques do not appear effective, a few of them do look promising.

McConnell, J. V. Learning theory. In R. A. Baker (ed.) *Psychology in the wry*. Princeton: Van Nostrand, 1963. A science fiction story in which an earthling psychologist finds himself a subject in learning research conducted by beings from outer space.

Premack, D. The education of S*A*R*A*H. *Psychology Today*, September 1970, 54-58. Previous attempts to teach monkeys to talk have not been very successful. Is this because monkeys lack the necessary vocal organs, or the necessary intelligence? To find out, Premack set out to teach Sarah, a chimpanzee, a written language that uses pieces of colored plastic for words.

Rice, B. Skinner agrees he is the most important influence in psychology. *New York*

Times Magazine, March 17, 1968, 27ff. An introduction to B. F. Skinner, who discovered many of the principles of operant conditioning and who pioneered in applying these principles to numerous human problems.

Skinner, B. F. *Walden two.* New York: Macmillan, 1948. Skinner's novel about a planned community, founded to some extent on conditioning principles.

Chapter Four

Darley, J. M. & Latané, B. When will people help in a crisis? *Psychology Today,* December 1968, 54ff. Why is it that crowds often merely watch when someone is in trouble? The authors report a series of carefully controlled experiments they carried out to test one possible explanation.

Deutsch, M. Psychological alternatives to war. *Journal of Social Issues,* 1962, 18, 97-119. The author summarizes much of the theoretical work psychologists have done on war, its causes and possible antidotes.

Meyer, P. If Hitler asked you to electrocute a stranger, would you? *Esquire,* February 1970, 72ff. An inside view of Milgram's disturbing version of the Asch conformity study, in which the experimenter instructs the subject to give another person stronger and stronger electric shocks.

Zimbardo, P. et al. A Pirandellian prison. *New York Times Magazine,* April 8, 1973, 38ff. What happens when college men play the roles of prisoners and guards in a mock prison for a week?

Chapter Five

Brecher, R. & Brecher, E. The happiest creatures on earth? *Harper's Magazine,* April 1961, 85-90. The authors describe what is known about the reward centers in the brain, and discuss the danger that such knowledge may be used to enslave mankind.

Davidson, B. Your eye can't lie. *Saturday Evening Post,* January 15, 1966, 76-79. It recently has been discovered that a person's pupil grows larger to stimuli he likes and smaller to stimuli he dislikes. Many practical applications have been suggested.

Krech, D. The chemistry of learning. *Saturday Review,* January 20, 1968, 45ff. This article discusses chemicals that influence learning, as well as those that are influenced by it. It concludes with the intriguing suggestion that certain chemicals, taken by injection or by pill, may eventually prove to be of practical value in facilitating human learning.

Wooldridge, D. E. How the machine called the brain feels and thinks. *New York Times Magazine,* October 4, 1964, 24ff. Can the living brain of a monkey, removed from the body, still feel and think? In answering this question, Wooldridge reviews most of the major knowledge about the brain.

Chapter Six

Geldard, F. A. Body English. *Psychology Today*, December 1968, 42-47. Using psychology's fund of information about the skin's sensory capabilities—its thresholds and discriminations—the author has developed language systems that utilize the sense of touch instead of hearing.

Hastorf, A. H. & Cantril, H. They saw a game: A case study. *Journal of Abnormal and Social Psychology*, 1954, 49, 129-134. When a film of a notoriously rough Princeton-Dartmouth football game was shown to students at the two colleges they perceived the number of rule violations committed by the two sides quite differently.

Melzack, R. Phantom limbs, *Psychology Today*, October 1970, 63ff. A particularly puzzling perceptual problem is the phantom limbs that amputees often feel after their real limbs have been removed and the pain that often afflicts these limbs. The author speculates on possible explanations of this pain and possible ways of treating it.

Murphy, G. Parapsychology: New neighbor or unwelcome guest. *Psychology Today*, May 1968, 52ff. The author describes some of the notable findings regarding extrasensory perception, and discusses what steps parapsychologists must take to become more acceptable to other psychologists.

Rock, I. When the world is tilt. *Psychology Today*, July 1968, 24-31. Why is it that subjects who wear distorting glasses eventually report that the world is beginning to look normal again? Rock describes where psychologists now stand in their attempts to explain this phenomenon.

Chapter Seven

Azrin, N. Pain and aggression. *Psychology Today*, May 1967, 26-33. The author recounts his accidental discovery that painful stimuli lead many kinds of animals to behave aggressively, and his efforts to discover the exact nature of this motivational phenomenon.

Dement, W. The effect of dream deprivation. *Science*, 1960, 131, 1705-1707. Is there a motive to dream? The author attempted to find out by preventing subjects from dreaming for several nights in succession and then observing whether they dreamed more frequently than usual during the following nights.

Harlow, H. F. The nature of love. *American Psychologist*, 1958, 13, 673-685. The author wittily describes his famous studies on what makes baby monkeys love (cling to) their mothers.

Herzberg, F. Motivation, morale, & money. *Psychology Today*, March 1968, 42ff. The writer, like many other industrial psychologists, follows the motivational theory of Maslow. He believes that today's businessman puts too much emphasis on the "lower" motivational factor of money, and ignores the "higher" motives such as responsibility, challenge, and the opportunity for growth.

Hoffman, M. Homosexual. *Psychology Today*, July 1969, 43ff. Is homosexuality a psychopathology? Definitely not, says Hoffman. He then outlines some of the normal ways in which it may occur.

Horner, M. Fail: Bright women. *Psychology Today*, November 1969, 36ff. Research on n Ach has been done mostly with men, because the early results for women were confusing. Why so? Horner argues that this is because many women have learned a strong motive to avoid success.

Chapter Eight

Domhoff, B. & Hall, C. S. The dreams of Freud and Jung. *Psychology Today*, June 1968, 42ff. This article analyzes the dreams of two psychiatrists who made extensive use of dream interpretation in their own treatment of patients.

Harris, T. G., Garcia, J., Mercer, J. R., & Watson, P. I. Q. abuse. *Psychology Today*, September 1972, 39ff. A group of articles arguing that IQ scores may be used to discriminate unfairly against minority groups.

Keniston, K. The alienated self. In K. Keniston, *The uncommitted.* New York: Harcourt Brace & World, 1965. In this chapter, Keniston describes the characteristics of the alienated individual, whom most readers will recognize.

Langguth, J. Dr. Berne plays the celebrity game. *New York Times Magazine*, July 17, 1966, 10ff. An entertaining glimpse into the personality of Eric Berne, inventor of the currently popular personality theory of transactional analysis.

Stoller, F. H. The long weekend. *Psychology Today*, December 1967, 28-33. This article is about the encounter group, that recent and popular innovation to help normal people see themselves more clearly and become more effective.

Chapter Nine

Bassin, A. Daytop Village. *Psychology Today*, December 1968, 48ff. Details a living-in treatment facility for drug addicts. A basic aspect of the program is that addicts and ex-addicts are used as treatment personnel.

Eysenck, H. New ways in psychotherapy. *Psychology Today*, June 1967, 39-47. A summary of the new and exciting attempts to apply the principles of conditioning to the treatment of neurotic disorders.

Galton, L. One of the great mystery stories of medicine. *New York Times Magazine*, November 6, 1966, 34ff. The story of the search for the causes of schizophrenia in body chemistry. Although many leads have turned up, the case has not yet been solved.

Lent, J. R. Mimosa Cottage: Experiment in hope. *Psychology Today*, June 1968, 51-58. This article describes a treatment program for retarded children which is based on behavioral principles. The children learn to do things for themselves instead of remaining completely dependent on others.

Orlinsky, D. E. & Howard, K. I. Inside psychotherapy. *Psychology Today*, July 1968, 50-57. Discusses the reactions of patient and therapist in psychotherapy.

Glossary

abnormal behavior.   Behavior that deviates from a norm or average.

activation.   The intensity or vigor of behavior, which is one aspect of motivation (cf. direction).

acute brain disorder.   An organic disorder that occurs as a result of a specific known accident or illness (cf. chronic brain disorder).

adaptation (sensory).   Refers to the influence of the level of recent stimulation on a threshold. For all senses, the threshold increases when the sense organ is subjected to a high level of stimulation and decreases when it is subjected to a low level of stimulation.

adjustment.   A general term referring to mental health.

adrenalin.   A hormone, secreted by the adrenal glands, which increases heart rate and produces other symptoms of excitement.

affective reaction.   A synonym for manic-depressive reaction.

all-or-none principle.   The principle which states that a neuron fires completely or not at all.

anal stage.   According to psychoanalytic theory, the psychosexual stage during which the anus is the zone most sensitive to pleasurable stimulation (cf. oral stage, genital stage).

antisocial reaction.   A type of sociopathic personality disturbance characterized by behavior that is impulsive and directed toward immediate self-gratification, without regard for social norms.

anxiety.   Apprehension, often due to anticipation of future danger.

anxiety reaction.   A neurotic reaction characterized by free-floating anxiety occasionally punctuated by acute anxiety attacks (cf. depressive reaction, phobic reaction, obsessive-compulsive reaction, conversion reaction).

approach-approach conflict.   When the organism is motivated to approach two different goals, and can't have both at once (cf. avoidance-avoidance conflict, approach-avoidance conflict).

approach-avoidance conflict.   When the organism simultaneously wants to approach and to avoid the same object (cf. approach-approach conflict, avoidance-avoidance conflict).

association areas.   Those areas of the cerebral hemispheres whose function is unknown. It is assumed that these areas serve to bring together information from the rest of the cerebrum for use in such higher mental processes as learning, memory, and thinking.

attitude.   A person's attitude toward a particular object or idea includes his feelings, cognitions, and behavioral tendencies with respect to that object or idea.

attribute.   A characteristic ascribed to a person or object by an observer.

autonomic nervous system.   The part of the nervous system that consists of sympathetic and parasympathetic divisions, and serves the internal organs and other non-skeletal muscles.

avoidance-avoidance conflict.   When the organism wants to avoid one outcome and at the same time wants to avoid its alternative (cf. approach-approach conflict, approach-avoidance conflict).

axon.   The part of a neuron that carries impulses to other neurons.

behavior.   The responses of an organism that are open to observation by all, e.g., speech, the pressing of a lever, a muscle contraction.

behavior modification.   A type of directive therapy in which learning principles are used to decrease the frequency of undesirable behaviors and increase the frequency of desirable ones.

behavioral approach.   An approach to personality which emphasizes learning principles.

biological drive.   A motive based on evident bodily conditions, such as the presence or absence of hormones, food, or water (cf. psychological motive).

blind spot.   The place where the optic nerve leaves the retina. Images falling on the blind spot cannot be seen.

body-sense area.   An area of the cerebral cortex located at the front of the parietal lobe. Electrical stimulation of this area results in reports of sensory experiences, e.g., "Something is touching my arm" (cf. motor area, visual area, hearing area).

cerebellum.   The part of the brain that is responsible for coordinating motor activities. Located below the cerebrum.

cerebral cortex. The outer layer of the cerebrum.

cerebral hemispheres. The right and left halves of man's cerebrum. Although capable of operating independently, they ordinarily are kept in close coordination by several connecting cables.

cerebrum. The largest and highest part of the brain. Located above the cerebellum.

chromosomes. Small particles found in pairs in every cell of the body. They carry the genetic determiners (genes) that are transmitted from parents to offspring. A human cell has 23 pairs of chromosomes.

chronic brain disorder. An organic disorder that develops slowly over time and is the result of gradual deterioration, e.g., senile psychosis (cf. acute brain disorder).

classical conditioning. The conditioning procedure in which a conditioned stimulus (e.g., a light) is first presented to the subject, followed by an unconditioned stimulus (e.g., food). After this procedure has been repeated over enough trials, the conditioned stimulus will itself produce the response (e.g., salivation) (cf. operant conditioning).

client-centered (nondirective) therapy. A type of psychotherapy, developed by Carl Rogers, in which the therapist attempts to provide a permissive atmosphere so that the client may discover and solve his own problems.

clinical psychologist. A psychologist, usually with a Ph.D. degree, who is trained to work with cases of abnormal behavior. The techniques available to him include testing, psychotherapy, and research, and exclude medical methods such as drug therapy and surgery (cf. psychiatrist).

closed therapy group. One which remains intact until the entire membership feels that it is time to disband (cf. open therapy group).

cognition. Processes of thinking and knowing. Language, memory, and problem-solving are usually considered to be among the cognitive processes.

cognitive dissonance. According to the theory developed by Leon Festinger, an unpleasant psychological state that occurs after a person behaves in a way that is inconsistent with his attitudes. To reduce dissonance, his behavior or attitude will tend to change.

compulsion. See obsessive-compulsive reaction.

concept learning. In theoretical terms, learning to abstract out those characteristics that are essential to a particular category, and to ignore the nonessential ones. In observable terms, learning to respond in the same way to stimuli that are examples of the particular category, in spite of their many differences.

condition (of an experiment). Every experiment includes two or more conditions—combinations of variables—in order to determine their effects on behavior.

conditioned response (CR). The response that occurs to the conditioned stimulus in classical conditioning. In Ivan Pavlov's salivary conditioning experiment, it was the number of drops of saliva the dog secreted to the bell.

conditioned stimulus (CS). The stimulus that later—after classical conditioning has occurred—comes to produce the response. In Ivan Pavlov's salivary conditioning experiment, it was the bell.

conditioning. Simple stimulus-response learning; i.e., learning to make a particular response to a particular stimulus. The two major types are classical conditioning and operant conditioning.

cones. Visual receptor cells that pick up images in color. More numerous in the center of the retina than at the periphery. More sensitive than the rods after adaptation to bright light.

conservation of quantity. According to Jean Piaget, a child has developed conservation of quantity when he realizes that changing the shape of a substance does not change its quantity. This occurs at about age seven.

constancy (perceptual). The tendency to perceive objects as unchanged under widely different conditions of stimulation.

continuity. The Gestalt principle that stimulus elements which are part of a smooth, continuous sequence tend to be perceived as a group (cf. principle of nearness, principle of similarity).

continuous reinforcement. Reinforcement for every correct response (cf. intermittent reinforcement).

control. A variable is controlled in an experiment by keeping it the same in the various conditions of the experiment. A control group or control condition is one that shows the influence of only the variables that were controlled in the study, because the independent variable is at zero strength.

conversion reaction. A neurotic reaction characterized by incapacitating bodily ailments that have no apparent physical basis (cf. anxiety reaction, depressive reaction, phobic reaction, obsessive-compulsive reaction).

correlation. A correlation coefficient (r) is a number which describes a relationship precisely. Correlation coefficients, which may range from $+1$ to -1, are positive for positive relationships and negative for negative ones; they are larger for stronger relationships and smaller for weaker ones.

credibility (of a communicator). Believability. The more credible a communicator, the more influential his messages will be.

critical period. A period during which certain experiences can influence development. Either before or after the critical period, however, these experiences will be ineffective.

cross-sectional method. A method of measuring trends in development which involves applying the measure to different people of different ages, usually at the same time (cf. longitudinal method).

culture. The behavior patterns shared by members of a society.

cumulative graph. A graph in which the total number of responses that have occurred since observation began is plotted against time. The steepness of the slope indicates how frequently the subject is responding.

custodial retarded. An individual with an IQ between 0 and 24 (cf. trainable retarded, educable retarded).

defense mechanism. A learned way of dealing with anxiety by reducing conflict and enhancing self-esteem. For the most part, people are not aware that they are using these mechanisms (cf. repression, rationalization, displacement).

delusion. A persistent belief that has no basis in reality, e.g., a patient's belief that he is Napoleon. Delusions of grandeur exaggerate the person's own importance, and delusions of persecution hold that others are plotting against him (cf. hallucination).

dendrite. The part of a neuron that receives impulses from other neurons.

depressive reaction. A neurotic reaction, often brought on by a severe loss, which is characterized by feelings of worthlessness (cf. anxiety reaction, phobic reaction, obsessive-compulsive reaction, conversion reaction).

developmental determinant (of behavior). A past event that influences present behavior.

differentiation. The process of one, unitary entity separating into several relatively distinct and independent entities.

direction. The goal orientation of behavior, which is one aspect of motivation (cf. activation).

directive therapy. A type of psychotherapy in which the therapist actively helps the client decide on his therapy goals and on a plan of treatment.

discrimination training. A procedure for teaching a subject who is generalizing to respond differently to the two similar stimuli. This is done by presenting the two stimuli and conditioning the response to one of them, but extinguishing it to the other.

displacement. A defense mechanism in which, because the individual's feelings (e.g., of aggression) toward their real target are blocked, he expresses them instead toward a safer and more available target (cf. repression, rationalization).

dream interpretation. A technique, used in psychoanalysis, that requires the patient to recall his dreams so that the analyst may look for clues to repressed motives in them.

drive. A biological motive.

ectomorph. One of three body types in William Sheldon's theory of personality. Characterized by a tall, thin, fragile body build (cf. mesomorph, endomorph).

educable retarded. An individual with an IQ between 50 and 75 (cf. custodial retarded, trainable retarded).

ego. According to psychoanalytic theory, one of the three parts of the personality. It consists of learned skills for overcoming barriers and thus more effectively satisfying the id (cf. id, super-ego).

electroencephalogram (EEG). A graphic record of the overall electrical activity of the brain, obtained by attaching recording electrodes to various points on the scalp.

embryo. A young animal in the womb, especially during its early stages (cf. fetus).

empathetic verbal report. A person's description of how he thinks another person is reacting to an event. Often assumed to reveal the person's own reactions.

endomorph. One of three body types in William Sheldon's theory of personality; characterized by excessive fat (cf. mesomorph, ectomorph).

epinephrine. A synonym for adrenalin.

extinction. The procedure of weakening a conditioned response by discontinuing reinforcement. In classical conditioning this involves continuing to present the CS, but not the UCS. In operant conditioning, it involves allowing the response to continue, but no longer reinforcing it.

fetus. A young animal in the womb, especially during its later stages (cf. embryo).

figure-ground perception. Perceiving a pattern of stimuli as a form (figure) that stands out against a formless background.

fraternal twins. Twins who developed from separate eggs, and whose heredity is thus no more similar than that of nontwin siblings (cf. identical twins).

free association. A technique used in psychoanalysis that requires the patient to say aloud everything that comes to mind.

free-floating anxiety. Chronic anxiety without a known cause.

frontal lobe. A region of the cerebral hemispheres, located in front of the parietal lobe (cf. parietal lobe, occipital lobe, temporal lobe).

functional disorders. Types of mental illness which have no known physiological or organic basis (cf. organic disorders).

galvanic skin response (GSR). A momentary increase in the electrical conductivity of the skin which, for unknown reasons, indicates an increase in emotion.

generalization. See stimulus generalization.

genes. Tiny segments of chromosomes that are considered the basic units of heredity. Genes are typically in pairs, one member of which is in the chromosome from the father, and the other in the corresponding chromosome from the mother.

genital stage. According to psychoanalytic theory, the final stage of psychosexual development, culminating in sexual union with a member of the opposite sex (cf. oral stage, anal stage).

Gestalt psychology. A theoretical position or "school" in psychology which emphasizes the importance of the organization of a stimulus pattern in determining how it is perceived.

halfway house. A residence for persons who have been discharged from mental hospitals, to help them readjust to society.

hallucination. An experience for which there is no known sensory input, e.g., hearing voices when no one is present (cf. delusion).

hearing area. An area of the cerebral cortex located in the temporal lobe. Electrical stimulation of this area results in reports of meaningless fragments of sound (cf. body-sense area, motor area, visual area).

homeostasis. A vital physiological balance within the body which is maintained by various homeostatic mechanisms, including homeostatic drives.

homeostatic drive. A drive that leads the organism to correct a physiological imbalance that could, if ignored, lead to its injury or death.

hormones. The internal chemical secretions of endocrine (ductless) glands. They are carried in the blood stream.

hypochondria. Extreme exaggeration of minor physical symptoms.

hypothalamus. A brain structure that regulates the internal environment.

hypothesis. A guess about the truth. A causal hypothesis takes the form "X influences Y," while a noncausal hypothesis takes the form "X is related to Y."

id. According to psychoanalytic theory, one of the three parts of the personality. It consists of unconscious drives (cf. ego, superego).

identical twins. Twins who developed from a single egg, and who therefore have identical heredity (cf. fraternal twins).

idiographic approach. An approach to the study of personality which seeks detailed understanding of a single individual (cf. nomothetic approach).

imprinting. The process by which many kinds of young animals form attachments to other members of their species. In imprinting, the animal becomes permanently attached to whatever kind of object (within limits) it experiences first during a certain early period of its life.

incentive. The organism's goal.

inner mental process. A psychological process, such as learning, motivation, perception, or thinking, that is theorized to go on inside the organism.

insight. In observable terms, the sudden solution of a problem.

instinctive behavior. Stereotyped behavior that is more complex than a single muscle movement. Although the behavior itself is not learned, the stimuli that control it may be influenced by experience.

intelligence quotient (IQ). A relative measure of intelligence, originally calculated by dividing a person's mental age (MA) by his chronological age (CA): IQ = MA/CA × 100. An IQ of 100 is average.

intermittent reinforcement. Reinforcement for only some of the correct responses that occur (cf. continuous reinforcement).

interposition. A cue for visual depth perception which occurs when one object appears to partially block the view of another.

inventory. A kind of measuring instrument consisting of a number of items that ask the subject about himself, e.g., the Minnesota Multiphasic Personality Inventory (MMPI).

kinesthesis. Sensitivity to position and movement of the body. Results from stimulation of receptors located in tendons, muscles, and joints.

learning. In observable terms, a change in behavior, for better or worse, that follows practice.

legal commitment. The patient's family, friends, or physician recommends his admission to a mental hospital, and a team of psychiatrists and psychologists at the hospital agree that he needs treatment (cf. voluntary admission).

longitudinal method. A method of measuring trends in development which involves measuring the same people at two or more different ages (cf. cross-sectional method).

manic-depressive (affective) reaction. A psychotic reaction characterized by exaggerated swings in the person's moods, from extreme elation to extreme depression (cf. schizophrenic reaction, paranoid reaction).

maturation. The unfolding of largely inherited characteristics with age.

maturational readiness. A state in which the organism is ready to benefit from particular kinds of training experience. Before this state is reached, the training is of little value, but any time afterward it is effective.

maze. A device often used in the study of animal and human learning, consisting of a correct path and blind alleys.

mean. The mean (or average) of a group of scores is obtained by summing all the scores and then dividing by the number of scores.

mental age (MA). A unit of measurement used in some intelligence tests. A child with a MA of 8 is one who obtains the same score as the average 8-year-old.

mesomorph. One of three body types in William Sheldon's theory of personality. Characterized by muscularity and well-developed bone structure (cf. endomorph, ectomorph).

methadone. A drug sometimes used in the treatment of heroin addiction.

motivation. The activation and direction of behavior. It is determined by motives and incentives.

motive. An internal urge or desire.

motor (*adj.*). Having to do with muscle movements.

motor area. An area of the cerebral cortex located at the rear of the frontal lobe. Electrical stimulation of this area results in muscle movement (cf. body-sense area, visual area, hearing area).

n Ach. Abbreviation of "need for achievement."

nearness, principle of. The Gestalt principle that stimulus elements which are close together tend to be perceived as a group (cf. principle of similarity, principle of continuity).

need for achievement. The psychological motive to perform well in any undertaking.

negative reinforcer. An aversive stimulus.

nerve. A bundle of axons belonging to many different neurons.

neural impulse. An electrochemical charge which travels along a neuron.

neuron. The nerve cell. Man's nervous system is made up of billions of neurons.

neurotic reaction (neurosis). The class of disorder that is less severe than the psychotic disorders. The common element in all the neurotic reactions (e.g., anxiety reaction, depressive reaction, phobic reaction, obsessive-compulsive reaction, and conversion reaction) is overwhelming anxiety.

nomothetic approach. An approach to the study of personality which seeks generalizations about groups of people (cf. idiographic approach).

nondirective therapy. A synonym for client-centered therapy.

nonsense syllable. A combination of letters that does not form a word. Used chiefly in experiments on memory.

norm (social). A rule for feelings, cognitions, or behaviors that is subscribed to by most of the members of a group. Norms may be conscious or unconscious, obvious or subtle.

object identity. According to Jean Piaget, a child who has developed object identity perceives objects as stable in two ways: (a) he realizes that an object that looks somewhat different because it is seen from two different viewpoints is in fact the same object, and (b) he realizes that an object that disappears from sight does not stop existing.

objectivity. If two observers independently applying a particular method of measurement to the same subjects at the same time agree closely in their observations, the measure has high objectivity; if they do not agree closely, the measure has low objectivity.

obsessive-compulsive reaction. A neurotic reaction characterized by frequently recurring, unavoidable thoughts (obsessions) and actions (compulsions) (cf. anxiety reaction, depressive reaction, phobic reaction, conversion reaction).

occipital lobe. A region of the cerebral hemispheres, located behind the parietal and temporal lobes (cf. frontal lobe, parietal lobe, temporal lobe).

open therapy group. One in which a member who feels he has reached his goals may leave and be replaced by a new member (cf. closed group).

operant conditioning. The conditioning procedure in which the trainer waits until the desired response occurs, then immediately presents or withdraws a positive or a negative reinforcer.

optic nerve. The nerve that connects the eye with the brain.

oral stage. According to psychoanalytic theory, the first psychosexual stage, during which the mouth is the zone most sensitive to pleasurable stimulation (cf. anal stage, genital stage).

organic disorders. Types of mental illness assumed to be caused by brain damage, e.g., acute brain disorders and chronic brain disorders (cf. functional disorders).

paranoid reaction. A psychotic reaction characterized by elaborate systems of delusions, usually delusions of persecution (cf. schizophrenic reaction, manic-depressive reaction).

parasympathetic division. The division of the autonomic nervous system that is dominant in calm, nonstressful moments (cf. sympathetic division).

parietal lobe. A region of the cerebral hemispheres between the frontal and occipital lobes (cf. frontal lobe, occipital lobe, temporal lobe).

perception. An individual's perceptions are what things look like to him.

personality. Personality characteristics are those enduring attributes of the person which affect his interpersonal behavior.

phobic reaction. A neurotic reaction characterized by an intense, irrational fear of a specific object or situation (cf. anxiety reaction, depressive reaction, obsessive-compulsive reaction, conversion reaction).

physiological motives. Synonym for biological motives. One of the five major categories of human motives, according to Abraham Maslow (cf. safety motives, social motives, self-esteem motives, self-actualization motives).

population (of subjects). A total set of subjects; any identifiable group, such as all white rats, all college sophomores, or all residents of the third floor of Smith Dormitory at Jones College (cf. sample).

positive reinforcer. A rewarding stimulus.

primary reinforcer. A stimulus that does not depend upon learning for its reinforcing properties, e.g., food, water.

proactive inhibition. Impairment of memory due to material learned before the material to be remembered (cf. retroactive inhibition).

projective test. A test in which the subject is asked to interpret some ambiguous stimulus, e.g., the n Ach test, the Rorschach inkblot test.

psychiatrist. A medical doctor who has gone through the regular medical training and then specialized in the treatment of abnormal behavior. Because of his medical training, he may use medical methods such as drug therapy and surgery (cf. clinical psychologist).

psychoanalysis. The method of psychotherapy, introduced by Sigmund Freud, that attempts to make the patient aware of his repressed motives.

psychoanalytic theory. The personality theory of Sigmund Freud and his followers.

psychological motive. A motive not based on any evident bodily condition (cf. biological drive).

psychosexual stages. According to psychoanalytic theory, a series of stages through which every normally developing individual passes. Each stage is characterized by a zone of pleasurable stimulation (cf. oral stage, anal stage, genital stage).

psychotic reaction (psychosis). The class of disorder that is more severe than the neurotic disorders. The entire personality of the individual is usually so profoundly disturbed that he is incapable of continuing his normal activities and must be hospitalized (cf. schizophrenic reaction, manic-depressive reaction, paranoid reaction).

rapid eye movements (REMs). Eye movements that usually occur during dreaming.

rating scale. A method of measurement which requires an observer to record his judgment of a person's behavior along some graphic dimension.

rationalization. A defense mechanism involving one's explanation of his behavior in ways that are more socially acceptable than the true explanation (cf. repression, displacement).

recall test. A test in which the subject must reproduce the correct answer entirely from memory (cf. recognition test).

receptor. An organ that is especially constructed to pick up information about a particular kind of stimulation, e.g., the eye and the ear.

recognition test. A test of memory in which the correct answer is supplied, mixed in with one or more incorrect answers, and the subject's task is to select it (cf. recall test).

reconstructive therapy group. One focused on bringing about major changes in the personality structures of the members (cf. supportive group, re-educative group).

re-educative therapy group. One focused on the development of more effective ways of handling particular situations (cf. supportive group, reconstructive group).

reflexes. Automatic reactions, in many of which the sensory neurons make contact with the motor neurons in the spinal cord without going to the brain, e.g., knee-jerk reflex, sneezing, and perspiring.

relationship (between two variables). A relationship is positive if there is a tendency for subjects who score higher on one variable to also score higher on the other; it is negative if the tendency is for those who score higher on one to score lower on the other. A relationship is strong if this tendency is a strong one, and weak if this tendency is weak.

reliability. A method of measurement is reliable to the extent that it gives similar scores each time it is used on the same subjects (cf. validity).

repression. According to psychoanalytic theory, a defense mechanism by which guilty impulses and memories are excluded from consciousness (cf. rationalization, displacement).

response. An instance of behavior.

reticular formation. A small collection of neurons in the brain stem, stimulation of which leads to an increase in the level of activation or alertness of wide areas of the cerebral cortex.

retina. The light-sensitive surface lining the back of the eyeball. Contains the rods and cones.

retinal disparity. A cue for visual depth perception which occurs when the images an object casts on the two retinas of an organism are different. The greater the retinal disparity, the less the perceived distance of the object.

retroactive inhibition. Impairment of memory due to material learned after the material to be remembered (cf. proactive inhibition).

rods. Visual receptor cells that pick up images in black and white only. More numerous in the periphery of the retina than at the center. More sensitive than the cones after adaptation to dim light.

role (social). A group of norms that make up one coherent set of duties and privileges.

safety motives. The need to have the environment be safe and stable. One of the five major categories of human motives, according to Abraham Maslow (cf. physiological motives, social motives, self-esteem motives, self-actualization motives).

sample (of subjects). The specific set of subjects selected from a population. One way to obtain a sample that is representative of a population is to choose the sample in a random manner, that is, a manner that gives every person in the population an equal chance of being chosen.

Scanlon Plan. An incentive plan for use in industry whereby part of the profits resulting from increased plant productivity is returned to the workers.

schizophrenic reaction. A psychotic reaction characterized by extreme apathy, inappropriate emotional responses, and withdrawal from social contact (cf. manic-depressive reaction, paranoid reaction).

secondary (learned) reinforcer. A previously neutral stimulus that has acquired reinforcing properties through association with a reinforcer (cf. primary reinforcer).

self. The subject's personality as he perceives it.

self-actualization motives. The need to strive to attain the fullest possible development of one's unique potentialities. One of the five major categories of human motives, according to Abraham Maslow (cf. physiological motives, safety motives, social motives, self-esteem motives).

self-concept. Synonym for "self."

self-esteem motives. The need to achieve, and to gain the respect of others. One of the five major categories of human motives, according to Abraham Maslow (cf. physiological motives, safety motives, social motives, self-actualization motives).

senile psychosis. A chronic brain disorder due to the gradual breakdown of brain cells with aging.

shape constancy. The tendency to perceive the shapes of objects relatively accurately regardless of the angles from which we view those objects.

shaping. A special operant conditioning procedure that consists of reinforcing closer and closer approximations to the desired response. It is used at the beginning of training in cases where the response to be conditioned occurs infrequently or not at all.

sibling. A brother or sister.

similarity, principle of. The Gestalt principle that similar stimulus elements tend to be perceived as a group (cf. principle of nearness, principle of continuity).

size constancy. The tendency to perceive the sizes of objects relatively accurately regardless of wide variations in the distances of those objects.

Skinner box. An apparatus designed by B. F. Skinner which is widely used to study operant conditioning. The rat presses a bar to obtain reinforcement.

social class. A social group that is defined in terms of its position in the social hierarchy, e.g., upper class (cf. social status).

social motives. The need to have warm and friendly human relationships and to belong to groups. One of the five major categories of human motives, according to Abraham Maslow (cf. physiological motives, safety motives, self-esteem motives, self-actualization motives).

social psychology. An area of psychology concerned with the influence of other people on the individual's behavior.

social reinforcer. A reinforcing stimulus stemming from other people, e.g., liking and disliking, helping and hurting.

social (or socioeconomic) status. One's standing in the social (or social and economic) hierarchy (cf. social class).

sociopathic personality disturbance. A condition characterized by the failure to learn from experience or to be aware of the consequences of one's behavior. Subcategories are antisocial reactions and addiction to drugs or alcoholic beverages.

supportive therapy group. One focused on helping members through some current crisis (cf. re-educative group, reconstructive group).

sympathetic division. The division of the autonomic nervous system that prepares the organism to deal with stress (cf. parasympathetic division).

synapse. The gap between the axon endings of one neuron and a dendrite of another neuron.

taboo. Something strongly prohibited by a culture.

temporal lobe. A region of the cerebral hemispheres, below the frontal and parietal lobes and in front of the occipital lobe (cf. frontal lobe, parietal lobe, occipital lobe).

thalamus. A brain structure, a major function of which is to receive incoming sensory information and relay it to the cerebral cortex.

threshold. A receptor's threshold is the faintest stimulus it can pick up.

trainable retarded. An individual with an IQ between 25 and 40 (cf. custodial retarded, educable retarded).

traits. Dimensions of personality, observable as general trends in behavior, e.g., intelligence, sociability, perseverance.

transient situational personality disturbance. A temporary breakdown of normal behavior due to a disturbing situation so unfamiliar to the individual that he has no learned way of dealing with it, e.g., battle fatigue.

transmitter substance. A chemical that transmits the nerve impulse across a synapse. It is released at the axon endings of one neuron and travels across the synapse to affect the dendrites of the next neuron.

types (personality). Categories—each consisting of a broad range of specific traits—into which total human personalities may be classified, e.g., introvert, extravert.

unconditioned response (UCR). The response that occurs to the unconditioned stimulus in classical conditioning. In Ivan Pavlov's salivary conditioning study it was the number of drops of saliva the dog secreted to the meat powder.

unconditioned stimulus (UCS). The stimulus that produces the response from the very beginning of classical conditioning. In Ivan Pavlov's salivary conditioning study it was the meat powder.

unconscious. A concept introduced by Sigmund Freud to refer to mental events which a person is not aware of, even though they may influence his behavior.

validity. A method of measurement is valid to the extent that it measures what it is supposed to measure (cf. reliability).

variable. A changeable aspect of a situation. An independent variable is the "cause" variable in a causal hypothesis, while a dependent variable is the "effect" variable.

verbal report. A statement in words by the subject; often an account of his inner mental processes.

visual area. An area of the cerebral cortex located in the occipital lobe. Electrical stimulation of this area results in reports of meaningless visual fragments such as a color, a long white mark, or flashing lights (cf. body-sense area, motor area, hearing area).

voluntary admission. When a person decides he needs treatment and voluntarily admits himself to a mental hospital (cf. legal commitment).

Answers to Questions

Chapter One

1. A. Example: Depression influences suicide.
   B. Example: Religious affiliation is related to suicide.

2. (Amount of) frustration; (amount of) aggression

3. A. Independent variable
      Dependent variable
   B. This is neither an independent nor a dependent variable, because the hypothesis is not a causal one.
      This is neither an independent nor a dependent variable, because the hypothesis is not a causal one.

4. A. Examples: Another person punches the subject, sideswipes his car, insults his wife, belittles him in public, etc.
   B. Examples: Hitting, shouting, swearing, etc.

5. 1. Create or find ready-made two or more conditions in which amount of alcohol consumed differs. (Example: On a Saturday night, the experimenter finds some subjects who have consumed a large amount of alcohol, and others who have consumed none.)
    2. Control other variables, such as sex, age, intelligence, body weight, and the material that is learned. This might be done by using only male subjects between the ages of 18 and 22, selecting the two groups in such a way that they both have the same average IQ and weight, and giving all subjects the same material to learn.
    3. Measure the amount each subject learns from studying the material provided. This could be done by giving him a series of multiple-choice questions on this material, and using the test score as his learning score.

6. A. The 50 foremen studied.
    B. Example: The concern a foreman in the auto industry shows for his men is related to the productivity of those men.
    C. Example: All foremen in the auto industry.

7. A. The 35 addicts you select for your program.
    B. All institutionalized heroin addicts.
    C. In a random manner.
    D. Example: Obtain a complete, alphabetized list of all institutionalized heroin addicts, put their names in a hat, and draw out 35 names.

8. Have two observers independently apply the conformity measure to the subjects in the experiment, and then compare their scores. If the scores agree closely, the measure is highly objective.

9. A. Ask some subjects how close they typically stand to others during a conversation; or, have an observer who knows the hypothesis observe how close the subjects stand to the others.
    B. Have an observer who does not know the hypothesis (or who is somehow prevented from knowing the sex of each subject) observe how close the subjects stand to the others.

10. A. Apply the measure to a group of teachers once, and then apply it again at some later time. (Or, if two different versions of the measure are available, they both could be given to the teachers at the same time.)
    B. If the two sets of measurements were highly similar, that would indicate high reliability. If they were not very similar, that would indicate low reliability.
    C. It would not imply anything about reliability. Instead, it would mean that the measure was not very valid.

11. It would mean that this test gives similar scores each time it is applied to the same subjects, but it is not measuring marital happiness.

12. Any three items that ask the subject about his own attitude toward pollution.
    Example: Are you in favor of or opposed to emission control devices on cars?
    (Check one.) _____ In favor of   _____ Opposed to

13. Example: Jimmy finds a small boy wrecking his tree house. What does Jimmy do?

14. Mean = 21/7 = 3

15. A. Positive
     B. Negative
     C. Set A
     D. $-.92$ $\diagdown$ $\diagup$ A
          1.00 $\diagup$ $\diagdown$ B

16. Not significant
     Significant

Chapter Two

1. $\dfrac{}{\underline{\checkmark}}$
    $\overline{}$

2. First obtain two or more groups of subjects having different heredity but the same environment, then measure the behavior under study.

3.

	Condition 1	Condition 2
Independent variable (similarity of environment)	Pairs reared in same family	Pairs reared in different families
Control variable (similarity of heredity)	Pairs of identical twins	Pairs of identical twins
	% schizophrenic	*% schizophrenic*
Dependent variable (similarity on schizophrenia)	1st members of pairs: 100% 2nd members of pairs: ?%	1st members of pairs: 100% 2nd members of pairs: ?%

4. 1. The behavior is stereotyped (e.g., given the right circumstances, the snake will strike at a stone or a tree).
    2. The behavior is more complex than a single muscle movement.
    3. The behavior itself is not learned.
    4. The stimuli that control the behavior may or may not be influenced by experience.

5. 1. If the children were the first objects the birds experienced during the critical period.
    2. The birds will become permanently attached to the children (e.g., they will tend to follow the children).

6. A. 2
    B. 1

7. This is an example of a critical period. (This environmental factor—measles—influences the embryo's development most if it occurs during the second or third month of pregnancy; it has little influence if it occurs either before or after that period.)

8. Cross-sectional   (It must have been cross-sectional if it took only one year to com-
                        plete; a longitudinal study would have taken at least five years.)
    Longitudinal
    Cross-sectional

9. A (Because these scores increase sharply at first, then gradually level off, just like
    the typical growth curve.)

10. 1

11. A. 2
     B. 2

12. 2

Chapter Three

1. __✓__ (The little girl's bicycling behavior changed following practice with the training
            wheels.)
    __✓__ (The piano student's playing of the Polonaise changed—for the worse—follow-
            ing practice.)
    _____ (The Spanish student changed her behavior, but no practice preceded this
            change.)

2. CS
    CR
    UCS
    UCR

3. A. First present fattening foods to the patient, then deliver a painful shock to him.
        Do this many times in succession, using many different fattening foods.
    B. CS: Fattening foods
        CR: Uncomfortable feeling (to fattening food)
        UCS: Shock
        UCR: Uncomfortable feeling (to shock)

4. The lefthand graph should be circled.

5. A. Examples: Praise, money, trophies, gifts, food, drink
    B. Examples: Disparagement, fines, jeers, electric shock, imprisonment, starvation

6. A. Present the tone to the subject, then puff air in his eye.
    B. Present the tone from time to time. Whenever the subject blinks his eye soon
        after it, put an M&M candy into his mouth.

7. Associate the words "good dog" with food by saying these words whenever you give
    him food.

8. A. 2 (This is a closer approximation to the desired response.)
    B. __✓__
        _____
        _____
        _____

9. A. 1
    B. 2
    C. 2

10. A. 2
    B. 2

11. 3 (The response would recover some, but not all, of its lost strength.)

12. A. 1
    B. 2 (The psychologist should decrease the frequency of reinforcement gradually, not suddenly.)

13. 2
    1
    3

14. 3
    1
    4
    2

15. She could add a snapping turtle to the classroom menagerie and then reinforce children's attempts to play with the harmless turtle, but not reinforce their attempts to play with the snapper. One way to do this might be to put the old turtle in an unlocked container, and the snapper in a locked one. Then children's attempts to open the containers to play with the turtles would be reinforced in the former case (the door would open), but not reinforced in the latter.

16. Concept (Various modern furnishings differ greatly in many respects—shape, color, etc.)
    Generalization (Various brown 1973 Mustangs are very similar in most ways.)
    Concept (Various tricky basketball plays differ greatly in many respects.)

17. Recognition test
    Recall test
    Recognition test
    Recall test

18. A. He could practice his social security number by repeating it to himself several times.
    B. He could search for meaningful associations for various parts of the number. For instance, if the number were 124-28-1707, he might break it up as follows:
        12 = Number of months in a year
         4 = Number of siblings subject has
        28 = Subject's age at marriage
        707 = Boeing 707 airplane

19. 2 (Because here memory is impaired due to activities—going to class—that occurred *after* the material to be remembered was learned.)

20. A ——— Solve most quickly
    B ——— Solve second most quickly
    C ——— Solve least quickly

Chapter Four

1. Example: Feeling: I dislike communism somewhat.
    Cognition: The Communists are trying to bury us.
    Behavioral tendency: I do not vote for Communist Party candidates or read the *Daily Worker*.

2. A. 2
    B. A
    C. 1
    D. A
    E. 2

3. The hostess could have changed into a miniskirt. (Only one "partner" drastically reduces the pressure to conform to the majority.)

4. A. 2
    B. 2
    C. 2

5. 1   (This group would probably have stronger positive and negative reinforcers for him because he would care more about the approval and disapproval of his barracks-mates than of trainees from other barracks.)

6. Each statement at the left matches the statement at the right immediately opposite to it.

7. Like most _____

    _____
    Like least _____

8. 2

9. 3

10. 1

11. A. 2
    B. 2

12. A. Example: The student agrees to defend the Vietnam war in a debate. (The clearest cases of dissonance are those where the individual voluntarily—not accidentally—does something inconsistent with his attitudes.)
    B. His attitude toward war would become somewhat less negative.

13. A. 2. (Because they all had just avoided playing with the toy, a behavior that was inconsistent with the fact that they liked it. In theory, this would produce dissonance, which they would then reduce by decreasing their liking for the toy.)
    B. 1   (Because they had weaker justification for avoiding playing with the toy.)

14. 1

15. ___✓___
     ___✓___
     _____

16. Yes
     No
     No

17. A. 1. High
             Low
         2. High
             High
         3. Low
     B. 2

Chapter Five

1. Motor neuron _____ Person can't move his little finger.
    Sensory neuron _____ Person can't feel his little finger.

2. 1. Synapse
    2. Dendrite
    3. Axon
    4. Cell body

3. 2

4. A

5. It would cease transmitting impulses.

6. 3

7. A. 2
    B. Each neuron follows the all-or-none principle; that is, it always fires at the same
        strength.

8. 2 and 3

9. 1

10. A. 2
    B. 2 (Because speech is controlled by the left hemisphere, and no information
        about the object was available in that hemisphere.)
    C. 2
    D. 1

11. Brain
    Spinal cord
    Spinal cord
    Brain
    Spinal cord

12. 2

13. 1

14. Measure for REMs while he is asleep.

15. ___ (This does not appear to be related to any biological drive.)

    ___✓___

    ___✓___

16. The behavior should occur less and less frequently.

17. The rat would be expected to press the lever more and more frequently.

18. Parasympathetic
    Sympathetic
    Sympathetic
    Sympathetic

19. Parietal

    Frontal

    Occipital

    Temporal

20. ___ (Since the hemisphere shown is the right one, it registers sensations from the left side of the body only.)

    ___2___

    ___3___

    ___1___

21. He will hear a rumbling sound. (It is an auditory area, and the result of electrical stimulation will be an unorganized sensation such as a rumbling, not a meaningful, organized one such as a song.)

22. D

Chapter Six

1. A. Example: My perception of my office desk is what it looks like to me—littered with papers that need to be graded, books and journals that need to be read, and notes about research ideas that need to be developed.
    B. Example: An observer (such as you, the reader) would have to infer what my perception of my desk was, on the basis of some behavior of mine (such as the written report presented in A).

2. 2

3. A. 2
    B. 1
    C. 1 (Because the images of such objects fall on the cones, which can pick up color.)

4. B

5. B

6. A. 1 (As can be seen in Figure 6-6, after only one minute in the dark the cones are still more sensitive than the rods.)
    B. 2

7. The floor plan on the left. (The nearness of the two areas would cause them to be perceived as a group.)

8. 1

9. In A the extraneous lines are not continuous with the 4, so they do not tend to be grouped with it. In B the opposite is true, making it difficult to distinguish the 4 from the extraneous lines in that drawing.

10. A. The black paper is one complete, uncut sheet.
    B. McCartney's face is in front and the black paper is in back (The black paper is perceived as more distant and as extending behind the face because it is the ground in this situation).

11. B (Because of apparent interposition; i.e., because B appears to partially block the view of A.)

12. A (This mosquito must be closer because the retinal disparity is greater.)

13. A. 1 (This would allow them to obtain accurate information about the distances of the circles.)
    B. 1

14. Jimmy _____ will probably perceive any interest you show in him as an attempt to hurt him.
    Walter _____ will probably perceive any interest you show in him as an attempt to help him.

15. A. 1
    B. 1
    C. 3

Chapter Seven

1. A. The boy's desire.
    B. The company of other people.

2. By depriving him of success; i.e., by seeing to it that he failed at several tasks.

3. A. 2
    B. 2
    C. 1 (It is homeostatic when it causes the organism to avoid injury or death.)

4. 1

5. ___✓___
    _____
    _____

6. He had eaten shortly before giving the blood.

7. ___✓___
    _____
    _____

8. To paraphrase the principle stated earlier for thirst, although the stimuli produced by the amount of water in the stomach are related to thirst, they are apparently not essential for thirst.

9. Because the sea water is saltier than their body fluids, causing them to become even thirstier when they drink it.

10. 2

11. _____✓_____
    _____

12. All of these alternatives are possible answers.

13. 1. Learning can influence what stimuli the organism is sexually motivated by.
    2. Learning can influence how the organism responds to sexual motivation.

14. The experiment suggests that sexual motivation is sometimes inhibited, and thus hidden from those who would measure it.

15. A. Several times in succession show the dog a car, then present a shock or some other negative stimulus. (This is a classical conditioning procedure.)
    B. CS: Car
       UCS: Shock
       CR: Fear
       UCR: Fear

16. A (Because her job deprives her of activity, she will probably be more active in her leisure time.)
    B

17. Most subjects spend more time looking at the righthand drawing in each pair.

18. 2

19. ____d____
    ____a, c____
    ____e____
    ____b____
    _____

20. A. Physiological, safety.
    B. Social, self-esteem, self-actualization. (In effect, these are currently not motives for this girl.)
    C. Attempts to increase self-esteem.

21. 1. Low concern
    2. High concern

22. A. 1
    B. 2

23. Approach-avoidance
    Avoidance-avoidance
    Approach-approach

Chapter Eight

1. 1. b
   2. a
   3. a

2. __✓__ The person is usually among the first to speak in a group situation.
    __✓__ The person is always late for appointments and meetings
    __✓__ The person's mood changes greatly from week to week
    __✓__ The person always drives a convertible
    __✓__ The person has no ash trays in his house
    __✓__ The person speaks in a loud, booming voice, dresses in wild colored clothes
         and associates with a reckless group of people

3. N
    I
    I
    N
    I

4. 2, 1, 4, 3

5. Observation of actions: Watching boy on the playground.
    Self verbal report: Interview with young boy.
    Verbal report of others: Asking boy about the fight between two boys in the school
    yard.

6. Superego
    Id
    Ego

7. A = 1
    B = 3
    C = 2

8. Bob feels that he and Jean had a good relationship, enjoyed each other's company,
    learned a lot about each other and themselves and that now it is appropriate for
    each of them to explore other interests.

9. The judgments about the two bits of information, body type and personality traits,
    were made by the same person and therefore not independent.

10. Trait level: Outgoing.
    Habitual response level: Joins new groups; often is the first to speak in a group
    situation.
    Specific response level: Greets people on his way to work.

11. __✓__ The number of times per week the client has had conversations with his parents.
    __✓__ The amount of time the client spends at home with his parents.

12. Trait theory
    Sheldon
    Behavioral theory
    Freud
    Trait theory
    Behavioral theory
    Rogers

13. 2
    5
    3
    4
    1

14. Independent variable: Degree of similarity in heredity.
    Dependent variables: Scores on intelligence test; ratings on personality traits.

15. 1. The observations made on the patients and relatives were not independent;
       therefore, the accuracy could be questioned.
    2. Very little has been said about the validity of his method of assessing adjustment
       status.

16. Developmental
    Current
    Current
    Developmental

Chapter Nine

1. __✓__ A person with an IQ of 57.
   __✓__ A person with an IQ of 142.
   __✓__ A person who risks his life to protect a stranger from an assailant.
   __✓__ A person who gives $75,000 a year to charity.

2. __✓__ An individual with an IQ of 57.
   __✓__ An individual who is so concerned about neatness and cleanliness that it inter-
       feres with some of his daily commitments.
   __✓__ A person who is regularly receiving therapy from a psychologist.

3. __✓__ A behavior of an individual that is so disturbing it leads him to seek help
       at the local mental health clinic.

4. Most likely: A 32-year-old twin living in a low income housing project. His brother
   has a history of adjustment problems.
   Least likely: A 52-year-old man living in a small town with his wife and three children.
   He has never experienced any major adjustment difficulties.

5. Displacement
   Rationalization

6. 1 =
   2 = a
   3 = d
   4 = c
   5 = b

7. __✓__ A person loses sleep because of vivid nightmares, and then has unpleasant social
       interactions the next day.
   __✓__ A person does not recognize people he has known for years.

8. Withdrawal
   Flattened emotional response
   Hallucinations: talking to a person who isn't present.
   Delusions: receiving messages about having special abilities; subject to irradiation
   effects.

9. Schizophrenic reaction: The boy shows detachment and withdrawal, very little emotion and experiences hallucinations and delusions.

10. Antisocial reaction
    Acute brain damage
    Transient situation personality disturbance
    Addiction: alcohol

11. Acute
    Chronic
    Acute

12.

	Within capacity	Beyond capacity
Custodial:	Smile at hospital attendant	Live alone
Trainable:	Sort objects by shape	Supervise the work of others
Educable:	Count money	College training

13. Psychiatrist
    Psychiatrist
    Clinical psychologist

14. 1
    3

15. Directive
    Nondirective
    Directive
    Directive

16. 1
    3
    4

17. Reeducative
    Reconstructive
    Supportive
    Supportive
    Reeducative

18. 2
    4

Index